ANATOMY OF DISINTEGRATION

WHAT BRAZIL REVEALS ABOUT THE GLOBAL FAR RIGHT

RODRIGO NUNES

Haymarket Books
Chicago, IL

Published in 2026 by
Haymarket Books
P.O. Box 180165
Chicago, IL 60618
www.haymarketbooks.org

ISBN: 979-8-88890-823-5
Hardcover ISBN: 979-8-88890-825-9
Epub ISBN: 979-8-88890-824-2

Distributed to the trade in the US through Consortium Book Sales and Distribution (www.cbsd.com) and internationally through Ingram Publisher Services International (www.ingramcontent.com).

This book was published with the generous support of Lannan Foundation, Wallace Action Fund, and Marguerite Casey Foundation.

Special discounts are available for bulk purchases by organisations and institutions. Please email info@haymarketbooks.org for more information.

Cover design by Kevin Barrett Kane.

Printed in Canada by union labor.

Library of Congress Cataloging-in-Publication data is available.
Library of Congress Control Number: 2026945953

10 9 8 7 6 5 4 3 2 1

MIX
Paper | Supporting responsible forestry
FSC® C103567

PRAISE FOR *ANATOMY OF DISINTEGRATION*

"*Anatomy of Disintegration* is a sharp, incisive analysis of the material and affective conditions that underpin the global rise of the far right. Compelling, provocative, and deeply insightful, this is essential reading for understanding the contemporary far right—and the transformative political possibilities that we must pursue instead."

—NAOMI KLEIN, coauthor of *End Times Fascism: And the Fight for the Living World*

"Where most bring a bludgeon, Nunes brings a scalpel. From observations of the 'lumpen elite' and crowds shouting 'We want my money!' to the exposure of the recreational nihilism and brand subjection that so many of us participate in, his analysis gives no quarter. A necessary book."

—QUINN SLOBODIAN, author of *Hayek's Bastards* and coauthor of *Muskism*

"In his razor-sharp analysis of Bolsonarismo, Rodrigo Nunes builds a globally relevant perspective on the far right from the point of view of the periphery. At once sobering and entertaining, I can think of few other works that so astutely and bracingly illuminate the challenges before us. A must-read."

—MELINDA COOPER, author of *Family Values: Between Neoliberalism and the New Social Conservatism*

"In its original Portuguese, *Do transe à vertigem* helped me more than any other work to understand the far right. Now, in an expanded English-language edition, Nunes speaks to a global audience on the topic of our very survival. Rodrigo Nunes is one of Brazil's most insightful and exciting thinkers, and *Anatomy of Disintegration* is essential."

—VINCENT BEVINS, author of *If We Burn: The Mass Protest Decade and the Missing Revolution*

"Tracing the history of the far right starting from the world's peripheries enables us to understand the centrality of processes that are time and again dismissed as 'marginal.' Using the notion of the 'anatomy' of social disintegration, Nunes offers an analysis of the ways in which neoliberalism reorganizes itself and, above all, accelerates. These are essential lessons for reflecting on the organic links between cycles of struggle that have challenged this logic of disintegration."

—VERÓNICA GAGO, author of *Neoliberalism from Below* and *Feminist International*

"Toggling between Brazil, the United States, and the world, this illuminating book provides an original and insightful analysis of the many facets of contemporary far-right movements, demonstrating how and why they have become a global phenomenon."

—MICHAEL HARDT, coauthor of *Empire* and *Multitude*

"Brilliant and counterintuitive, *Anatomy of Disintegration* dissects the emergence of Bolsonarismo in Brazil and exposes its key tropes of individualism, punitiveness, and order above the law. Eschewing as too simple the label 'fascism,' the book demonstrates how a focus on the Global South can shed light on the rise of the far right in the United States and Europe. A powerful diagnosis that makes for an urgent call to action."

—BERNARD E. HARCOURT, author of *The Counterrevolution: How Our Government Went to War Against Its Own Citizens*

"Undoubtedly one of the most valuable contributions to the ongoing effort to understand fascism in its contemporary configuration."

—SUELY ROLNIK, author of *Molecular Revolution in Brazil*

"*Anatomy of Disintegration* offers the sharpest analysis of what empowers the far right in our current media environment. By looking at these issues from the South, from the particular case of Brazilian politics, it uncovers many features of what most of us encounter, but often fail to identify, within our more familiar Northern political stages. Its clarity and depth of conceptualization, putting affective infrastructures at the core of the problems, brings precious help for progressive movements to redefine new (and better) strategies in front of very alarming threats."

—**YVES CITTON,** author of *The Ecology of Attention* and *Mediarchy*

"Through the lens of Bolsonarismo, Rodrigo Nunes zeros in on the challenge that the enduring success of the far right forces the left to face in Brazil and beyond: How do we reckon with the appeal of political actors who promise radical positive change while reassuring their own supporters that they, and only they, won't need to change their ways? To put it in the words of the author, how do bold leftists convince a majority of people that instead of hating particular categories of players, they should hate the game, when their opponents thrive on telling voters that hating other players can spare them the hazardous work of changing the game? To start answering that question seriously and intransigently, *Anatomy of Disintegration* is a must-read."

—**MICHEL FEHER,** author of *Rated Agency: Investee Activism in a Speculative Age* and cofounder of Zone Books and Diagrammes

ANATOMY OF DISINTEGRATION

To Liz, Tião, Mati, Hannah, Flora, Stela, Antônio, Rosa (all three of them), Antonia, Violeta, João, Bento, Sarah, Uirá, Amélie, José, Nuno, Dora, Clara, Maya, Ali, Nina, León, Tomás, Mai, Tom, Miguel, Letícia, Raduan, Lourenço, Iolanda, Madalena, Lis, Agnes, Livy, Clarice, Mia, Teté . . .

Heirs to what courage we may muster.

CONTENTS

INTRODUCTION

This book originally took shape between September 2019 and February 2022, a two-and-a-half-year period that coincided with the lion's share of Jair Bolsonaro's term as president of Brazil and the COVID-19 pandemic. Its gestation, however, was slightly longer and more complex. The germ of some of the ideas developed here had been with me at least since the 2018 general election, when work on another book prevented me from offering a quick response to the radically new conjuncture.[1] But that reduced capacity to weigh in on the (literally) everyday controversies of the early Bolsonaro years perhaps contributed to making possible a different way of absorbing not just what was happening in Brazil but the historical moment as a whole, and particularly the broader resurgence of the far right across the world. Behind every gesture, speech, and measure of the new government, what interested me most behind each gesture, speech, or measure of the new government was not so much its meaning and intention but the dynamics in which it was embedded. If my more ponderous pace of work at the time made swift interventions harder, the opportunity that it presented, on the other hand, was that of treating Bolsonarismo, the global rise of the far right, and the political polarizations of the last ten or so years as complex, many-sided realities.

Throughout, then, it is as if the object outlined in the initial chapter—Bolsonarismo and the global far right—is expanded laterally and vertically, its synchronic and diachronic, national and international context filled in, singling out the different social and political strands that go into its composition, situating the others with whom it interacts (the left, the liberal "center"), identifying the processes through which these different poles, their identities and strategies, were constituted over time. This approach follows from a methodological wager: that to truly understand such phenomena, we must avoid the temptation to reduce them to a smallest common denominator or a single explanatory scheme. What we must try to do instead is to reproduce in thought the very course of their constitution—one that works through accretion more than through organic growth, that takes place over multiple temporalities endowed with their own rhythms and logics, and that ultimately results in complexes that exist together even though they are not necessarily internally consistent. To do so, this book keeps on coming at these realities from different angles, adding layers and expanding a few chosen elements, gradually building a picture whose complexity can hopefully render justice to that of its subject matter.

The results of this wager are visible in two further decisions that the book makes. One has to do with the naming of its object: I prefer to use the more neutral term *far right* over the stronger alternative, *fascism*. This is not, of course, meant in any way as minimizing the gravity of the threats we are currently facing. My first reason for skirting the fascism conversation concerns my misgivings about what seems too facile an association between the seriousness of the problem and the seriousness of the language. It seems to me that, a lot of the time, this discussion takes place as if a decision on the name automatically afforded a clarity of political vision that I am not convinced it can actually possess. What do we expect to follow from it? A policy of mandatory popular front alliance with the center in order to defeat the main enemy, as in the 1930s? How different would that be from what the left was already doing in most places in the years when the far right was in the ascendant? Or is it the conclusion that all roads but armed resistance are closed—which appears at the time of writing as highly premature? It is not that the name we give things does not matter, but that we should approach the pólemos pragmatically: when it is impossible to obtain consensus around a name, especially around those as sensitive as *fascism* or *genocide*, it may happen that the dispute around the name will end up obfuscating—or worse, becoming a convenient way to evade—the effort to understand the processes to which it refers. More important than agreeing on a name, I believe, is agreeing on the contours of the object, and it is to the latter task, therefore, that I dedicate myself here.

Apart from suspecting that the stakes of the debate are, in fact, lower than is often implied, my other motivation for circumventing it comes from the desire to avoid two complementary dead ends.[2] The more obvious one is the analogical reasoning that compares whatever we have before us with a list of characteristics drawn from the experiences of the 1930s, particularly in Germany and Italy. The poverty of this approach is transparent, as there is no consensus on what precise characteristics constitute the essence of historical fascism, nor on whether they are all equally important, nor on how many of them (and which) a political formation today must display before it can be properly called fascist.[3] More importantly, the impulse to find comparisons with the past often gets in the way of actually looking at what is in front of us right now. The other dead end is an excessively philosophical concept of fascism as "black hole," "cancerous body,"[4] "suicidal state,"[5] "autoimmunitarian paroxysm,"[6] or a social formation that "does not so much self-transform as self-destruct."[7] Here, there is a distinctively circular logic in forging the notion out of a singular example (German National Socialism) and turning its presumably contingent fate (it could have avoided self-destruction had it not lost the war) into a necessity, as if by marching toward total annihilation Hitler and his ilk had done nothing but take to its natural conclusion a destiny inscribed in all similar political processes from the start. The upshot is the idea of an order that is, in some intrinsic and fundamental way, self-undermining and ultimately incapable of normalization and survival. This, I would suggest, denotes a political imagination that predates neoliberalism and the triumph of what Ruth Wilson Gilmore has memorably called the "anti-state state."[8] What the latter demonstrates is the possibility of an order that continues to reproduce itself despite—and to some extent *because* of—its constant self-undermining, for as long as it continues to build up its repressive capacities at the same time as it makes the effectively lethal parts of its "suicide" ever more unevenly distributed.

Once again, this is not to deny that there is something deeply suicidal about the contemporary far right in a context of mounting climate catastrophe and social reproduction crisis. Yet this is less a radical rupture than the creeping social Darwinism of decades of transformation of state, economy, subjectivities, and social relations taken to its logical consequences—and is, in fact, perfectly continuous with the way in which vast numbers of people already experience the world. To put it bluntly, what is suicidal in today's far right comes not from fascism, as some mysterious "outside" of politics, but from neoliberalism, and perhaps we understand the contemporary far right better if we see its ultimate horizon not as an enigmatic strange attractor that drags everything toward ruin but as something rather more prosaic and similar to what we already have.[9] If it is true that it consists in an acceleration of the social disintegration produced by neoliberalism, its goal is not disintegration per se, nor is, therefore, acceleration an end in itself. Even those points that appear to be steps back—such as rhetorically broad but practically very targeted defenses of the national economy or welfare chauvinism—are tactical moves required to attract a social base and fractions of capital more than they are nonnegotiable strategic orientations.[10] The purpose is never really simply to rush forward toward apocalypse or to reverse breakdown; it is rather to ensure that disintegration carries on at a pace that allows it to be managed for private interests, which means going neither so far nor so fast that its present managers will not be able to land on top.[11] Whether that game can indeed be played indefinitely is, of course, a different matter.

A second decision that follows from the effort to do justice to the multiple aspects and temporalities of what we are living through concerns the question of how to relate the resurgence of the far right to the achievements of and potentials for a politics of liberation, especially considering how the former tends to invoke a communist threat that is conspicuous by its absence from our times. Typically, answers to this question vary along two axes: time (whether far-right politics are a reaction to or a preemption of an emancipatory threat) and intensity (whether that threat is revolutionary or reformist, more or less successful, strong or weak). Since what historical fascism referred to as "communism" in the 1920s and 1930s had a much more tangible referent—the Russian Revolution of 1917 and the failed German (1918–19) and Italian (1919–20) attempts that followed it—it is common to see the emergence of figures like Adolf Hitler and Benito Mussolini as a response to the failure that simultaneously tried to solve the crisis of capital by incorporating some demands and mobilization from below. We thus have Antonio Gramsci's characterization of fascism as a form of "passive revolution" and Walter Benjamin's oft-quoted (but apocryphal) assertion that "every rise of fascism bears witness to a failed revolution."[12] In 1970, Nicos Poulantzas would revisit that period to highlight the "failed" part, stressing that the reaction only came after the danger posed by the working class had been extinguished. George Jackson made a similar point around the same time, except he was referring not to the interwar years but to his present; whereas Angela Davis, drawing from her former teacher Herbert Marcuse, preferred to characterize that present as one of "preventive counter-revolution." Reading the debates of the 1970s in light of the phantasmatic nature of today's red scare, finally, Alberto Toscano suggests "preventive counter-reform" as a more adequate way of grasping the feebleness of the actual danger behind current right-wing fears.[13]

Naturally, what is key to all these analyses is the existence and intensity of a challenge to capital at the level of the economic "base" of society. But thinking in such terms risks collapsing the several timelines that converge on our present into a single one, and minimizing the potential of victories that could be too hastily dismissed as merely "superstructural," the intensity with which they are experienced by supporters and opponents alike, and how the reaction to them can be instrumental in shoring up the "base." When the far right mobilizes anxieties around gender and sexual diversity today, it is at once stoking fantasies around "cultural Marxist" plans to undermine the moral foundations of society, instrumentalizing resentment against even the most timid inclusion policies of the last couple of decades, and tapping into phobic reactions to more than seventy years of changes brought about by the sexual revolution. The fact that those changes still meet with resistance today, or that they came about without a radical break with capital and the state, does not make them any less momentous, nor does it mean that conservatives are not correct in feeling that this a fight that they have lost, at least for now, in several parts of the world. Likewise, when the white supremacist nightmare of the "Great Replacement" is mobilized in the United States, it is simultaneously a frightened rejoinder to recent waves of protests that have thus far failed to break the existing racial order, a delayed counteraction against the advances made by the Civil Rights Movement, and a move to simultaneously stop those advances from going any further and, as much as possible, roll them back. Both panics, finally, contribute to entrenching existing class power. In a sense, far-right reactions are always "posthumous and preventive," as Angelo Tasca put it in the 1930s: pushing back against victories that could not be made complete and trying to ensure that they cannot become the basis for subsequent offensives.[14]

Thinking of the problem in these terms also changes how we confront another question, on the relationship between the resurgence of the far right from the middle of the last decade onward and the cycle of struggles, beginning in 2011 with the Arab Spring, that immediately preceded it. Should we see the former as a backlash against the challenge mounted by the latter or as a move to take advantage of its weakness? This allows me to explain something about the scope of this book. While it is possible to see a slow growth of the far right taking place since the late 1990s—with the victories of Viktor Orbán in Hungary (1998) and Lech Kaczyński in Poland (2005), as well as parties like Bharatiya Janata (India), Front National (now Rassemblement National, France), Lega Nord (now only Lega, Italy) and Freedom Party (Austria) gradually increasing their share of the national vote—I believe a qualitative shift did take place in the mid-2010s, with 2016 as the point of inflection. That was the year when what I am calling the *contemporary far right* really entered the scene, and did so with a bang by claiming major upsets in two of the world's most powerful countries: the United Kingdom, with Brexit, and the United States, with Donald Trump. What changed then was not only the speed with which it grew and the resonance that its ideas started to acquire but also the fact that this assault was being led by forces that were in many ways new, fluent in the language of the internet and of younger generations, and oriented more toward emulating and learning from one another than toward attempting to build from the traditions of the past, even in cases in which some lineage could be traced back to postwar neofascism or other such origins.[15]

This change, in turn, strikes me as impossible to separate from the mass protests of the early 2010s, not just in the sense that the material from which both moments draw is the same—the social malaise left in the wake of the 2008 crisis—but also in that one helped pave the way for the other in three significant ways. First, the repression and decline of the Arab Spring, *indignados*, Occupy, and so forth served to reinforce feelings that the dice were loaded, institutions were unresponsive, and the system was incapable of reforming itself; the failure of that early anti-systemic charge bred in many an even stronger anti-systemic sentiment, as well as a certain contempt for the naïveté and politics of the first wave. Second, the social composition of those mobilizations—young, urban, socially progressive—and their diffuse demands for political and economic equality did also stir a negative reaction among sectors of the population that the far right then managed to exploit. Finally, there is no doubt that global and national elites recognized that the defeat of that upsurge left behind a situation that would remain highly volatile, which explains why they would start divesting from their ever less electorally viable centrist representatives and regrouping around the emergent forces of the right.

Yet what these elites saw was not just danger but opportunity. That they had managed to wait out the largest wave of protest in human history, and that things could carry on afterward pretty much as before, exposed something important about the nature of power today: the fact that political systems have become accustomed to running on very low legitimacy, that active consent from populations is no longer an indispensable necessity, and that public opinion and demonstrations on their own are increasingly unlikely to attain the level of strength required to bend governments to their will. (The insouciance with which politicians and media have since ridden roughshod over opposition to the genocide in Gaza is further evidence of that.) This meant that the best defense for those elites was indeed to go on the attack.[16] An economy that cannot include or provide for vast numbers of people, the concentration of economic and political power and the entrenchment of social disparities, a world made increasingly unpredictable and exiguous by climate change, the huge asymmetry of military capacity between state and people—everything appears to conspire in the direction of an "end of mediation" for which increasingly authoritarian forms of rule are naturally the most adequate.[17] It is in light of this double tendency, both defensive and offensive, that the consolidation of the contemporary far right must be read: not so much a last resort as the anticipation of an endgame.

The main questions with which this book grapples are not about the specific sequence of events that led to that consolidation in each country but have to do instead with the conditions in which a social base for the far right could develop and grow. In other words: What explains the far right's appeal? What makes it so attractive to so many people today? The fact that we find the same phenomenon in several parts of the world shows that at least some of these conditions must be very widely shared. Thus, while we may notice relevant differences in the short term—opposition to protective measures against COVID-19 may have cost Trump and Bolsonaro reelection, for example, whereas Alberto Fernández's extremely cautious approach to the pandemic in Argentina helped popularize Javier Milei's libertarianism—looking at processes taking place over longer, slower periods can help reveal more general causes. This is why it is relevant to situate the contemporary far right within the global context opened up by the 2008 financial crisis, which is itself a chapter of a period that began with the rise of neoliberalism in the late 1970s. This, in turn, must be located as an event within the longer history of capital, which, finally, exists within the larger span of the earth's geobiophysical system, the stability of which—and we shall see how this is hardly alien to the problems with which we are dealing—climate change is in the process of putting in check.

My emphasis on the Great Recession does not derive from a simplistic economic determinism that assumes a linear relationship between worsening living conditions and increased social mobilization. Rather, it follows from the realization that, beyond their immediate material effects, the events of over fifteen years ago ushered in a historical moment in which the intensification of some of neoliberalism's most poisonous tendencies coincides with a crisis of legitimacy for neoliberalism—and, by extension, for political systems and parties that remain incapable of calling it into question. It is this broader context that serves to explain why politics worldwide have tended toward the extremes in the last decade, disrupting what had been, since the full consolidation of neoliberal hegemony in the 1990s, its "natural" center of gravity. It also helps us understand the recrudescence of the "culture wars" that accompanied the emergence of figures like Margaret Thatcher and Ronald Reagan in the 1980s and that are in most places today mobilized by the far right to defend an even more extreme form of privatization of risks and suspension of social protections against the "progressive" or "normative" neoliberalism—to borrow the labels advanced by Nancy Fraser and Will Davies, respectively—that was dominant from the 1990s until 2008.[18]

The crisis of legitimacy of neoliberalism has both a symbolic and a material aspect. The symbolic aspect stems from the way in which state response to the financial collapse, which protected those who caused it and transferred the costs of the economic rescue to people at large, exposed the convertibility of economic into political power that makes the promises of a strictly meritocratic and self-regulating order inevitably false. Contrary to what the German ordoliberal Wilhelm Röpke claimed, inequality is not, in the end, the same for everyone. But the other thing that 2008 exposed was the void beneath the feet of the global economic system. If the financialization introduced from the 1970s onward was an attempt to sustain the profits of capital and the consent of the population in a scenario in which the postwar expansion was beginning to run out of steam, what the debacle at the end of the last decade has shown is that not only does the underlying problem remain unresolved, but the latest solution found to "buy time" has generated its own set of dangers.[19] On the one hand, the global economy's growth rate has been falling continuously for five decades. On the other, since the second half of the 1990s we have witnessed what Robert Brenner calls the "extraordinary spectacle of a world economy in which the continuation of capital accumulation has come *literally* to depend upon historic waves of speculation," financed by the supply of cheap credit that has simultaneously buried families and corporations in debt and made the global system much more prone to crises.[20] If they did not destroy faith in this arrangement altogether, the revelation of this fragility, the lack of an alternative recipe to put in its place, and the increase in underemployment and precariousness that came with the postrecession recovery have both made promises of future prosperity less credible and demonstrated how easily they can be rescinded. (Just remember that, in the United States alone, over six million families who had been lured into the speculative property bubble by the mirage of home ownership faced foreclosure filings between 2007 and 2010.)[21]

This crisis of legitimacy, however, does not necessarily imply a retreat from neoliberalism. On the contrary, the austerity of the last decade represented its intensification, and the fiscal expansionism instigated by the COVID-19 pandemic—itself foreshadowed by the trillions injected in the banking sector through quantitative easing—has not really represented a change of direction.[22] This is partly explained by the relative mismatch between political institutions and society. Given that the crisis of legitimacy has not translated into a sufficiently strong challenge to the ascendancy of financial and corporate capital, the latter continue to be able to impose their will on the population, and it is precisely because they have seen their power waver, but not fall, that they are now using it to step on the accelerator instead of the brake. But there is another mismatch that goes on within society itself or, rather, within each individual: The symbolic and material shock to the authority of neoliberalism is partially canceled out by neoliberal hegemony in the field of affects—and attention to this affective dimension of social life is another constant in this book.

What I am referring to is the dimension constituted by the effects that the experiences individuals go through have on their pleasures, displeasures, and desires, establishing, over time, loves, hates, fears, hopes, objects of repulsion and admiration, and so forth. To the extent that affects are the product of interactions, and interactions are always conditioned (and to a certain extent fixed and standardized) by the material arrangements that determine our place in the world, as well as by institutions such as the family, the police, and wage labor, the affective is never simply private: It is always social. This does not mean, however, that affect should be treated as a raw, immediate fact. In reality, affect is always in a circular relationship with the systems (again, never merely individual) through which we interpret and justify what happens to us. The regularity of our experiences produces affects that consolidate evaluative schemes, but these evaluative schemes can continue to operate even when elements of lived experience begin to contradict them—and the mass of disinformation available today can certainly help alleviate cognitive dissonance as that contradiction mounts.

It is this inertial force of habit that explains the mismatch mentioned above. Ours is a time in which coexist, side by side, a widespread feeling that, for various reasons, things cannot continue as they are (and that, if they do, it is simply because those who benefit from them have sufficient power to impose their will on everyone else); and the sentiment that things could not be otherwise, sustained by the extent to which the way we live, relate to one another, and understand ourselves is intimately constituted by mechanisms such as consumption, individualism, competition, discipline, and the "entrepreneurship of oneself." If contemporary capitalism's promises of a good life seem increasingly suspect, our "passional servitude" to the current state of affairs remains deeply rooted—even among those who consciously oppose it.[23]

This conflict produces monsters, such as denialism (in the sense I give to the word in chapters 1 and 2), the casual nihilism of the troll (chapter 4), and the proliferation of scams and con tricks characteristic of the "political entrepreneurship" that has marked the rise of the far right (chapter 3) and increasingly ubiquitous in contemporary culture. In fact, if we were to reduce the two paths opening up from the current conjuncture to simple formulas, we could say that, while the left would have to propose an alternative game to the one that has been exhausted, the far right simply has to assume that, when competition becomes more and more a matter of life and death, getting rid of other competitors becomes a valid option. In short:

Don't hate the player, hate the game versus *Don't hate the game, hate the other players.*

Some further consequences that follow from the choice to pay attention to the affective dimension permeate this book. To begin with, the emphasis on the necessity of a certain perspectivism for politics. If affectivity constitutes us as individuals endowed with habits and dispositions that are both unique (because they belong to our singular experience) and widely shared (with those whose living conditions are similar to ours), it is to be expected that the political space will not look the same depending on where one is looking from. This means that ideas, practices, slogans, and public figures can appear in different ways to different people, and understanding the system of these variations is essential to knowing how to move between different points of view. This is a crucial element in understanding Bolsonarismo (chapter 1), and even more so political polarization (chapter 4 and 5), which involves the tendency of different perspectives to organize themselves increasingly in opposition to one another. It is also one of the reasons why the concept of "affective infrastructure" matters (excursus 2). Two corollaries of this approach, which appear in more than one analysis proposed here, are the fundamentally comparative aspect of class experience and the distinction between programmatic and identitarian radicalization.

The first of these points refers to the fact that the comparisons people make—between their current living conditions and their previous situation, and between their expected position and that of those in their immediate vicinity—are decisive for how they identify their interests and respond politically to different scenarios. This is what explains why protests such as those Brazil saw in 2013 can occur not because things have gotten worse but because expectations have risen; why even groups whose lives have improved can feel worse off if others around them appear to have benefited more (chapter 3); and why the far right's maneuver of associating the losses that many have accumulated with the small relative gains made by historically marginalized groups can be so efficient (chapters 1 and 5).

The second point, in turn, draws attention to the risk of confusing adhesion to left-wing principles and values with observance of a set of external markers that make up an identity: linguistic codes, aesthetic preferences, objects of love and hate. However fluid the boundary between those two things may be, the ability to differentiate between them is important for reasons that are touched upon in different ways in chapters 4, 5, and 6. One is that, by making it possible to identify situations in which the obstacles to communication are more at the level of associative thinking and prejudices than of content, this ability helps both avoid the form in which a message is communicated from preventing it from reaching its recipients and discover possibilities for dialogue and convergence even when our interlocutors do not speak exactly the same language as we do. Another is that it reveals the error, very common on the left, of treating political identities as fully constituted packages, such that, from a difference in vocabulary or taste, it would be immediately possible to infer a complete set of beliefs and convictions. As I suggest in chapter 1, it is important to distinguish between degrees of support for the far right; and as chapter 5 puts it, only those who see political orientation as a central element to their own identity tend to expect all their positions to be consistent with one another. Most people, for whom politics are less relevant, tend to be less consistent, which is exactly why their ideas and attitudes may contain contradictions that can be exploited.

Finally, discerning between the two different types of radicalization helps us see that often the excessive emphasis that is placed on political identity is a way of compensating for either a lack of capacity to effectively influence a conjuncture or the lack of a program that differs substantively from the status quo. In the second case, we have the liberal capture of so-called identitarian agendas by a "progressive neoliberalism" that is all the more strident in extolling the moral virtues of its politics of recognition the less it has to propose from the point of view of redistribution. In the first, we have the capture of desires for transformation by a "communicative capitalism"[24] that tends to make the public expression of individuality—built on a series of belongings—into a substitute for political action: *Participating* is equivalent to *being seen participating* in the media and social networks (chapter 4). Both are easily recognizable aspects of our present.

To be clear, opposing "program" to "identity" does not imply an incoherent return to a rationalism according to which it would be enough to present a set of convincing proposals in order to win people over. (On the contrary, pointing out the way in which affectivity conditions the reception of messages serves precisely to prevent persuasion from being conceived as a simple matter of reasoning.) The issue here is, rather, twofold. On the one hand, an identity has little appeal, or even a negative one, for those who do not already see themselves in it. If what is at stake is attracting those who do not share it, what needs to be offered is not the symbolic comfort of belonging but ideas that actually make sense to people; that is, that offer them the plausible prospect of a better life, as well as the desire (and some sense of the means) to achieve it. That is what "program" represents in this context. On the other hand, what counts as plausible cannot be measured solely against what people are already willing to consider as such but must also take reality into account, and what reality demands today cannot but seem "extreme" compared with the political and economic arrangements that we currently have. This is what "radicalization" refers to, and it is in this sense that a "programmatic radicalization" appears as the means for exploring the conflict between the crisis of legitimacy of neoliberalism and continued affective adhesion to it.

Here we find what are, perhaps, the two main recurring themes of this book. The first is the one that identifies the most important mismatch of our time as that between a consensus established three decades ago on what is "realistic" to defend and a profoundly transformed reality. Hence the refusal to accept the game that pits the "realist" against the "utopian" in order, instead, to reclaim realpolitik itself: Faced with environmental collapse and the concentration of economic and political power that we have today, *it is the realism of thirty years ago that has become unreal*, and what once seemed absurd often contains a grain of reason. This applies even to the far right: As I sometimes point out in the course of the book, there is a sense in which it can be said to be more of a rational reaction to the current state of affairs than the belief that everything could simply continue as before. After all, it at least implicitly assumes the ever-increasing costs of keeping things in their place and prepares its followers for an ever-bloodier fight of all against all.

If being a realist today necessarily means setting oneself ambitious goals, the second major theme of this book is the rejection of an alternative between operating within the limits of what is possible and acting in conformity with that ambition. It is true that not everything is possible at any given time. However, this is only valid as an argument against boldness if we forget that politics is first and foremost a dispute to define the limits of what is possible, and that doing what can be done now does not have to be an excuse but must rather be a *means* of getting closer to what we are not yet capable of doing. The last fifteen years have been a period in which the unthinkable has not stopped happening, and the far right has understood better than anyone else how to use the many crises of the present to bring the unspeakable to the center of public debate and make the inconceivable commonplace. Dealing with it, and with the even worse barbarism that lies ahead if we just let things continue their current course, will require unrivaled effort and the capacity to ensure that realism about what is possible is increasingly aligned with realism about what is real—that is, necessary.

THE POINT OF VIEW OF THE PERIPHERY

Attempts to make generalizations from what happens in the United States and Europe to the rest of the planet do not, as a rule, meet with much surprise; these are, after all, generally assumed to be the most advanced edges of world history, where processes that will eventually spread to other regions first take hold. Most of the literature on the lethal danger surrounding democracies that has flourished in the last decade implicitly assumes these central countries as the normative standard from which others—and increasingly themselves—can be measured as deviations. Starting from a place like Brazil, on the other hand, does not enjoy the same air of self-evidence and seems to require some explaining. Countries on the periphery are supposed to be somehow quirky and unique, partaking in what is universal only through the ways in which they have caught up with their developed counterparts, and otherwise assumed to be locked in a particularity that prevents them from offering anything generalizable. The irony, in this case, is that a tradition within Brazilian social thought has for some time elaborated an argument not only as to why that is not true but that those may, in fact, be precisely the places from where to start.

After the defeat of historical fascism in the Second World War, the division of the world into two competing geopolitical blocs pushed both sides to work on their sales pitch to those countries that had hitherto lain in the margins of the global market. Whereas the Soviet bloc offered the international comradeship of the exploited and the imminence of world revolution, its capitalist rivals held up the promise that, if they stayed the free market course, all nations could one day attain the same level of material well-being that the richest countries enjoyed. This prospect was at the center of the different approaches that became collectively known from the 1950s onward as "modernization theory."

Almost immediately, a loose group of thinkers from Latin America and Africa began to build a critique of it.[1] Development was not a race, they argued, in which each country had their own lane to run down and could reach the finishing line regardless of when they began, but rather more like chess, the position of each piece conditioning the moves available to all others. This gave the first countries to set out on the capitalist road a first-mover advantage: While their own early takeoff had been made possible by colonialism and slavery (and the access to cheap labor and nature that these afforded), the integration of former colonies into the global market had been based on unequal exchange from the start, subordinating whatever development they could have to the needs and interests of development taking place elsewhere. The fact that one could speak of a center and a periphery within capitalism was, therefore, no mere factual, transient contingency. Not only had the constitution of the subordinate pole been the exact same process through which the dominant one established itself, but the fact that the former could only grow within terms dictated by the growth of the latter meant that, even as the periphery progressed, the very relation of dependency reproduced itself. This entailed that the development of the periphery could only ever be "dependent," "limited," or "underdeveloped."

That was not all. The assumption that modernization in all spheres of life—political institutions, labor relations, culture—would follow naturally from economic progress was simply not true. As Francisco de Oliveira's classic text from the early 1970s put it, in a place like Brazil, "capitalist expansion takes place . . . through the introduction of new relations in the archaic and the reproduction of the archaic in the new": "a symbiosis and organicity, a unity of contraries, in which the 'modern' thrives and feeds off the 'backward,' if we still wish to retain those terms."[2] Thus, for example, in the country's mushrooming urban centers, it was the spread of self-built informal settlements ("favelization") and the offer of cheap services like domestic work (itself a legacy of slavery) that, compensating for insufficient accumulation and infrastructure, enabled the high pace of industrialization observed from the 1930s to the 1960s.[3]

But this dialectical twist on the dialectics of the modern and the archaic had a further twist in store. By the late 1980s, it was modernization tout court, not only in the postcolonial world, that was coming to seem a mirage. In capitalism's very core, rights and institutions that had been thought to be everlasting achievements were being rolled back; from that point on, it would be ever clearer that astonishing material advancement could exist side by side with levels of exploitation and inequality until recently deemed to be part of the past. Economic growth was no longer a guarantee of any of the things that were supposed to come with it—including, increasingly, democracy. What if what had been mistaken as the inevitable march of progress, the direction toward which the arc of history bent, had in fact only been a blip produced by three decades of uninterrupted expansion after the war—and what the future had in store was, in fact, as some had begun to predict, a progressive "Brazilianization" of the world?[4]

If that were so, a group of Brazilian thinkers concluded, it was no longer just the case that the periphery was a space forever destined to be stuck between the future and the past. In its permanent, uneasy but organic, functionally dysfunctional amalgamation of the modern and the archaic, the developed and the under- or de-developed, it was, and had indeed always been, the future. "[A]t the historical hour when the country of the future [Brazil] seems to no longer have any future," Paulo Arantes wrote, "we are singled out, for better or worse, as the future of the world."[5] Not, and this was crucial, in the simple sense that the once modern core was backsliding, but rather in that, having been a society overpoweringly determined from the outset by the dictates of economic reason (its constitution as a locus of production for the nascent world system), Brazil foreshadowed a world in which brute exploitation became the ever more dominant social logic. "We are once again in the vanguard, except now of disintegration."[6]

This "Brazilianization" (or, in more general terms, peripheralization) thesis states, in a nutshell, that "*the world's horizon of expectation* is no longer informed by the center, but by the peripheries."[7] That is, both by the peripherical areas that proliferate in the metropolises of a "planet of slums"[8] and by the former colonies that have from birth been "perfect laboratories for new forms of capitalist exploitation integrating authoritarian control of surplus populations, the management of unresolvable social conflicts and a new police state compatible with parliamentary democracy."[9] (Gaza being, of course, the most extreme form yet experienced of such laboratories.) What this suggests is that the likes of Brazil, Argentina, El Salvador, and so on may actually help us see more clearly the direction in which the contemporary far right points than can places like the United States and Western Europe, whose still relatively dominant position in the international division of labor allows for promises of national redemption that dull and disguise the features of what is likely to come: the privately managed breakdown of a world beset by climate collapse, the rampant growth of inequality and superfluous populations, and the proliferation of protected enclaves, sacrificial zones, and areas of contested sovereignty at both the supra- and the infranational level.

CHAPTER 1

OF WHAT IS BOLSONARO THE NAME?

> [O]ne might refer to the fascist movements as the wounds, the scars, of a democracy that, to this day, has not lived up to its own concept.
>
> —**Theodor Adorno**, *Aspects of the New Right-Wing Extremism*

WHAT'S IN A NAME?

Let us begin with a lesson that can be universally applied: It is essential to distinguish between electoral support and social base. Not everyone who votes for the far right necessarily identifies completely with the far right—*though they may come to.* Stopping them from doing so is, in fact, one of the key reasons why it is both analytically and politically important to make that distinction.

To speak of *Bolsonarismo*, then, is not the same as speaking of Bolsonaro voters. Evidently, whatever we can call Bolsonarismo must have been a factor in Jair Bolsonaro's election in November 2018, but the former army captain's victory was overdetermined in all sorts of ways, and the electoral coalition that brought him to power was broader than any phenomenon we can accurately describe with that name.

But here is another lesson that can be generalized. Smaller than Bolsonaro's actual or potential electorate, Bolsonarismo is at the same time bigger than Bolsonaro himself, neither created by nor solely dependent on the individual from whom it borrows its name. (The names *Trump* and *MAGA* increasingly capture the same distinction in the context of the United States.) This means that the link between "leader" and "movement" is synthetic rather than analytic, and its strength hinges not on some essential bond but on the contingent fact that, having found himself at the crest of a groundswell at a critical time, Bolsonaro ended up with more power to shape it than anyone else. In short, Bolsonarismo is a real convergence of different trends in Brazilian society, with the potential to consolidate itself as a major force for quite some time, but the arrangement of political forces that expresses it is neither coherent nor necessarily stable. In fact, one of its key sources of instability is precisely Bolsonaro and his sons, owing to their divisiveness, shady connections, and constant attacks on potential challengers to their control over this political capital.

Bolsonarista thus refers to a social segment that acquired an explicit political orientation in the last ten years or so through an interactive relation with leaders like Bolsonaro, even if the fact that the latter came to dominate that segment is itself contingent. How big is it? Considering Bolsonaro's approval ratings never dropped much below 30 percent, it could be estimated at the very least as the solid, unwavering half of that percentage; that was the calculation proposed by statistician Reginaldo Prandi at the end of June 2020.[1] Despite totaling less than one-sixth of the adult population, this group would still have a disproportionate political weight by virtue of the high electoral floor that it offers, its commitment, and its permanent engagement. Though composed of atomized individuals not organized in any major political structures, but rather mobilized mostly through social media, it is a vocal, militant core from which the gravitational pull of the far right radiates to the rest of Brazilian society. Yet Bolsonaro's performance in the 2022 elections, when he consistently outdid the polls' predictions, and the results of research conducted in 2025 suggest that this number may be higher.[2] It would, of course, be a huge mistake to expect it to remain constant: However much of a fluke the election of figures like Jair Bolsonaro, Donald Trump, and Javier Milei may have been at first, the tendency over time is for the identification with them to consolidate and intensify, and for its power of attraction to grow and bring more people into its orbit. The distinction between electoral support and social base matters precisely to the extent that it allows one to devise strategies to minimize contagion between the latter and the former.

Insisting on a contingent, synthetic link between Bolsonaro and Bolsonarismo might beg the question of why call the latter by the former's name. But following Ernesto Laclau's remarks on naming as retroactively constitutive of its object, we could turn the question on its head and reply that it is exactly that contingency that justifies this choice.[3] Not, of course, that Bolsonarismo emerged fully formed the moment the name was uttered. For polemical and ontological reasons, Laclau tends to exaggerate the passivity of things and the spontaneity of leaders, minimizing the horizontal ties that pull people together in favor of a shared vertical bond with the figurehead or the empty signifier. The truth tends to be more prosaic: Instead of naming as the foundational act that inaugurates a linear causal chain, what occurs is a feedback process through which people begin to gravitate toward one another and represent themselves as doing so until one or more representations "stick." While the political operation "at the top" was essential to giving it shape, Bolsonarismo should be seen as the coming together, under the aegis of the political factions that coalesced around Bolsonaro's campaign, of social trends that had for some time been imbued with a certain mutual tropism, and in that campaign encountered for the first time a common identity and a shared leadership. And while they are certainly far from constituting a consistent theory or worldview, they have a lot of common ground to connect them.

Most accounts of Bolsonaro's rise to power tend to remain at the more superficial level of the sequence of events that led to his triumph. While it can enrich our understanding of the political decisions that produced Bolsonarismo, this approach is insufficient when it comes to identifying the deeper social shifts that were precipitated by these decisions and also made them possible. A comprehensive look at Bolsonarismo must work on more than one time scale and take into consideration at least four different levels of analysis: the different *discursive matrices* that came together in its formation; the *common grammars* that ensured these matrices' communication and mutual compatibility; the *affective conditions* or collective moods that gave them something to latch on to; and the *organizational infrastructure*—encompassing churches, radio and TV shows, YouTube influencers, WhatsApp groups, click farms, social media bots, etc.—that they rely on. This chapter will focus primarily on the first two, with a nod to the third, while the following excursus will touch upon the last. My goal here will be twofold. First, to present Bolsonarismo as a phenomenon that can take on different meanings depending on the position that one occupies within it; second, to highlight what is generalizable in this story. To the extent that similar conditions can be found elsewhere, that of which Bolsonaro is the name is in no way a uniquely Brazilian phenomenon.

ELECTIVE AFFINITIES?

What, then, are the elements that went into the composition of Bolsonarismo? Sociologist Gabriel Feltran provides a useful starting point by listing three discursive matrices he calls "police militarism" (support for law-and-order policies and the extrajudicial use of force), "Evangelical anti-intellectualism" (rejection of science and formal education in favor of religion and personal experience), and "entrepreneurial monetarism" (an "entrepreneur of oneself" ethos for which precarity equals autonomy).[4] This is doubly useful, as it not only pinpoints long-term tendencies that Feltran has identified in his fieldwork on the periphery of São Paulo but does so by resorting to the concept that Eder Sader advanced in his analysis of the early 1980s' "social movement boom" out of which the Workers' Party (PT) emerged.[5] The same caveat raised earlier about Laclau applies here: To speak of discursive matrices is not to claim some fundamental priority for language over embodiment or affectivity but to propose that we understand the two spheres as being in a circular, reciprocal relation. Language has the power to give names to things that are already vaguely sensed in everyday experience and resonates to the extent that it does so; in so doing, however, it renders that experience communicable, enhances its publicness, and reframes sensibilities accordingly.[6] Discursive matrices should therefore be considered as generative not only of statements but of affective structures (likes and dislikes, hates and loves, objects of admiration and repulsion; what Spinoza would call *ingenia*), identification and belonging, ways of understanding and narrating oneself—all the latent conditions for what may or may not develop into fully conscious, mobilized political subjectivity.

Yet Feltran's conclusions, valuable as they are for showing the fertile ground Bolsonarismo has found among the poor, are needlessly constrained by the way he generalizes (or fails to generalize from) his ethnographic findings. As he himself recognizes, anti-intellectualism is not exclusive to the evangelical population and is just as visible among the predominantly Catholic upper class. As for militarism and entrepreneurialism, though they are each a single matrix shared by rich and poor, they take on such different connotations depending on class and racialization as to result in very distinct subjective positions: It is not because people are using the same words that they are saying the same thing. In short, Feltran's observational bias puts him at risk of (correctly) countering the idea that

Bolsonarismo is merely "a mobilisation of the elites against the poor" with the (incorrect) suggestion that "sectors of finance, agribusiness, religious and rural elites" joined this "totalitarian movement" late in the game, "possibly without realising what they were doing."[7]

A formulation like this misses three crucial things about Bolsonarismo. First, its character as a cross-class alliance around a few common identitarian and political reference points that have, until now, far outweighed the contradictions among the divergent interests that it brings together. Second, the fact that what makes this balancing act possible is both the pervasiveness of certain discursive matrices and their having enough grammar in common as to be compatible with one another. Thus, although there may be an upper- and a lower-class militarism or anti-intellectualism, the two sides can still understand and identify with one another, especially when set against what they oppose (criminality, drug use, unbridled sexuality, leniency with "marginals" of all kinds, leftist indoctrination, etc.). This means, third, that we should not speak as if there were a preexisting movement to which some groups latched on to in 2018 but rather think of what happened as the confluence of different vectors, "from above" as well as "from below," that already had much in common. The wealthiest 10 percent of the electorate was in fact the first sector Bolsonaro won over, very early on, in 2018; and if the Brazilian 1 percent did not have him as their first choice, they had no qualms about embracing him when it became clear he could win. To sum up, Bolsonarismo is a cross-class project held together at the top by politics and at the base by strong elective affinities. Although the points of convergence and the exact class composition will inevitably vary from place to place, this is another point we can extrapolate to the far right elsewhere.

This means that we can distinguish three different types among the discursive matrices that compose the far right. There are those that are restricted to a particular class or group; those that are widely shared but whose meaning remains constant across groups or classes; and those that are shared but take on different meanings depending on one's position in the social structure. As we have seen, anti-intellectualism, militarism, and entrepreneurialism all cut across strata, but the latter two belong to the third type.[8]

In what regards militarism, the difference is obvious. For those living in dangerous areas, the hankering for unrestrained state violence supposes a clear demarcation between the "working people" and the "criminals" in the neighborhood, with some collateral casualties in between. For those in well-off areas, on the other hand, policing is about protecting them from the poor, making the gray zone of potentially disposable life much larger. As for entrepreneurialism, whereas for the rich it often acts as a meritocratic narrative disguising inequality of opportunities, among the poor and much of the middle class it is more akin to what Verónica Gago has called "neoliberalism from below." This ambivalent dynamic, through which individuals engaged in inventing strategies of survival in an environment reconfigured by neoliberal policies come to understand themselves according to "the logic of the microentrepreneur," is in fact a major factor in the sea change that Latin American politics has seen in recent years.[9] Largely unchallenged and often encouraged by the progressive governments in the region, this "mass self-entrepreneurship"[10] was effectively reinforced by the growth of informality and indebtedness during the Pink Tide years, making neoliberalism even more "anchored in territories, strengthened in popular subjectivities . . . expanding and proliferating within popular economies."[11] Phenomena like Bolsonaro in Brazil and Milei in Argentina are partially understandable as the encounter between a radicalized version of the 1990s "neoliberalism from above" and a neoliberalism from below that flourished during the neodevelopmentalist interlude of the first decade of this century, which continued to pose the market as the primary arena for the pursuit of recognition and material satisfaction. As Rosana Pinheiro-Machado and Lucia Scalco show, the empowerment produced by PT's "inclusion through consumption" was so imbricated with the capacity to buy things that, once the economic downturn took that capacity away, many of "the very citizens that had symbolized Brazil's rise" under PT readily shifted allegiance from Luiz Inácio Lula da Silva to Jair Bolsonaro.[12]

Not only does Bolsonarismo openly espouse entrepreneurialism, it is an entrepreneurial phenomenon in its own right—another way in which, as we shall discuss in the fourth chapter, it is paradigmatic of the contemporary far right. The quintessential Bolsonarista is neither rich nor poor but a member of a downwardly mobile "lower upper middle class" (to borrow George Orwell's turn of phrase) among which "failed businessman" is perhaps the most common occupation. Extremely sensitive to negative fluctuations in the economy, they are by that same token especially prone to a politics of resentment that blames others for their frustrated expectations. Since 2014, many have followed a career path that went from becoming a right-wing influencer on social media to going into politics. Eighty-five percent of the senators and 47 percent of federal representatives elected in 2018 were first-timers, most of them successfully riding on Bolsonaro's "outsider" discourse—which was effective even though the former army captain had been a congressman since 1991. Among these were twenty-two policemen or members of the military, a retired porn actor, and an heir to the Brazilian royal family.

CONSTRUCTING THE UPSTANDING CITIZEN

Despite being more socially circumscribed, two other matrices play an important role in establishing narrative connections among the others: economic libertarianism and anticommunism. Whereas anti-intellectualism, militarism, and entrepreneurialism developed in parallel across social strata, in these two the direction of diffusion is more clearly flowing from the upper classes to the poor. Besides, their propagation is more obviously the result of coordinated action.

The seeds of the staggering resurgence of anticommunism in Brazil started being sown during PT's first term in power. At a time when the economy was booming and most people's material standards were improving, red scares manufactured with the aid of the media were among the few weapons in the opposition's armor. The contrast between these and the embracing of Lula by the international establishment produced a cognitive dissonance that conspiracy theories about a global leftist plot would subsequently help solve. It was the social media–fueled spread of the latter that operated the shift from Cold War discourse as a tool in parliamentary struggle to anticommunism as an overarching geopolitical narrative pitting Trump and Bolsonaro as the Asterix and Obelix of the struggle against "cultural Marxism-driven economic globalization."[13] The very fact that no concrete threat existed made this discourse only more efficient, as its "abstractness" meant that "anything that somehow [did] not fit [could be] subsumed under [an] all-purpose term" like "communism" or "globalism."[14]

While market libertarianism is in one sense merely the theoretical counterpart to entrepreneurialism, it merits independent consideration because of its importance as a rallying point for a young, university-educated middle class that played a protagonist role in the events leading to Bolsonaro's election. This too was a process that began shortly after PT came to power, the creation of Instituto Millenium in 2005 being a major landmark. Backed by some of the most powerful financial, industrial, and media groups in the country, this think tank worked to popularize ultraliberal ideas and, alongside players like Instituto Mises Brasil (founded in 2007), contributed to a veritable editorial boom in the field. (A boom in conservative literature was happening around the same time.) This created the environment in which young, media-savvy libertarian activists started to organize, drawing on grants from international funders like the Cato Institute.[15] The most important of these groups, the Students for Liberty–trained Movimento Brasil Livre (Free Brazil Movement, or MBL), emerged in

2014 as the right-wing answer to Movimento Passe Livre (Free Fare Movement, or MPL), which kick-started the June 2013 protests that, initially against a raise in bus fares, grew to question the government's commitment to social justice and severely damaged its popularity. Two years later, MBL was key to organizing the marches calling for the impeachment of Lula's successor, Dilma Rousseff; in 2018, it elected seven members of congress.

At first, this sector's selling point was the cosmopolitan, socially liberal attitude that set them apart from the traditional right: "Liberal in economics and in social mores" was how its proponents described themselves. As power beckoned, however, they increasingly converged with social conservatives, not only finding areas of cooperation but adopting some of the same discourses and tactics. Conversely, their newfound clout was one of the factors that pulled Bolsonaro, whose economic views had previously appeared to lean statist, toward an ultraliberal agenda. Despite the former army captain's unequivocal authoritarian tendencies, they continued to support him with varying degrees of enthusiasm, invoking a distinction between the government's "technical" (economic) and "ideological" areas as an excuse. With their progressive incorporation of a "culture war" agenda and the traditional right's increasingly radicalized neoliberalism, the two have become less and less distinct, which may explain why the new right lost ground to more established forces: In the 2022 elections, the number of MBL congressmen fell to two.

The most widely shared of Bolsonarismo's discursive matrices, anticorruption discourse, illustrates the power of libertarianism and anticommunism in tying

Bolsonarismo's different strands together. In Brazil, corruption has long worked in the public imaginary as a sort of metaproblem, the magical cause that, once eliminated, would cure all other ills. In this account, the weight of structural constraints and differences in political orientation are entirely disregarded in favor of a voluntaristic, individualized vision of politics: The country would be prosperous and there would be money for everything if only there were honest individuals in charge.

Although Brazilian elites have used anticorruption rhetoric to destabilize progressive governments in the past, until not long ago it was widely understood that misappropriation of public funds was endemic to the political profession. Having usually been far from positions of power, left-wing parties were, if anything, deemed more trustworthy. Yet the vast institutional sleaze uncovered in 2014 by the now-infamous Operation Car Wash that eventually led to Lula's imprisonment presented libertarians and anticommunists with a unique opportunity to promote a new narrative.[16] It combined a Hayekian mistrust of social justice as "[amounting] simply to the protection of entrenched interests" with the notion that the left's universal modus operandi is to buy off interest groups, such as minorities and artists, in order to install corrupt totalitarian regimes.[17] The sheer size of the schemes Operation Car Wash revealed thus functioned as evidence not of PT's definitive integration into the country's political elite but of how far it had advanced in its plan to "turn Brazil into Venezuela"—exactly as the right had been warning it would for a decade.

It helped that one of the largest corruption scandals in the country's history unfolded in parallel with one of its worst economic crises ever, indelibly connecting the two in most people's minds. If there was a recession, the thought went, this was not due to bad economic policy or a global slump but to an unprecedentedly large attack on the state's kitty. It became easier on this basis to cement the association between left-wing governments, sleaze, and economic inefficiency, even though the scandal actually involved all mainstream parties. The political advantages of this account were obvious. In one fell swoop, it turned what was deemed to be a universal, endemic problem into a particularly left-wing vice; it painted even PT's cautious reformism as part of a communist threat, making anything but the most promarket libertarianism potentially suspicious; it legitimized opposition to progressive policies by reframing it as resistance against a slide toward tyranny; and it nurtured a feeling of imminent danger that created the demand for urgent, radical action.

The final element in the Bolsonarista constellation is another discursive matrix that plays an important role in tying together the rest: social conservatism. Like anticommunism, it came from the fringes of the political spectrum and was progressively mainstreamed by politicians and media vehicles interested in denting PT's popularity. Unlike anticommunism or market libertarianism, it did not spread downward but was already well established across all classes. Spurred by the advances made by women and the LGBTQIA+ community under PT, on the one hand, and by fabricated moral panics, on the other, it too relied on a sense of urgent threat to expand and mobilize. Growing steadily over the Lula years, the defense of "family values" first proved to be a force to be reckoned with the "gay kit" episode in 2011, in which the PT government quickly ceded to the religious right's disinformation campaign against a proposed sexual education program.[18] By 2016 it was so strong that many invoked it as a reason to support the impeachment of Rousseff, one congressman in particular claiming to be acting against "programmes that aim to make children change sex and learn sex at school." Needless to say, no such programs existed.

As Isabela Kalil has noted, Bolsonarismo's greatest achievement was to make all these different elements—militarism, anti-intellectualism, entrepreneurialism, anticommunism, market libertarianism, anticorruption discourse, social conservatism—converge around a single figure, the "upstanding citizen" (*cidadão de bem*).[19] If there is an empty signifier that represents the Bolsonarista base to itself, it is that.[20] On the other side of the antagonistic frontier, the concept of *mamata* (from *mamar*, to suckle) does the same work when it comes to identifying the enemy. Meaning "easy life" or "undue advantage," *mamata* can apply to anything from perceived leniency with criminals to the exorbitant salaries of politicians and the judiciary; from labor rights to the supposedly charmed existence of artists and academics; from the job stability of civil servants to sexual freedom and the questioning of traditional gender roles; and from the misuse of public funds to affirmative action at universities. Its capacity to establish equivalences between basic rights and elite privileges, and to present the former in terms of the latter, is key to building the class alliance on which Bolsonarismo depends. Its constitution of a continuum between private and public morality allows it to be the *point de capiton* that makes changes in societal attitudes resonate with rising crime rates, corruption, progressive social policy, and even contemporary art as gathering evidence of a single process of moral decadence that it behooves the upstanding citizenry to stop.[21]

It bears repeating that, although these discursive matrices overlap at various points, not every Bolsonarista (let alone Bolsonaro voter) subscribes to all of them with the same intensity, or at all. Not only are there inconsistencies among them, but none of them is fully consistent either. This matters little, as the power of the metanarratives that establish their connection lies in association more than logic, and coherence derives less from any actual content than from the feeling of being on the same side in a struggle.[22] Whether one believes or not in all that is said about the enemy is less important than believing that there is an enemy and it must be defeated. And precisely, what these metanarratives promise is more than just certainty amid change and sensory overload. The perception of imminent existential threat that they cultivate intensifies subjective commitment, presents their adherents in a heroic light, and frames politics as a fight to the death in which all means are justified in advance.

ON RACE, GENDER, RELIGION, AND NATION

Why not include racism among the various discursive and behavioral matrices that compose Bolsonarismo? This is a question that I have been asked a few times. The connections between historical fascism, colonialism, and racism have, after all, long been explored by thinkers of the African diaspora, such as Aimé Césaire and W. E. B. Du Bois.[23] More recently, Alberto Toscano has observed that racial fear is often an essential mediator in gaining popular support for a political project aimed at reducing all state capacities apart from those that have to do with repression.[24] Bolsonaro himself, a descendant of Italian settlers, is no stranger to making casual racist remarks and railing against the excesses of "political correctness"; more importantly, racism is unsurprisingly widespread among his supporters, especially in the Brazilian South and Southeast, and along the extractive frontier of the North and Midwest.

The answer hinges on what I perceive to be a difference between the Brazilian case and that of places like India, Germany (and other European countries), and the United States. In India—the closest equivalent to German National Socialism among the contemporary far right—race plays a central role in building political cohesion: The construction of a Hindu nation at the exclusion of Muslim and other minorities is the avowed goal of Narendra Modi and the Sangh Parivar, the group of organizations that includes the ruling Bharatiya Janata Party. In Europe, antimigrant sentiment has long been not only key to the right's electoral success but a major way in which far-right talking points have been mainstreamed, including by the center left. This often takes the euphemistic form of worries about assimilation and "cultural" differences, but the racial connotations of the discourse of parties like Alternative für Deutschland are so transparent that even a supposed fight against anti-Semitism can be put at the service of the persecution of foreigners and Germans of African and Asian origin.[25] Finally, openly white supremacist groups and dog whistles in varying shades of explicitness are intrinsic to the MAGA movement and certainly an essential part of Trump's appeal for many in his base. In all three cases, the more or less overt promise of racial segregation and a state built on an ethnic basis is not only present but arguably—even if in different degrees—the most important element in shaping the "we" that is being called into being in each case.

In Brazil, by contrast, neither racism nor xenophobia is as central to tying together the far right's different strands and signaling who is "in" or "out." This obviously has nothing to do with the country or much of the far right not being racist—they are—but is probably a consequence of the country's racial composition. Whereas the fraction of the Brazilian population that declared itself as Black at the last census was 10.6 percent (to the United States' estimated 14.4 percent), numbers go up to 55.9 percent when we tally those who describe themselves as Brown; and while Brown identity is no doubt a disputed terrain, this inevitably acts as an obstacle to the political viability of any project that would unambiguously center white supremacy.[26] In Argentina, on the other hand, Black, Indigenous, and migrant populations appear not to be sufficiently big to make them into major enemies for the far right. Racism operates differently in these cases: Instead of being foregrounded, it is silently assumed as a structural force that determines the concrete content of explicit discursive matrices. This is how the latter can play an *objectively* racist role without necessarily requiring subjective adhesion to racism. Thus, for example, Bolsonaro's advocacy for arming "upstanding citizens" so they can defend themselves from "criminals" may be articulated in ways that are not offensive to Black and Brown voters and still signal something to white voters attentive to the ways in which those two categories are statistically racialized. This makes it easier for Black people in Brazil to imagine themselves among the population protected by the far right than it is for those in the United States to do, which in turn helps explain why, even if the Black vote for Trump in 2024 was the highest ever for a Republican candidate (15 percent), it was still significantly lower than the 39 percent Bolsonaro polled among Black and Brown people in the run-up to the 2022 elections.[27]

What this suggests is a broader lesson about the far right: that contrary to what is often thought, the production of scapegoats and internal enemies, which is undoubtedly essential to this kind of politics, does not necessarily have racism and xenophobia as its primary vehicles but may find other expressions in situations in which the populations to be racially excluded are either too large to allow for a majoritarian project or too small to generate a repertoire of associations that can be exploited.[28] Yet this immediately raises a question about the role of the nation in these constellations. It is true that appeals to patriotism and mythologized past identities are intrinsic to the language that the far right speaks, but is it really the case that, as Richard Seymour has argued, "[w]hat unites the seemingly senseless and random outbursts of individual and collective violence in recent years . . . is the nation-state"?[29]

When the contemporary far right emerged in the last decade, analogies with historical fascism and more attention to what was said than what was done led many to see it as a retreat from globalization and a return to the national sphere. Yet the practice behind the discourse was a lot less straightforward, and it sufficed to look at the Brexit campaign to notice it: While tapping into British imperial nostalgia and nationalism as a convenient stand-in for racial fears, its architects clearly envisaged the exit from the European Union as a way of making the United Kingdom even more open to global finance and commodity flows. Equally, the ample use that Trump has made of tariffs and other protectionist measures in his first and—much more aggressively—second term does not seem to add up to much of a consistent long-term plan. In his hands, these instruments have been deployed in a rather more haphazard and piecemeal fashion, variously functioning as bones thrown to his electoral base (the incentives to the steel industry), steps to cement strategic alliances (the "AI action plan"), blunt geopolitical weapons (the "Liberation Day" announcements and his blackmail of Brazilian institutions to halt Bolsonaro's trial for an attempted coup), and ways of using the United States' imperial might to perform shakedowns for his own family's private gain (the US$1.5 billion deal for the Trump Organization that preceded a trade agreement with Vietnam in 2025, among others).

It is thus necessary to distinguish, first of all, between nationalism as a source of political enthusiasm that is mobilized by the far right and as an actual program. In the latter regard, it is obvious that there is little on offer at the moment that compares to the 1920s and 1930s. Secondly, it is important to differentiate between those places in which appeals to the nation come wrapped in more or less overt, more or less total promises of an ethnostate or an "ethno-economy" and those in which references to the fatherland are secondary elements to, or window dressing for, the desires and interests that really matter.[30] This is what happens with the Brazilian, Argentinean, Chilean, and El Salvadoran far right, where an outwardly patriotic rhetoric, often associated with the military, is combined with a foreign policy of automatic alignment with "the West" (read Trump and Israel), an elite disdain for the national (and a fawning admiration of all things "First World"), and an unquestioning acceptance of one's subaltern insertion in the international division of labor. (In the case of El Salvador, the latter extends to becoming a provider of carceral services for the United States, capitalizing on Nayib Bukele's sole achievement as president, namely, reducing gang violence at a steep human rights cost.) What these examples indicate is that, as with race, the centrality of the nation for the far right is not a given and will vary from country to country according to such factors as ethnic composition, historical memory, and geopolitical clout; "commitment to muscular national capitalism" is largely absent among many representatives of the contemporary far right, especially on the periphery.[31] They also show us that reality is a lot more complex than any linear "return of the nation-state" narratives would allow. While it is true that we are witnessing a recoil from the turn of the century's triumphant globalization narrative, especially after COVID-19 and the war in Ukraine, even the most strident "anti-globalism" of our times is best understood not as a simple reassertion of the nation-state but as a new scramble to find survival strategies, build alliances, and hoard political and economic power, at the supra- as well as the infranational level, in a world haunted by economic stagnation and looming climate catastrophe. If the nation is often invoked in this process, this does not necessarily make it what the process is *about*.

Another question that might be asked of my characterization of Bolsonarismo is why I have not included antifeminism and opposition to so-called gender ideology among its discursive matrices. To be clear, I understand these to be already covered by the catchall term *social conservatism*. What I would add, however, is that not only are they absolutely central to the contemporary far right, being among its most reliable constants, but the investment in traditional gender roles constitutes most of what we have in mind when we speak of "social conservatism" and is essentially what is left once such things as strong beliefs in discipline, social deference, and a strict education are cast aside. This coming together of misogyny, homo- and transphobia, pedophilia panics, incels, tradwives, and the manosphere is, of course, very telling. Anxiety around the dissolution of the gender binary and the breakdown of the patriarchal order is the extremely condensed symptom of a number of different processes: a crisis of social reproduction that transfers ever more costs and responsibilities to families and, perforce, women; the experience of emasculation that arises from being unable to meet even basic benchmarks once expected of breadwinners; the fear of losing out to minorities who have made however small advances in a world of intensifying competition; and the resentment at a tolerance and fluidity perceived as the luxury of an educated cosmopolitan elite. The comfort with which the far right beckons is not just the compensatory desublimation of a license to lash out at the imaginary beneficiaries of perverse enjoyments from which one is barred but the misplaced hope that, if one can only reestablish the familial (and familiar) certainties of a previous era, the very material other sources of uncertainty in our world can be kept away.

Finally, one last question I have been asked is why not include religion, and particularly Pentecostalism and neo-Pentecostalism, among the social tendencies that come together to compose Bolsonarismo. It seems to me that talking about religiosity or a specific religion would be an inaccurate way of framing the issue, especially if we were to leave out the (far from negligible) contribution of conservative Catholicism to the far right.[32] "Anti-intellectualism" and "social conservatism," on the other hand, appear to cover the most important elements that are usually associated with religious Bolsonarismo without suggesting that they are exclusive to believers, let alone to this or that religion. This is not to deny the importance of churches, especially evangelical ones, in forming the Bolsonaro base; but to suggest that this importance is more organizational and contingent, resulting from the formation of an ultraconservative leadership in this milieu, than an inevitable consequence of doctrinal content. With that, we avoid the double risk of treating evangelicals as a monolithic bloc and of making them solely responsible for problems that are actually much broader in scope.

Focusing on the organizational aspect also helps deflate simplistic narratives of ignorant congregations duped by their leaders. Being a constant presence in their communities allows evangelical groups to have an impact on the well-being of their base that an absent, underfunded state apparatus often cannot match. To join a church in the peripheries of Brazil and elsewhere is to find not only religion but often also support to deal with childcare or addictions, training and help finding a job, literacy programs, networks of mutual aid, a social life.[33] This lends the political messages that eventually run through these circuits at once greater credibility and a high degree of redundancy, since it ensures that the same ideas will be coming at the faithful via friends, family, radio shows, WhatsApp groups, and the pulpit. Besides, as the theologian André Castro has suggested, a vision of the world as a terrain of spiritual battle accelerating toward a final conflict is less far-fetched than it sounds to those inhabiting the wreckage of aborted modernization. Whereas the gap between the promises of social integration and its realization could once be occupied by Liberation Theology's prophetic offer of immanent redemption through struggle, an apocalyptic message is probably more appropriate to a time when the everyday experience of capitalism is "ever more distant and disconnected from the notion of progress."[34]

A COMMON GRAMMAR

Although *mamata* has a very Brazilian flavor, the operation it makes possible is the far right's quintessential conjuring trick everywhere: promoting the confusion between anxiety around the loss of *rights* and the fear of losing *privileges*. This is what has allowed it in the last decade to gather the support of both those sectors that have few material concerns but resent the advances made by some groups and those that are haunted by falling standards and the prospect of no longer enjoying conditions they once had. In that, it was evidently abetted by the fallout from the 2008 crisis coming on the back of years of a "progressive neoliberalism" that combined a "plutocratic economic program" that left millions of people behind with a "liberal-meritocratic politics of recognition" that offered mostly symbolic improvements to so-called minorities.[35] The concomitance of severe losses for some and modest gains for others is what helps the far right convince the "losers" of globalization that if they are being deprived of *rights*, it is because others—women, migrants, ethnic groups, LGBTQ+ people, etc.—are gaining *privileges* off their backs: and, conversely, to portray the challenge to privileges that some groups enjoy over others, such as racism and sexism, as an encroachment on the their freedom and rights.

It is this triadic structure of right populism—not "the people" versus "the elite" but the people against an elite that unduly favors some other group—that explains how, in the United States, a billionaire could establish himself as the candidate of the common man against an "establishment" consisting of Hollywood actors, newspaper columnists, Black Lives Matter activists, and graduate students on social media.[36] It also makes the confluence of social conservatism and no-holds-barred neoliberalism a lot easier to explain. When the loss of certain privileges by some (white, male, heteronormative, etc.) is associated with the conquest of rights by others (affirmative action, for example), the desire to see the status quo restored finds a natural ally in the rejection of redistributive policies.

Not that this confluence should surprise us too much. In places like Brazil and the United States, the coming together of social conservatism and neoliberalism has long been prepared, on the one hand, by the "prosperity gospel" of neo-Pentecostal churches, which provides divine justification for the accumulation of wealth and "reinforces the Calvinist tenet of individual responsibility for material success,"[37] and, on the other, by a "neoliberalism from above" that has never ceased to invest the family as disciplinary institution, counterweight to the market's disaggregating tendencies, safety net that could take on functions previously exercised by the state (education, health, well-being), and part of a dispositif for the privatization of risk.[38] Ultimately, however, what Bolsonarismo and Trumpism help us see is that if neoliberalism and neoconservatism can be relatively easily welded together by politics, it is because they share the same moral grammar.

Once again, to speak of "grammar" is not to stay at the level of language only. A grammar, following Ludwig Wittgenstein, is part of a form of life. Thus, if the way one lives conditions what one can say about the world, what one can say about the world provides the grounds for decisions and institutions that condition the way one lives.[39] Indeed, the moral grammar of the far right at once reflects how its adherents see the world and demands that the world be remade according to that vision. Its key elements are *individualism*, *punitivism*, and *the valorization of order above the law*.

Ideas like self-reliance and becoming an "entrepreneur of oneself" are of course among the highest values posited by neoliberal discourse. But in a world reconfigured by these ideas, they are also essential to the strategies required to navigate relationships, institutions, and work and are integral to how individuals perceive themselves. As safety nets shrink and uncertainty grows, the sheer "strain of risk-bearing" forces people to internalize the idea that they are solely responsible for their own fate.[40] By rendering invisible both the interdependencies that sustain individual trajectories and the structural constraints that hold them back, this individualistic grammar voids the notion of a social space beyond the immediate private sphere: There are only individuals and (at best) their families, as someone famously put it. This not only deprives people of the language in which to address structural injustice but induces them to interpret positive changes in their economic environment as their own achievement and structural demands as special pleading: "[I]f they have to battle through life alone, then everyone else should too."[41]

Perversely, individualism is an ideal that works as well in success (narrated as heroic self-realization) as it does in failure (in a "therapeutic" mode that restores dignity by locating emotional development in adversity).[42] In our societies, individual sovereignty is the site of "cruel optimism" par excellence, the frustration of its expectations only making its grip stronger.[43] Inadequacy is therefore less likely to lead to a reformulation of the ideal than to a doubling down that can be turned inward as self-aggression and outward as resentment and negative solidarity.[44]

This is where the grammars of individualism and punitivism intersect. On the one hand, the neoliberal emphasis on individual responsibility recovers a nineteenth-century tradition of moralization of poverty, in which the absence of protections and the recrudescence of social and economic coercion are justifiable as means of tempering the fiber of the marginalized so as to prepare them for the "adult life" of economic agents.[45] (The offense that many people in Brazil experienced upon discovering that recipients of Bolsa Família would also use their income for leisure or medium-term investments has much the same meaning.)[46] On the other hand, in a world where everyone feels they are (and ought to be) out on their own, nonconformity is seen as eschewing personal responsibility or seeking special treatment and is therefore worthy of punishment.[47] Punitivism thus has a prophylactic sense—making people go through hardship is good for them—as well as a properly retributive one. In the end, everyone is aways potentially deserving of punishment, which means that, besides discipline itself, disciplinary mechanisms also inculcate the naturalization of disciplining: the generalized sentiment that one can—and must—be subject to having one's behavior corrected at any given time.

As a product of internalized discipline, punitivism is highly respectful of established authority, social roles, and divisions; organized crime and social movements are potentially equally loathsome and despised. Among the rich as well as the poor, the punitive animus is directed against those at the base of the social pyramid more than at those at the top, whose transgressions can be shrugged off as part of their reward for having "made it." It is here that individualism and punitivism intersect with a notion of order as something above, and ultimately against, the law.

Many have identified this as a founding trait of Brazilian culture of which Bolsonaro is merely the latest, obscene flower.[48] It goes back to the early days of the country's formation, when local landowners were at once representatives of state power and the most powerful men in their areas, fostering the confusion between public and private interests.[49] The agrarian, slaveholding structure of the plantation economy not only divided society into individuals endowed with rights and pieces of common property but meant that even free men often owed their fortunes to attracting the favors of the property-owning elite. This meant that liberal discourse and a modern state apparatus developed not by supplanting but by appeasing, and often providing cover for, that archaic structure of command.[50] Even after the abolition of slavery—which Brazil was one of the last countries to enact—the permanent and assured exercise of one's rights was a privilege reserved to those of a certain social standing. Punishment, conversely, was certain only for those whose status did not exempt them from observing the same rules as everyone else.

In a society in which the guarantee of equality before the law is a privilege, the demand for order is thus usually not about applying the law but about revoking the rights of those who do not "deserve" them and granting special treatment to those who do. This was visible in the way the media and the public cheered Operation Car Wash on through its numerous procedural infringements, which have exposed its legal results to revision and annulment even if its political effects are irreversible.[51] It is also visible in four themes dear to Bolsonarismo: the call for "human rights for the right humans,"[52] not criminals; the flexibilization of gun laws, which amounts to privatizing the sovereign power over death; the dismantling of environmental protections, understood as obstacles to entrepreneurship; and the crusade against speed cameras and traffic fines, seen as impinging on car owners' liberties.[53]

But the placing of order above the law is in no way a Brazilian exclusivity; given the two countries' shared origin in slavery, it is unsurprising that the far right in Brazil and in the United States should be so similar in this regard. Yet it is not only the past that makes this exceptionalist logic generalizable: The growing concentration of economic and political power revives and reproduces it in our times. On the one hand, the premodern logic that sees the right to flout common rules as the greatest right of all fits in well with the libertarian absolutization of individual freedom. This was made explicit by the rejection of movement restrictions and mask enforcement during COVID-19 by the likes of Trump and Bolsonaro, which the latter then followed on by insisting that "nobody can force anyone to take the vaccine" once one was available. On the other hand, as this type of order supposes not the formal equality of laws but the arbitrary exercise of authority, it combines perfectly with the defense of a "private life of power" premised on a traditional distribution of roles between men and women, white and nonwhite, straight and not straight, etc.[54] As Wendy Brown has noted, nihilistic revanchism against the inroads made by oppressed groups "releases the will to power not only in subjects, but in traditional values themselves, baldly revealing the privilege and entitlement they encode."[55] "Those who can, rule; those who know better, obey," as the Brazilian saying goes—or, as Thucydides would have it, "the strong do what they can and the weak suffer what they must."

This too is a moral grammar, but one indexed less on codes than on the power of a "strict father" to lay down the law.[56] This confluence of the pre- and the postmodern, traditional authority and the neoliberal voiding of the social, creates the basis on which the ruling elite and the excluded can meet. It is a meeting between those who have given up on waiting for the democratizing promises of modernity and those no longer even nominally interested in pursuing them; those who have ceased to expect accountability and equality and those unwilling to make concessions to such values. It is in this sense that today's far-right movements can be understood as the scar of a democracy that has failed to live up to its concept, as per the Adornian aphorism I have chosen as the epigraph for this chapter. They converge around the paradoxical dream of a state of nature presided over by a paternal figure at once strict (with those who are not "upstanding citizens") and permissive (with those who are); in which authority is both exercised decisively from above and devolved to local powers that are free to act in their own sphere of influence (the pastor, the landowner, the cop, the paterfamilias, the crime or paramilitary boss); and in which conflicts of jurisdiction are nonetheless unlikely, because "everyone knows their place." The supreme leader thus really is at once a "father of the horde" and a "great little man."[57] If he is entitled to a surplus of obscenity, it is not because of any intrinsic quality that he possesses but simply because he "made it to the top." He is therefore free to use his position in his own favor, *as any of us would*. ("If I can give my son steak, I will," as Bolsonaro said of his intention to make his middle son the Brazilian ambassador to the

United States; or, as Trump said in a 2016 debate when confronted by Hillary Clinton on getting around paying taxes: "That makes me smart.")

This state of nature is clearly not the same as the one Hobbes had in mind, in which individuals were more or less evenly matched. The contemporary far right's horizon is that of a *differentially distributed state of nature*: a total abdication of any responsibility for the mediation of social conflict in a situation in which disparities are given free rein and, like conflict itself, tend to grow. It combines the right of the group in power to impose its will in such matters as social mores and free speech with an extremely laissez-faire attitude toward the exercise of power—including brute force—wherever power differentials exist. It is thus a wager on the acceleration of the social disintegration produced by late capitalism, but a controlled wager in that it still seeks to ensure that the agents that have the power to do so at different scales can maintain the capacity to privately manage this disintegration in their own favor.

The problem, of course, is that such a dream cannot really work for all who invest in it. If dog-eat-dog is made the rule, dog *will* eat dog, and the strong will feed on the weak. It is at this point of convergence, then, that Bolsonarismo, and even more so Bolsonaro's election, reveals itself as a huge misunderstanding. Whereas some (mostly poor) supporters tended to see Bolsonaro as the sheriff who would restore respect, others (mostly middle class) perceived him as a self-made chancer like themselves, who would make life easier for other go-getters. The elite, finally, identified him above all with that figure from the plantation whose function was historically superseded by the army and the police. Unable to find a viable candidate among their own ranks, they chose to elect the *overseer*, and as long as he fulfilled his duty of containing demands from below while ensuring ever more draconian conditions for capital accumulation at the top, he could manage his political capital as he pleased. A dangerous bargain, to be sure, as the overseer was given free rein to combine this political capital with the armed support of overseers like him in the police, paramilitary, and armed forces; but one that paid off for some time, and could still do so again.

As we have seen, however, Bolsonarismo is not reducible to either a national atavism or a simple repetition of historical fascism. It is a very contemporary tragedy, the conditions for which are given far and wide today and tend to worsen as political and economic inequality grow and the effects of climate change intensify. Some form of overseer capitalism may well be part and parcel of that "Brazilianization" with which the developed world has for decades been menaced from time to time.

DARK MOODS: THE RATIONALITY OF THE IRRATIONAL

Among the thorniest problems in analyses of historical fascism is the interplay of deceit and desire, rationality and irrationality at its heart. To what extent were people duped into doing certain things? To what extent did they actually come to desire them—and how conscious were they of doing so? Were irrational justifications such as conspiracy theories mere attempts to rationalize antisocial urges run rampant? Was stirring and acting out these urges merely a cover for base interests and calculations, such as appropriating the wealth of persecuted groups? Although it is not hard to notice that there is a certain "phoniness" about fascists—a category that "applies to the leaders as well as to the act of identification on the part of the masses"—it is not always easy to tell who is faking what to whom, and when.[58]

Thinking through these questions demands that we consider the discursive matrices and grammars on which the far right relies in relation to the affective conditions that give it something to latch on to: the shared affects or moods that enhance receptivity to its politics and make it appear as a plausible answer in a concrete situation. Given that the resurgence of far-right politics is a global phenomenon, we should expect to find the same affective conditions in several different countries and be able to trace them back to processes taking place globally. And indeed, everywhere we look today we will find feelings of humiliation in the face of joblessness, underemployment, poverty, and debt; abandonment and being taken for granted; fear of losing one's place in the world; abjection and wounded male pride; desensitization toward the suffering of others (and even one's own); resentment against groups perceived as benefiting from transformations that occurred in the last decades; and the diffuse, unfocused anti-systemic sentiments that follow from that. It is not hard to see the processes set in motion by neoliberal globalization and accelerated by the 2008 crisis at the root of all of these. Yet there are other components to our present ambient mood that are less salient because the changes to which they respond unfold on a time scale that is longer and less immediately obvious. Among these, I would like to focus on one in particular that provides an interesting angle on the issue of phoniness; I will call it *denialism*.

What I am calling by this name does not, however, refer exclusively to the lies that fraudsters and conspiracy theorists consciously spread. It encompasses first and foremost the public that consumes those and what attracts this public to them in the first place. My intuition here is that the state we describe as "being in denial"—an unconscious attempt to protect oneself from a traumatic experience or thought by refusing to recognize its reality, or what Freud called "disavowal"—creates a demand for the commodity that conscious "denialists" supply. A booming market for the latter should, therefore, lead us to suspect an increase in the former. This would mean that it is no coincidence that a sizable fraction of the Brazilian upper class would turn to those who blamed social conflict on "cultural Marxism" when the modest gains made by historically marginalized groups forced them to confront their place and role in the country's extremely unequal social structure. Disgusted by the sight of his face in the mirror, Caliban chose to believe those who said the mirror was broken. Likewise, it is no coincidence that the rise of leaders who eschew even the usual insincere platitudes about the environment comes after states and markets have, decade on decade for almost forty years, failed to adequately address global warming. It may be easier to imagine the end of the world than the end of capitalism, but it is much less costly psychologically to just wish its reality away.

As we shall see in greater detail in the next chapter, the perverse rationale for believing irrational narratives such as antivaccine conspiracies or "anti-globalist" diatribes is that they do not fail to acknowledge how dire the overall state of affairs is but do so by offering the comfort of fantasies that promise relatively simple solutions. In doing so, they can channel anti-systemic sentiments, starting with the feeling that there is something fundamentally wrong with the world, in circumstances where virtually no one believes that systemic change is really possible. Now, if the structural conditions that create an ever-widening gap between rich and poor cannot be changed, what is left for those at the bottom is to fight over increasingly meager scraps. And it is precisely for that situation that the alternative reality the extreme right presents in lieu of the disavowed traumatic content prepares its followers. By locating the source of the various contemporary crises in the misappropriation of resources by various "others" (countries, ethnicities, nationalities, religions, cultures, genders, sexualities), and thus framing the distributive conflict as a war against them, it makes the persecution of the weakest justifiable and neutralizes in advance the psychological burden generated by the excesses that may be committed or endured. It is a "conservative politics of antagonistic reproduction," as Alberto Toscano aptly summarized it, in a world in which social reproduction tends to become ever more antagonistic.[59]

In denialism, then, we find what is ultimately the greatest, most ironic misunderstanding on which the far right relies: the fact that it seals an alliance between those gearing up for surviving in worsening conditions and an elite increasingly at ease with the idea that, as Bruno Latour put it, "the earth no longer has room enough for them and for everyone else."[60]

CHAPTER 2

THE PRESENT OF AN ILLUSION: ARE WE IN DENIAL ABOUT DENIAL?

If you are reading this, you have probably lived through two once-in-a-lifetime crises already: the COVID-19 pandemic and the 2008 financial meltdown.

For many, the latter's definitive image was not panicking stock traders or the workers at bankrupt investment banks filing out of their offices with their personal belongings in boxes. It was Alan Greenspan, one of the chief architects of the deregulation that had made the subprime catastrophe possible, confessing to the US Congress that he had been forced to revise one of his most fundamental assumptions: that the search for profit would never override the survival instincts of supposedly rational economic agents. Exposed in its very logic by market irrationality, stripped of its normative claims by the brazenly unmeritocratic denouement of the crisis, lacking a plausible new deal to offer to the vast majority of people, neoliberalism seemed to be hemorrhaging legitimacy from all sides. Like many around that time, I too found it hard to believe that it could survive the shock. And yet, almost two decades and several further shocks later, neoliberalism staggers on, mechanically muttering the same old slogans with glazed eyes.[1]

At the start of the COVID-19 pandemic, some were cautiously optimistic: Surely the second major global crisis in just over a decade meant that real change might finally be in the cards. There were credible reasons for thinking that. The disease, this thinking went, would underline the risks of global capitalism's long logistical chains, the importance of public services, and the many interdependencies among people and states, highlighting the value of cooperation. The virus was bringing the cold shock of the real back into a public debate increasingly contaminated by conspiracy theories and antiscientific fantasies. Finally, the ensuing economic downturn would throw rising inequality and the unresolved issues left by the Great Recession into sharper relief, resulting in conditions akin to those that erupted into the Arab Spring and the 15-M and Occupy movements in 2011.

It is true that, in the first months of the pandemic, dogmas were temporarily jettisoned and governments adopted policies—fiscal expansion, investments in public health, temporary suspensions of rents and evictions, and measures to guarantee wages and jobs—that would have been anathema just a month before. Even Jair Bolsonaro, who had campaigned on an economic program of extreme market libertarianism, was pressured into creating a short-term basic income for the most vulnerable. From the start, however, these measures came wrapped in demands for more austerity once things returned to normal. What is more, they were vastly compensated at the other end by policy that follows the 2008 playbook in pursuing the well-being of big corporations and financial institutions above all.[2] In general, governments continued to minimize the scale of what was happening and how long it could go on so as to eschew a conversation about what would have to change were we to really protect people's lives and livelihoods for the duration of a protracted crisis.

Of course, powerful movements could still have risen to demand a different solution this time. (In the United States, with the George Floyd protests, it felt for a moment like they would.) But it should be noted that the expectation that the virus would act as a solvent against disinformation was unfortunately proved unfounded. If anything, what many considered irrefutable evidence seemed only to accentuate irrational beliefs at the far-right end of the political spectrum. The gap between the realities inhabited by different parts of the population appeared to become so large that the leaders of countries like Brazil and the United States, although these countries were among those that fared the worst during the pandemic, managed at least for some time to retain much of their popularity even as they mobilized their social base against protective measures, scientific institutions, vaccines, and health workers. For Donald Trump's hardcore supporters, his merits were so obvious that only a fraud involving the entire American establishment, including part of the Republican Party, could explain his subsequent electoral defeat. In Brazil, while defeat in his particular war against reality would eventually have a political cost for Bolsonaro, it should not be forgotten that there was a moment in 2020 when he not only regained the support he had lost in the first months of the pandemic but became *more* popular than he had been since the start of his presidency.[3] The elasticity that allowed the likes of Donald Trump, Jair Bolsonaro, and Boris Johnson to bounce back, even after blows that would have sufficed to end the careers of other politicians, is in fact what requires further explanation.

LIMIT AND PUNISH

If there is one thing that the last decade ought to have taught us, it is that strong objective factors do not automatically translate into powerful movements, let alone into the spontaneous discovery of the correct line by the masses. Even if we may still see major social explosions in the coming years, there is no reason to believe that they will take forms that will be easily recognizable to the left or that they will be immune to instrumentalization from the right.

This is usually the point at which the conversation might turn to fake news and propaganda, and it is undeniable that part of Bolsonaro's and Trump's surprising resilience even outside of government stems from the fact that they possess a far more efficient informational infrastructure than do their opponents to get their version of facts across. Yet the path I wish to pursue here is a different one. It consists in relating the mystery of these two resiliencies—that of far-right discourse and the one displayed by neoliberalism post-2008—not just to show how they communicate and feed back into another but equally to point out what lies behind the sway of disinformation and constitutes the terrain in which it flourishes.

To put it bluntly: If the far right has managed, using lies or otherwise, to mobilize the anti-systemic feelings of people who feel they have been failed and left behind, it is because those sentiments *exist.* In other words, it is only because many people sense that there is something profoundly wrong about the existing economic and political system that the far right's message can take hold. Combating this message, therefore, is not just a matter of fighting deception; it is ultimately about addressing the issues that are at the source of those feelings. This cannot happen, however, for as long as we are in denial about those issues.

Let us start with the first mystery. Those who believed radical change was inevitable after 2008 underestimated two factors. First, they did not foresee the extent to which our political systems have become inured to running on low legitimacy. In the absence of any sustained challenge to their power, elites seem to trust their capacity to continually outmaneuver the majority of the population regardless of whether or not they are actually trusted. This was made possible by the concentration of political power that has followed directly from the concentration of economic power since the 1980s, but equally by decades of institutional reforms that have served to subtract ever more areas, particularly fiscal and monetary policy, from any sort of social control—the design of the Eurozone, for example, the anti-democratic nature of which was made explicit by the 2015 Greek crisis, or the "expenditure ceiling" introduced in Brazil after the impeachment of Dilma Rousseff in 2016.[4]

The second factor is the sheer inertial force of neoliberalism's disciplinary mechanisms—labor precarity, reduction of social protections, private debt, etc.—and the reprogramming of subjectivity that they serve to constantly (re)produce. While these have no doubt become more draconian in an age of austerity and uberization, we should not forget that neoliberalism has always had a retributive or punitive dimension, which is manifested in its intimate connection with crisis situations, famously summed up by Naomi Klein in the expression "shock doctrine." Crisis is neoliberalism's greatest disciplinary device: Every time one breaks out, neoliberalism not only uses it to accentuate the economic coercion to which people are subjected but does so by reactivating the foundational myth with which it narrated its own rise in the 1970s and 1980s—that of being the rational and technocratic cure for the excesses of a previous period, which exempts it from debate and converts it into the only available alternative. It matters little that most crises we experience today are in effect a product of neoliberalism itself: We are no longer living in a crisis of management but in an era of management by means of crises.

If today's neoliberalism seems to take on increasingly "punitive" characteristics, as Will Davies has observed, this is because the calls for belt-tightening are no longer accompanied by anything more than a pale prospect that they may one day be loosened again.[5] Discipline has become starker even as—or precisely because—the normative claims behind it have become more suspect. If sacrifice was once presented as a way to make life better, it now appears increasingly as an end in itself: the sheer imperative to adapt to a horizon of lowering expectations. This tendency reached its culmination with the pandemic, when official discourse in places like Brazil and the United States literally began to say that people had to choose between the economy and life. As Texas Lieutenant Governor Dan Patrick pungently put it in 2020, "There are more important things than living and that's saving this country"—that is, the economy.

That this was politically possible, that it did not destroy the careers of such leaders, is a sign of how much, since the end of the golden age of real or promised welfare protection of the postwar period, populations have become accustomed to declining expectations. When Michel Foucault called liberalism "the general framework of biopolitics," what he was saying is that it was with liberalism that, for the first time, state management of the processes related to the life of the population was posed as based on a cost-benefit calculation (the greatest effect at the lowest cost), with the market as the ultimate judge of its success or failure.[6] But what he did not notice at the time is that there is an asymmetry between "greatest benefit" and "least cost": While the former is vague and has no defined threshold, the latter does—it is zero. What neoliberalism has done over four decades is to increasingly measure "greatest benefit" by its proximity to "zero cost," with the upshot that the best public intervention ended up being, by definition, that which costs nothing—that is, no intervention at all. By exempting themselves, as far as possible, from the duty to intervene to protect life, Trump, Bolsonaro, Johnson, and others tested the extent to which this logic has already become naturalized; the result is grim.[7] Nothing is more symbolic of this transformation than the way in which the expression "herd immunity" changed meaning during the pandemic: From designating the immunization achieved at the end of a public vaccination effort, it came to be used mainly by those who intended it as the protection that results from letting a disease freely wreak its havoc across a population.

One of the reasons why Bolsonaro's overall ratings were up 10 percent at the height of the pandemic—despite him losing a sizable chunk of his upper-class support—may of course be the very basic income program he had initially opposed. Another reason, however, was that, for the poor voters who came to approve of his government, framing the issue as a choice between life and the economy *was objectively true.* Since inequality made quarantining an unattainable luxury for them, posing the situation as a choice between potentially dying from COVID-19 and potentially starving to death showed that Bolsonaro understood their reality more profoundly than did the hypocrites telling them to stay at home when they had no option but to go out to work.

The painful reality is that, in cases such as this, the story that the far right tells effectively makes *more sense* to a lot of people than whatever the other side are saying. This is because it corresponds more clearly to the world as most people encounter it on a daily basis; it resonates with lived experience. For many, being told that life is a series of dark trade-offs in a deadly struggle over finite resources does not sound far-fetched at all. What is more, it agrees with the disciplining effect that these experiences effectively have: the deeply entrenched feeling that this is all there is, that nothing else is possible, that the fundamental facts of how we live could not change.

For this is the great irony and paradox of far-right politics: What it proposes is a very conformist kind of revolt. Even as it purports to be an attack on elites—understood not in economic but in cultural and political terms, which explains how a billionaire could campaign as a champion of the common man in the United States—the future the far right projects is very much like the present. As far as social structure is concerned, their vision is quite resigned to the status quo. What it promises is, in short, an anti-systemic politics for people who do not really believe the system could change in any major way: Everything stays essentially the same but yields better results for some of those feeling left out now.

This takes us back to the point about denialism, in the sense proposed in the first chapter, as a dimension of our present condition that is yet to be fully appreciated.

FLEEING WITHOUT LEAVING THE SPOT

There is no doubt that the sheer volume of disinformation available today is a factor. Entire ecosystems of mutually reinforcing sources exist to interfere with individuals' capacity to form sound beliefs, and the algorithms of our most popular online platforms constantly pull us toward these parallel worlds. Something we failed to consider earlier on about the internet is that belief, being a necessarily social phenomenon, has a statistical nature: Once the amount of bad information crosses a certain numerical threshold, it is hard for the system as whole to bounce back.

This is because, as William James pointed out, truth is a credit system: We "trade on each other's truth," accepting things we have not experienced directly, in the assumption that someone down the line has actually verified them—and that, if enough people appear to believe them, it is because some have at least gone through the trouble of making sure others have carried out that verification.[8] In the early days of the internet, one of the best arguments made for it was that it would enable us access a surfeit of good information that established gatekeepers—the press, the publishing industry, the government, academia—prevented us from encountering. That was, of course largely true, but at the time, much of that information had at least undergone some degree of quality control, often following the same conventions that those very gatekeepers set. The problem now is, firstly, that by slashing publishing costs, the internet has made it possible for anyone to publish information of any kind. What this means is, secondly, that there is an intrinsic risk to treating "being on the web" as tantamount to integration in those chains of delegated trust that James talked about—though that is still what most people in the world instinctively do for at least some of the time. Thirdly, and by the same token, those chains have become much more easily falsified: All it takes is for enough sources, by mistake or by design, to treat the information provided by another as trustworthy, and the referred legitimacy will produce the appearance of verifiability down the line. Fourthly, and finally, whereas in the past much of the information coming into the web was being produced elsewhere and according to different standards, nowadays much of it is based on material found online, which makes delegated trust dicier and quality control harder to enforce. (Increasingly, in fact, it will be produced by AI reading AI material trained on information found on the web.) The upshot is that, as disparate statements and "alternative facts" about the broadest range of subjects proliferate, all of which are lent credence by others who share, cite, or otherwise endorse them, everything begins to seem just as likely to be true as anything else. If, as Bruno Latour and Steve Woolgar defined it, scientific procedure consists in reducing equiprobability to a minimum (making a statement or result much more likely than an opposite or alternative one), what the internet has done—and would have likely always done, regardless of being instrumentalized by malicious actors—is raise equiprobability across the board.[9] This is the so-called age of post-truth in a nutshell.

But the fact of all discourses becoming equally believable still does not explain *why* some are believed—especially those that might strike us as most implausible.[10] If our processing of information is itself constrained by a number of cognitive biases that respond, in turn, to unconscious needs, the question we need to ask ourselves is, therefore, *What needs do the far-right's narratives meet*? And this is where we must note the connection that is implied by the expressions "being a denialist" and "being in denial." When we call a member of the oil or tobacco lobby a "denialist," we are saying that they know that what they deny is real; in other words, that they are consciously lying. When we describe someone as being "in denial," on the other hand, we suggest they are unconsciously protecting themselves from a traumatic experience or thought—the process that

Freud named *Verleugnung*, or disavowal. Should this not lead us to suspect that this is the itch that the far right scratches—that a growing need to disavow the state of the world, which the lies of the far right and other "merchants of doubt" are highly effective at placating, is a dominant mood of our times?[11]

To be sure, the right does not paint a rosy picture of the present. On the contrary, theirs is a narrative of civilizational conflict, in which a fantasized spirit of the Crusades is retooled to fight such enemies as migrants, independent women, and Black people. What is remarkable about this narrative, however, is how it displaces the real threats looming on the horizon into distorted, fun-house-mirror versions of themselves. Thus, the problem with democracy is not political elites everywhere who are beholden to the interests of corporations and financial markets but a secret cabal of pedophiles planning to institute a world government and the arcane "deep state" that protects it. (The fact that such a cabal was found to exist does not make this any less of a fantasy; this subject is addressed again later.) The problem with the economy is not that capital accumulation has become so autonomous from production as to make the very rich relatively indifferent to the vicissitudes of the real economy but that migrants and minorities are being given undue privileges. Finally, the problem with the environment is not climate change but the weaponization of science by a political agenda bent on changing our lifestyles and preventing growth.

Yet we have learned from Louis Althusser that ideology "represents the imaginary relationship of individuals to their real conditions of existence."[12] If the reality of one's conditions of existence becomes increasingly traumatic, should a flight further out into the imaginary not be expected? The truth behind the violent picture that the far right paints is that we are living in an age of diminishing horizons, in which everyday experience is increasingly colored by the diffuse sensation that, all things remaining equal, what the future holds is ever worse conditions of reproduction for ever more people. Fewer jobs, less income, less access to basic goods and services; more risk and less protection. Climate change, economic stagnation, growing precarity, weak democratic oversight, global pandemics—those are the things humming in the background or moving at the edges of our fields of vision. The far right addresses this atmospheric dread by at once recognizing that yes, we are before an abyss, and fabulating an abyss that is less traumatic than the one we actually face, since its causes and fixes, though painful, are comparatively simple. In so doing, it also displaces responsibility, attributing real, observable effects to imaginary causes or to things that are, in fact, other symptoms of the same underlying problems—thus becoming highly instrumental to anyone who wishes to disguise their own role in creating the traumatic content to be disavowed. If they always come down to "not knowing what to make of the symptoms," as the Italian novelist Wu Ming 1 notes, the right's "diversionary narratives" simultaneously function as a grounding wire, "which discharges tension and stops people being hit by the awareness of the need for systemic change," and always "appear to aim at the top, but strike at the bottom."[13]

To the extent that it speaks to this pervasive anxiety, the far right's "dreamwork"[14] will sound much more truthful to many than any arguments claiming that things are generally getting better and this is only a bad patch that we will soon pull through provided we continue to do more or less the same as before—which is essentially the message of the right's liberal and centrist counterparts. But it also does more. On the one hand, it generates psychological compensations over, above, and regardless of any actual material gains: feelings of belonging, recognition, relief from the cognitive dissonance produced by the discrepancy between one's own beliefs and the mass of other information available, moral and intellectual superiority for being among the few who recognize where evil truly lies and is willing to stand up to it. By forging identification with figures who constantly expose the lies and hypocrisy of "elites" and the "establishment" and appear fully prepared to wield their force—whether state backed, media based, or physical—against those who deserve it, these narratives also offer regular doses of the affect of winning, served via social media posts, TikTok videos, and governmental acts, even while there is precious little winning to be had in one's everyday life.

Yet it would be an overstatement to say that it "isn't the economy, stupid. It isn't even physical survival."[15] Even if it may be never entirely conscious, there *is* a perverse material rationality at the heart of the seemingly purely irrational impulse to "destroy a neighbour"[16] or "take back control" to the point of self-harm.[17] As Theodor Adorno wrote regarding the "functional character" of prejudice, one "may well assume that the fear of being superfluous looms large" in anti-Semitism as well as in any other form of hostile disposition toward particular groups (including "communists" or, more broadly, the left).[18] Thus, by locating the cause of the problem in the misappropriation of resources by various "others," and the solution in a fight to exclude those others from access to resources, the far right tells a story well suited to a world of intensifying competition at the bottom. For people who already feel that they live on the edge of the state of nature, talk of civil war, however delirious it might be, could make perfect sense: It not only describes the world as it already is experienced to a large extent but offers a certain competitive advantage by legitimizing moving first against the "enemy"—usually a direct competitor in the struggle for survival. As Adorno also remarked, it ultimately does not matter if one really believes that the other is the devil as long as one enacts the belief that the other must be defeated at all costs.[19]

This is how the far right's fantasies can be said to offer, in their own twisted way, a reasonable response to the insanity we are currently building. In a world that can no longer reproduce itself in the same conditions, and where social reproduction therefore tends to become more like a struggle of all against all, the fantasies naturalize that state of affairs by simultaneously placing it outside the scope of what can or must be changed, allaying the emotional cost of accepting it, and preemptively justifying the need to take it further—whether through vicious welfare cuts, mass deportations, intensified international competition or, at the limit, violence and war. Trying to reduce the interpellatory power of these fantasies to a mere effect of fake news is an attempt to disavow this basic reality. And since the attempt to evade the truth of our present predicament is a decisive affective dimension of our times, it should be no surprise that those who wish to resist mounting insanity and a politics that seeks to accelerate it would be entangled in disavowals of our own. We too are denialists; what else might we be in denial about?

NONE SO BLIND

At the start of this chapter, I alluded to the fact that the myth of spontaneity is a mirage that still leads many radicals astray. Obviously, no one denies that objective conditions have an effect on what people do and think, or that sharp, sudden changes can transform the very limits of what is thinkable and doable at a given time. The problem is when people believe that, out of the various ways in which such transformations can go, they will inevitably go our way. By convincing us that a certain outcome can come to pass regardless of our efforts or capacity to produce it, this idea fulfills the obvious compensatory function of rationalizing away our organizational weaknesses and fear of becoming organized. But if banking on that outcome a decade ago was a mistake, it borders on folly today, in an environment in which the far right is a real, active force.

Literally nothing can guarantee that whatever anti-systemic revolts may occur in the coming years could not be captured by the right and end up reinforcing the system they are protesting against. To return to something said above: If the far right demonstrates an enormous capacity to win narrative disputes, such as those surrounding the COVID-19 pandemic, at least among its captive audience, it is because it has an informational infrastructure far superior to that of its opponents; as long as we do not admit it, we are in denial. And it is not just the Telegram and WhatsApp networks or the digital influencers arraigned and led by presidents like Trump, Bolsonaro, Modi, Milei, and Bukele but the fact that the stories that circulate through them arrive at people through others they know and trust, at church, in their families, in their social circles. Breaking through the informational redundancy that the right wing enjoys today therefore requires not only the creation of wider and more effective communication networks but also a regular and reliable presence in people's lives.[20] This, in turn, requires organization.

If we can say that spontaneity is the illusion of radicals, liberals, on the other hand, often appear to be suffering from an illusion of a different kind. It consists in drawing false symmetries between political extremes and idealizing the centrist consensus that prevailed until 2008. Ultimately, this attitude boils down to supposing that people have taken temporary leave of their senses, but everything can carry on as before as soon as the sensible guys are once again in charge. This is to ignore that wealth distribution and political representation have become so lopsided as to demand an overhaul that cannot but seem radical compared with what we have now and that, on an issue like the environment, the time for gradualism is long gone: Winning slow, as the saying goes, is as good as losing. To the extent that it continues to ignore the magnitude of the tasks that lie before us, and thus contributes to the conditions on which the far right thrives, this may well be the most dangerous form of disavowal around today.

AFFECTIVE INFRASTRUCTURES

The last ten years or so have seen "affective infrastructure" gain traction as a way of talking about political organization on the left, in relation to the party, for example, or the commons.[1] More often than not, the term functions less as a clear-cut concept than as an operator allowing those who use it to do different things without necessarily attempting to provide a definition of it. Although it is not always clear how literally or metaphorically the word "infrastructure" is meant in each context, what is common to the various uses it has been put to is the sense of it as something that simultaneously limits and enables, a set of constraints and affordances that sustain some affects while staving off others: "both that which partially causes and can never transitively 'determine' that which happens."[2]

Can the same idea be applied to contemporary far-right formations? And can it be done without turning "infrastructure" into a mere metaphor? The first step would be to think of affective infrastructures as nested and partially overlapping realities, so that we can see phenomena like Bolsonarismo and MAGA as affective infrastructures in their own right, while being at the same time contained in broader infrastructures, and containing, in turn, zones that could be singled out as specific infrastructures themselves (for example, those of the "manosphere," of the religious right, of Groypers, and so on). A society can thus be conceived as "a skein, a cacophony, a battleground"[3] in which some affective conditions are widely shared while others are particular to certain groups, sustaining some dissonance against a background of underlying consonance or commonality; and the same would apply to the far right, as an ensemble of parts that do not quite all fit perfectly together but still chime with one another on some deeper level (which, to push the musical metaphor further, we could call a pedal point, that is, a sustained bass note that pulls everything together).

What allows us to identify them in those terms? First, a communicational infrastructure. This encompasses such things as WhatsApp and Telegram groups, YouTube channels, social media profiles, influencers, allied voices and outlets in legacy media (radios, newspapers, TV channels). In the case of Bolsonarismo, much of this scaffolding was built from the bottom up, either directly as spaces in which to discuss politics or as social spaces that then acquired that character, in the years running up to the 2018 elections. Ultimately, however, these efforts would all be incorporated and expanded into something more organized and pyramidal from that presidential campaign onward. This resulted in a system of top-down diffusion and bottom-up feedback in which the general lines of discourse and action filtered down from the president and the group of aides who coordinated his social media, being developed and translated into more local contexts by those further down the chain; while responses, themes, and material produced at the base traveled up to the top, where they might be amplified, adapted, or recycled by more influential nodes. This process of vertical integration appears to occur wherever the far right starts to coalesce outside institutional politics before it finds a way to cross over into it. But the infrastructure of the contemporary far right also includes nondigital spaces, in both the physical and the social sense, such as gatherings like the Conservative Political Action Conference, churches and church groups, social and sports clubs, friends and family networks that are connected in one way or another to the main stem of the communicational network-system. We could thus see far-right ecologies as varying along two axes: one in which their infrastructures may tend more toward the online (as in Brazil) or the offline (as in India; the United States, with organizations such as Turning Point USA, Proud Boys, and Oath Keepers, is something of an intermediate case); and another according to whether they tended to grow around their own parties or institutions (India, Hungary, Italy, France) or only gradually acquired a center, typically at the moment of entering electoral politics, often by taking over previously existing structures (the United States, Brazil, Argentina). Either way, what matters from an affective perspective is that both digital and nondigital spaces enable regular practices and encounters that create and reproduce certain affective habits, as we shall see.

All of this is evidently built on material infrastructure, both public and private: mobile phones, computers, cables, servers, antennas, electricity, printers, buildings, and whatever facilitates and organizes their use. This reference to a specific material support is, I would argue, what justifies treating affective infrastructure as a concept that indicates more than just a shared affective condition. Obviously, it is not the case that affective conditions or structures of feeling can exist without relying on material supports, not least bodies endowed with the capacity to affect and be affected. It is useful, however, to have a concept that foregrounds that reliance and opens it up to closer examination, putting the spotlight on a concrete material infrastructure with its own determinate architecture (and what that affords and constrains), as well as on the specific practices that activate it.

Now, what is it that enables us to characterize a certain material support as an affective infrastructure? It is, first of all, the fact that what circulates in it is not just information or goods and services but also affects. By means of repetition (of frames, messages, practices, encounters) and recursion (adjusting said frames, messages, practices, and encounters to changes in the group or its environment), an affective infrastructure locks participants in certain affective patterns, sustains the intensity with which these are felt, and thus reproduces a certain relation of the group to itself and to its various out-groups (which may be compressed into a single, compact figure of the "other" or "enemy"). It is through that, rather than through merely rhetorical means, that an affective infrastructure can produce the "chains of equivalence" that split the social field into two camps, "us" and "them."[4] Affective and discursive patterns interact so as to define objects of love and hate, admiration and repulsion, fear and hope, emulation and aversion, as well as the relations between them and certain dispositions and possible courses of action. Finally, affective infrastructures also function as media for positive-feedback effects that ramp up the intensity with which certain emotions are experienced, resulting in phenomena of affective synchronization (in which large numbers of people find themselves simultaneously experiencing the same strong feeling) that may or may not lead to individual and collective discharges (in the form of protests, online behavior, or stochastic violence, for instance).[5]

This gives us a hint as to how affective infrastructures might be individuated—that is, on what grounds we can draw a boundary around a certain part of the sociotechnical assemblages that constitute a society and call it that way. Obviously, both the material support and the affects that an affective infrastructure latches on to, feeds off, and sustains belong to society at large; it is because they already exist and are structurally or conjuncturally reproduced that they can be seized upon. What, then, makes them predicable of that particular infrastructure and not just of a general "mood" or "affective condition"? The answer lies in the fact that affective infrastructures possess a certain degree of closure and self-reference. That is, even if what they do is essentially fold affects and materials that are already "out there," they involve the effort to establish and maintain an "inside" through iteration (of patterns and investments), identification (with those patterns, with other participants, with leaders), and orientation (regarding themselves, their others, and the courses of action that this polarized relation suggests). This is also what allows us to distinguish affective infrastructures from infrastructures designed for the circulation of information and affects, such as digital platforms: While the latter can function as media for the formation of affective infrastructures, they do not possess the requisite level of consistency that would make them describable in that way.

Something that follows from conceiving affective infrastructures in this way is that they should be understood as media in their own right: not only in the sense that they are at once the means for the propagation of information and affects and the milieu through which these propagate but also in the sense that one can speak in optics of a translucent medium, that is, one that transmits the waves that go into it, but not without some loss or distortion. This is precisely one of the things that characterizes these infrastructures as an "inside": by means of affective biases that select and/or modify what passes within, they mediate between those who participate in them and information and affects coming from the outside. Borrowing a concept from Spinoza, we could say that they amount to a collective *ingenium*, that is, a particular affective constitution that predisposes the individuals who participate in it to respond to outside stimuli in certain ways; or, to put a more contemporary spin on this early-modern notion, we could say, in Simondonian terms, that they amount to a transindividual zone of individuation for the singular *ingenia* of participants.[6] This means that affective infrastructures entail some form of perspectivism, a thought that has important practical consequences for politics. If messages and actions will signal different things and trigger different reactions according to the affective infrastructure(s) to which one belongs, we must understand that, paraphrasing Roy Wagner's well-known bon mot, sometimes our misunderstanding of others will not be the same as their misunderstanding of us, and we may very well mean dissimilar things even if we are using the same words or, conversely, our very disparate grammars may conceal the same concerns.[7] Thus, when talking to those who are not yet necessarily on "our side" (while not necessarily being "the enemy" either), we must worry less about whether they are using the right words than about the sentiments they are expressing, what that says about their *ingenia*, and how we might be able to communicate with them more effectively.

Using a concept that has been usually employed to talk about political organization on the left in order to talk about the right serves to highlight that the two are not as intrinsically different as the former might like to believe. This can be shown through three distinct levels of analysis. The first concerns the passivity and alienation produced by the dominant sociotechnical arrangements in the society in which both left and right affective infrastructures take shape: In both cases, organizing is a response to broadly shared feelings of subjection, frustration, and powerlessness that both sides of the political spectrum, each in its own way, seek to address. The second level concerns the ratio of passivity and activity within the infrastructure itself. Regardless of its political orientation, an affective infrastructure always provides its participants with the means to experience their own collective capacity to act, to feel it wax and wane as it affects and is affected by the world. At the same time, this inevitably depends on some degree of passivity, from greater or lesser submission to leaders or to written and unwritten rules to the technical alienation of dealing, for example, with digital platforms one neither fully understands nor controls. Whether its goal is liberation for all or domination for some, political participation always feels liberatory, just as much as it always involves submitting oneself to constraints. It is only at the third level, that of an affective infrastructure's outward orientation and objectives, that a distinction can really be made. This is where it is possible to judge whether it is in the direction of greater collective activity and emancipation or, on the contrary, greater passivity, alienation, and subjection. It is here, then, that one can finally pose "the fundamental problem of political philosophy," "the one that Spinoza saw so clearly, and that Wilhelm Reich rediscovered: 'Why do men fight for their servitude as stubbornly as though it were their salvation?'"[8]

CHAPTER 3

OUR BRAND IS CRISIS: ENTREPRENEURIALISM AND THE FAR RIGHT

On February 14, 2025, Argentinean president Javier Milei took to the platform formerly known as Twitter to champion LIBRA, an obscure cryptocurrency he assured his 3.8 million followers would funnel investment into his country's enfeebled economy. Within hours, the token soared in value from near zero to almost $5 and then collapsed to under $1, causing $251 million in losses and leaving 86 percent of those who bought in poorer—while a fortunate few walked away with $180 million in gains. The debacle led to calls for Milei's impeachment and an investigation into whether the head of state had willingly taken part in a pump-and-dump scheme to enrich a small coterie of traders with inside knowledge. Donald Trump would face similar suspicions two months later. That was when the North American president, who had already launched his own crypto venture and meme coin since his election, went on the same platform to announce, in typically over-animated capital letters, that it was "A GREAT TIME TO BUY"—signing the message off with the initials "DJT," which also happen to be the Dow Jones ticker for Trump Media & Technology Group. Less than four hours later, he would announce a U-turn on his flagship tariff policy, leading to a stock market rally that caused his own company's stock to shoot up by 22 percent.[1]

More than just a sign of increasingly barefaced kleptocracy or of the devaluation of public office at the hands of social media populists, these events are a condensation of the different ways in which entrepreneurialism intersects with the contemporary far right, shaping some of its most distinctive features. These intersections can be analyzed at three different levels: that of mass psychology, that of mutations in the forms of political organization, and that of broader trends in contemporary political economy that the far right both responds to and feeds off.[2] At the first level, we can examine the role that widespread identification with the figure of the entrepreneur has played in far-right agitation by providing not only some of the ideological and affective material with which it works but also a shared point of reference for the building of cross-class alliances. At the second, we can look beyond the pro-entrepreneur content of this agitation to view it as an entrepreneurial phenomenon in its own right, and the "political entrepreneurs" who engage in it as a fundamental element in contemporary far-right organization in several countries. Finally, at the third, we can see these political entrepreneurs themselves as indicative of changes associated with assetization, precarization and the pervasiveness of finance and the attention economy—which are in the process of reconfiguring laboring activity as well as the very meaning and valence of entrepreneurship.

TRIUMPH OF THE WILL

Let us start with the first point, on entrepreneurialism and the class composition of far-right support. For the cross-class coalition that has led the far right to electoral triumph in countries like the United States, Brazil, and Argentina to be possible, it was necessary for certain images and words to produce identification among very disparate sectors of society. *Entrepreneur* was one of these signifiers. After all, it is a term that can not only encompass very different realities—from the executive to the informal worker, from the chain store owner to the small trader—but also, by representing an object of aspiration, may refer to reality as much as to desire. In a world in which people are constantly urged to admire entrepreneurs and to see things from their point of view, it is not surprising that candidates who present themselves as the champions of free enterprise should appeal to rich and poor alike. They are, after all, drawing on something that has, as Stuart Hall puts it, "secured a traditional resonance over time and left [its] traces in popular inventories."[3]

The entrepreneur was first given its due as a leading character in the market economy at the height of the Enlightenment, with the posthumous publication in 1755 of Richard Cantillon's *Essai sur la nature du commerce en général*.[4] This pioneering work outlined some of the most enduring traits of this figure, as well as some of the question marks that would surround it from then onward. For Cantillon, the entrepreneur is someone "who exercises business judgment in the face of uncertainty."[5] As such, it is a function, not a position or social rank: There are those who have capital but do not risk it, as there are those who risk capital that is not theirs. To be sure, some access to capital is of the essence, but given the centrality of uncertainty to his definition, and the ubiquity of uncertainty in our lives, Cantillon would be the first to see the concept expand in all directions. Production, commerce, arbitrage, art, liberal professions—even, curiously, mendicancy and robbery—all of these are areas in which entrepreneurs are to be found.

It was the subsequent triumph of industrial capital that cemented the association between this figure and the sphere of production, most notably in the work of Joseph Schumpeter, for whom the "fundamental impulse that sets and keeps the capitalist engine in motion comes from the new consumers' goods, the new methods of production or transportation, the new markets, the new forms of industrial organization that capitalist enterprise creates."[6] A golden age of capitalist expansion from the nineteenth to the mid-twentieth century invested these heralds of economic dynamism with a heroic allure and imbued them with a moral, even civilizational meaning: Through their innovations, they made not only money but history, and set a model of ingenuity and spirit to be followed. It is this aura that we can still find today around the giants of the tech industry, be they true visionaries or, like Elon Musk, only rich enough to buy other people's breakthroughs.

As the 1970s ushered in a rollback of industrialization and social protections in most parts of the world, it was instrumental that one could simultaneously democratize the figure of the entrepreneur and continue to moralize it—that it could appear at once as the ultimate truth of human behavior, something that people must be trained into becoming, and the thing it would be a failure not to become. By recasting every individual as an investor and defining *entrepreneurship* as practically synonymous with human activity, Theodore Schulz's and Gary Becker's human capital theory and the Austrian school of Ludwig von Mises and Friedrich Hayek fulfilled that role, making good on Cantillon's original intuition of the concept's generality.[7] For Mises, "entrepreneur" ultimately means "acting man [seen] exclusively from the aspect of uncertainty inherent in every action," and therefore "every actor is always an entrepreneur." But why stop there, if all action can be described as the allocation of finite resources towards competing goals with uncertain results? Gerard Radnitzky would go on to claim that "all life, beginning from bacteria, exhibits 'entrepreneurial spirit.'"[8] Around the same time, management guru Peter Drucker revived Schumpeter's hero for an age of constant change and endless adaptability, in which, even if not everyone was in a position to create disruption, it was imperative that all develop the skills and discipline to respond to it.[9]

This is the background for the cult of the entrepreneur of the last four decades, which is enshrined not only in the dominance of such ideas in the public debate but also in the policies through which these ideas have recreated the world in their image—and that, by favoring the market as a mechanism for allocating resources to the detriment of social rights and public services, have privatized risks and raised economic insecurity and coercion, fostering an ever-intensifying sink-or-swim social logic. Especially in places like the United States, Latin America, and West Africa, this state of affairs was given a further boost by the growing influence of evangelical churches preaching the so-called "prosperity gospel" and the boom of the self-help and coaching industries.

But their ubiquity may not be the only explanation for these ideas' continuing appeal. Even under normal conditions, of course, the market always produces many more losers than winners. Indeed, the fiction that it would be a space in which individuals flourish solely on merit usually serves to obscure all the advantages on which winners actually depend: intergenerational wealth, good connections, privileged access to political power, and so forth. But a large part of the power of entrepreneurial ideology stems precisely from the fact that the impossibility of realizing it tends to strengthen rather than weaken identification with it. When success is believed to depend solely on individual effort, failure is experienced not as a sign that the dice are loaded but as guilt, shame, and a call to try even harder. Success and entrepreneurship itself thus become objects of what Lauren Berlant called "cruel optimism": the attachment to a promise of happiness that not only fails to materialize but prevents us from achieving happiness, and to which we return again and again in the hope that "this time it will be different."

Accumulated over decades, this repetition produces negative solidarity (the feeling that "if I have to go through this, so does everyone else") and resentment (the hatred that arises from the experience of not getting what one imagines one deserves). Much of the material that Donald Trump and other far-right leaders have found at their disposal comes from this. What their discourse can offer is relief from individual blame—failure, which would normally be the responsibility of the individual, in this case is not—without acknowledging the action of social structures on our lives. The valuable function that scapegoating and conspiracy theories play is to attribute personality and intentionality to impersonal forces that condition personal trajectories: If you failed, it is not because the system distributes opportunities unequally but because specific agents wanted it so. In this way, the demand for justice comes to be equivalent to the demand for the "equality" of an idealized market, free from the harmful actions of more or less hidden subjects, and actions to disempower and imperil those who have supposedly been unduly favored (like trans people or migrants) appear as leveling, rather than further unbalancing, the playing field.

Affects like resentment and negative solidarity are an integral part of the *longue durée* of the neoliberal reprogramming of subjectivity—the internalization of what we can call, following Verónica Gago, "neoliberalism from below." Naturally, they tend to grow in intensity as economic conditions worsen, particularly among those who are most exposed to downward social mobility and rapidly shrinking horizons of expectation. The fact that the most likely outlet for these people today is the ultra-precarious world of the gig economy will only tend to reinforce that. Under its conditions, seeing oneself as entrepreneur—rather than worker, exploited or poor—is instrumental both to navigating a world in which one bears all risks and to sustaining self-esteem in the face of hardship and overwork. Government regulation, from taxes to obligations put on bosses to even the laws of traffic, appears as a hindrance to economic activity, whereas the existential threat of losing one's car, motorbike, or phone makes promises of heavy policing, laxer gun legislation, and greater leniency with killings carried out in defense of property more enticing. Tellingly, the rise of the far right in Brazil coincides with a 979.8 percent rise in the number of people working for digital platforms between 2016 and 2021, and one can find among Argentinean Uber drivers some of Milei's most dedicated supporters.

THE LOWER UPPER MIDDLE CLASS

But such moments of economic crisis are also what allows the far right to connect these feelings as they occur at different levels of the social structure to a different form of resentment that can grow even in times of relative prosperity—and whose main point of origin we can locate in a class stratum that we might call, borrowing an expression from George Orwell in *The Road to Wigan Pier*, the *lower upper middle class*.

When Trump won his first election, the upset was often almost entirely attributed to the mythical "white working class" of regions deindustrialized by decades of neoliberal globalization. As much as members of this social segment may have actually defined the outcome of the vote in their own districts, this analysis confused anecdote and fact by ignoring that only 25 percent of Trump voters matched the profile of a white person without a college degree and with household income below the national average, or by failing to take into account that many poor voters relative to the national average were relatively well off compared with the areas where they lived ("nationally poor but locally rich," as one study put it).[10] Similarly, in Brazil, while the left focused on the millionaires who supported Bolsonaro, and the right tried to present itself as the true voice of the people, the hardest core of Bolsonarismo could be found among people who enjoyed a relatively comfortable status but were constantly haunted by the specter of losing it. Although their incomes place them in the middle or upper middle class, they lack the wealth of accumulated assets and the cultural and social capital of others with similar standards of living, in a world in which such assets, not the wage, are increasingly a prerequisite for securing a middle-class existence.[11] These deficiencies make them particularly sensitive to status differences and exposed to fluctuations in the economy. The fruit of recent upward class mobility, or heirs of families that saw their wealth dwindle over time, they find themselves permanently in a neither-here-nor-there position: high consumption, but at the cost of private debt; university degrees, but with mediocre grades or from low-prestige institutions; business ownership, but never operating with a completely comfortable margin and often resorting to tax evasion and other illegal resources to meet the bottom line.

This "lumpen elite" status makes them a hotbed of resentment directed both upward and downward. Upward, they begrudge a cultural elite that masters codes that elude them (and which they see as mere arbitrary markers of social distinction), a social elite that has the connections they lack (and which presents itself as a closed network of cronyism), and an economic elite that possesses the wealth they crave (which is an object of envy and emulation at the same time). Downward, they rue the threat of losing their own markers of distinction: exclusivity in access to consumer goods such as international travel, spaces such as the university, or services such as domestic work, for example.[12] This status anxiety in turn implies a high sensitivity to disruption to what Corey Robin called "the private life of power," and which we can understand by extending W. E. B. Du Bois's idea of a "psychological wage of whiteness" to speak also of class and gender relations.[13] The resentful often find emotional compensation in the possibility of feeling superior to the waiter, the maid, the Black (in the case of the white), the woman (in the case of the man), the gay or trans (in the case of the cis straight)—and therefore resent any risk of not being able to enjoy these advantages or of losing them.

In Brazil and other Latin American countries, the lower upper middle class did not fail to benefit from the years of prosperity under the Pink Tide but saw their gains suffer relative depreciation compared to the gains of the richest and the symbolic and material advances of the poorest.[14] It was in this environment that figures like Jair Bolsonaro, his own "guru" Olavo de Carvalho, and Javier Milei found the fertile ground on which it was possible to tie together, around the idea of a grand conspiracy against Western values, the frustrations of the *concurseiro* who did not pass his exams (and went on to blame racial quotas), the man who failed to correspond to the alpha male ideal (and came to blame feminism), the adult who felt intellectually diminished (and began to blame cultural Marxism), as well as the unsuccessful businessman whose disappointment was now recast as the outcome of redistributive policies.[15] It was thus that feelings of failure and impotence could find not only an explanation but a space for recognition, support, and organization. In Brazil, the coalescing of the new right that took place from 2013 onward, with its occasionally delirious protests and moral panics around universities and contemporary art exhibitions, was perhaps the greatest mental health program the country ever saw. And before taking hold in other classes, it was among the lower upper middle class—by then feeling the pinch of the economic downturn—that it first found a home.

This process, however, would have not been possible were it not for scores of figures whose business, carried out from their perches on social and legacy media, turned out to be far-right agitation. This is where we reach our second level of analysis: the business of far-right organization and the need to understand leaders like Trump, Bolsonaro, Milei—and the entire political-media ecosystem that supported their rise to power—as not only pro-entrepreneur but as entrepreneurial in their own right.

Unlike the United States, where a powerful right-wing media ecosystem had been building up for quite some time, this process was even more evident for how quickly it took place in countries like Brazil and Argentina, where the far right rose on the back of acute, rather than slow-burn, economic decline. As political and economic instability revealed the existence of a market niche, hundreds of bankrupt businessmen, decadent rockers, failed actors and actresses, disreputable journalists, "activist" sub-celebrities, struggling stock traders, lifestyle coaches, police and military officers seeking to supplement their incomes found the opportunity for a new career. Whether through the monetisation of YouTube channels and Instagram profiles, the conquest (or reconquest) of profitable legacy media gigs, the creation of movements capable of capturing resources of nebulous origin and destination, or the sales of various services and products, this colourful fauna of "conservative," "patriotic," "liberal," and "anarchocapitalist" agitators constituted a circuit of (mostly) online entrepreneurs that doubled as a counterpublic and, increasingly, as a political movement.

What is characteristic of these political entrepreneurs is that they take the basic principle of the influencer economy—the conversion of attentional into economic capital—and, making politics into its object, add political capital to that cycle of endless convertibility: Content becomes clout, which becomes money and political influence, which can be reinvested into more content, and so on. Becoming a personality in this field brings not only the capacity to influence people's opinions but the prospect of a career in politics, which in turn brings notoriety and a loyal audience, feeding back into social media performance, and so forth. Even in public office, politics is still carried out with the attention economy in mind, less about the boring slog of policy than it is about stunts to be edited into internet-friendly, bite-sized chunks. All the while, and even if it does not lead to career change, political entrepreneurship remains tied to the pursuit of monetary gains, both direct (invitations to conferences, advertising and publishing contracts, sale of products like T-shirts and stickers, access to public funds) and indirect (tax write-offs, loans and grants, access to authorities).[16]

Here lies an organizational feature of the contemporary far right that many commentators, lost in their obsession with interwar-period analogies, have failed to grasp: Rather than merely *lacking* the mass organizations of historical fascism, the far right in most countries today possesses its own *distinct* organizational logic, the basic cell of which is the political entrepreneur. Instead of riding to power on the back of a top-down structure designed along paramilitary lines, figures like Trump, Bolsonaro, and Milei have relied extensively on the mobilizing, recruiting, and ideologizing carried out by an ecosystem of individuals and organizations that existed independently but eventually came to see them as vehicles for their own ends — political and/or otherwise.[17]

This convergence of agents for whom political goals and economic incentives aligned eventually coalesced in structures akin to a pyramid scheme: a multilevel edifice of influencers of different sizes, each descending layer presiding over a smaller public, which may ultimately be that of a single church, friend group, or family. The relationship among the different layers is always symbiotic, those higher up depending on the diffusion that those on lower levels provide, while offering leadership, discursive frames, a general model, or even just a focal point in exchange. The places at the top are reserved for those who are capable of crossing over into institutional politics and as such can consolidate the gains of the movement and open new vistas and opportunities for the ecology as a whole; but, as in multilevel marketing, most of those who join at the bottom do so in the hope of emulating the success of entrepreneurs higher up the ladder.

In order to feed the "cruel optimism" that underpins the belief in entrepreneurship, it is essential that wannabe far-right leader-influencers play the role of aspirational objects. On the one hand, however much their new career may hide the failure of a previous one, they must present themselves as winners in the competitive world of the market, great exponents in their respective fields, authorities whose manifest merits only failed to be recognized on account of some malicious plot or thought police. (Like Bolsonaro's guru Carvalho, who fashioned himself as one of the world's greatest philosophers relegated by a cultural Marxist academic establishment to selling online courses, Argentina's Javier Milei fancies himself as a Nobel Prize–level economist denied his due credit thanks to the no-holds-barred radicality of his thinking.) On the other hand, if their clout and different kinds of capital start to grow, they, like the rich Instagram coach or the prosperity gospel pastor driving around in his shiny new car, come to embody not only the promise of "making it" but a proof of the veracity of their own discourse and of the viability of their chosen path.[18]

SHILLING THE RUBES

"There are strong indications that, at its present state at least, [far-right] agitation is as much a racket as a political movement," wrote Leo Löwenthal and Norbert Guterman in a classic study of the rhetoric used by right-wing propagandists.[19] The year was 1949. Historian Rick Perlstein has shown a promiscuity between commercial interests and political goals so long standing in the fundraising practices of the United States' conservative movement that it becomes impossible to say where one ends and the other begins. "They are two facets of the same coin—where the con selling 23-cent miracle cures for heart disease inches inexorably into the one selling miniscule marginal tax rates as the miracle cure for the nation itself."[20] Quinn Slobodian has remarked on how investment newsletters from the 1980s and 1990s merged business and propaganda and suggested that "the history of libertarianism in the United States cannot be separated from the business of selling collectible coins," with the likes of Ron Paul and Glenn Beck among those who used fears of fiat currency meltdowns to turn a profit from sales of gold.[21] Apart from the defense of the armed forces' corporative interests, Bolsonaro's twenty-seven-year trajectory as a congressman was practically restricted to the promotion of miracle resources like graphene and niobium and of a so-called cancer pill that was banned by the Brazilian National Health Security Agency.[22] In keeping with his modern image, El Salvador's Nayib Bukele closely aligned himself with cryptocurrencies, in which, like Trump, he is of course also an investor. As Perlstein concludes, there are several ways in which the right as a social movement resembles pyramid schemes or the infamous "multilevel marketing" of companies such as Amway—itself a long-standing magnet for members of the lower upper middle class in their search to shore up or enhance their social status.

"It must not be forgotten that the agitator banks on an audience composed of 'dupes,'" Löwenthal and Guterman noted.[23] That "common life experience" of being "insecure, dependent and bewildered" because one feels cheated by more powerful forces is at once a source to be tapped into politically and a weakness to be economically exploited.[24] Using digital platforms rather than soapboxes or more traditional forms of organizing, today's political entrepreneurs connect a demand (frustrations, anxieties, traumas, desires) with a supply (support, explanations, solutions, scapegoats). The basis on which this encounter develops is the emotional fragility generated by the inability to fulfil one's own expectations in a society where everyone is enjoined to strike out and make it on their own, a fertile ground for opportunists and profiteers of all kinds. What better disguise for a confidence artist than being the one who understands that fragility and reveals the real culprits behind it? As Naomi Klein recently observed, a figure like Steve Bannon "is not really offering his listeners any real alternative to the corporate predation he rails against ... he is just fleecing them in more small-time ways."[25]

Now, the notion of meritocracy has always struck a precarious balance between two fairly incompatible ideas, the ostensibly democratic promise that everyone can win through their own effort and the aristocratic celebration of those who actually win as endowed with above-average mettle and vision—as in Schumpeter's extolling of the entrepreneur as the agent of "creative destruction," a revolutionary whose achievements lie "outside of the routine tasks which everyone understands."[26] Things gets even more complicated when one admits—as one must in order to conjure any pretensions to justice, whether individual and moral or social and collective—that whatever rewards the market distributes "will of necessity be determined partly by skill and partly by luck."[27] In a disarmingly candid passage, Friedrich Hayek ponders the "real dilemma" of whether "to encourage in the young the belief that when they really try they will succeed, or [to] rather emphasize that inevitably some unworthy will succeed and some worthy fail;" for while "few circumstances will do more to make a person energetic and efficient" than the first belief, it also leads to "an air of self-righteousness" in those who do win, and "must appear as a bitter irony and severe provocation" to those who feel they deserved better.[28]

Closer to aristocratic genius than to democratic hard work in the caprice of its distribution, luck relativizes the connection between investment in human capital and return: It is possible to give it all without making headway just as it is possible to strike oil without breaking sweat. One can then see how the meaning of entrepreneurship can slip between industriousness and looking for the jackpot around the corner, and the praise of hard graft can slide surreptitiously into the valorization of grift. This semantic indeterminacy becomes even more evident when we move from Schumpeter's epic narrative to Hayek's more modest one, in which the hero is not a radical innovator but someone who knows how to exploit privileged information. For Hayek, the market is a large information processor that communicates beneficial differences in the conditions of production through price variations. It is the fact of knowing something others do not, such as where cheaper labor or transport can be obtained, that allows an agent to sell at a lower price. In this way, they will be both deriving an economic reward from their knowledge and bringing a useful novelty into the system. It is thus that, Hayek writes, "where only a few know yet of an important new development," it will be "the much maligned speculators" who "will see to it that the relevant information will rapidly be spread by an appropriate change in prices."[29] The shortest path to success is thus the discovery of a small marginal gain or of the next big idea. The problem is, of course, that where there are many people looking for a shortcut, there will always be someone whose shortcut is to convince others that they have found it; unsurprisingly, "the secret they don't want you to know" is one of the most popular titles for online videos.

The passage from the production-trade axis to finance adds another layer to this dynamic. While in the first case the gain brought about by privileged information is immediately verified in the cheapening of the product, the payoff from an investment is typically out in the future: Bet on the idea today and win later for having found it first. Financial markets put the next big thing theoretically within everyone's reach but at the same time make it so that profitable business, pyramid scheme, miracle cure, confidence trick, and conspiracy theory all share the same essential form: The promise that information now restricted to a small circle will soon prove to be a revolutionary truth and generate pecuniary and/or psychic gains for those who dared embrace it first. The difference between a missed opportunity and a million-dollar gamble—or belonging on the right side of history—could thus reside in the audacity of "freelance thinking," to borrow the phrase that disgraced political entrepreneur extraordinaire Tucker Carlson used to describe QAnon.[30]

The similarities run deeper still. As with pyramid schemes, the best way to make money in finance is to be the first in and the first out. Since the value of an asset depends on people's perception of what it will be worth, those who invest first have the opportunity to see their initial investment gain in value until the asset is valued so high that it can no longer deliver the expected return. Then it is time to sell, before the market reaches the same conclusion and the price starts to fall. This trajectory describes all speculative bubbles in history, from the Dutch tulip mania in the seventeenth century to the housing market crash that brought down the world economy in 2008, but these exceptional moments reveal nothing more than the way finance normally works.[31]

While this logic has remained unchanged since the birth of financial markets, two major changes have occurred in recent decades. The first is that the feedback loop between public perception and monetary value has been significantly shortened: The two now interact much faster. By connecting markets and nations across the world, late twentieth-century globalization created a world where money never sleeps and financial assets are continually subject to the mood swings of an international audience responding in real time to social media and 24-hour news broadcasts. It is thus that a gesture as small as Portuguese football star Cristiano Ronaldo's hiding two bottles of Coca-Cola during a press conference can have an almost immediate impact on the brand's stock.[32] The second is that the means and techniques for manipulating perception have undergone a boom, and there are ever more expedients and tools available to anyone who wants to inflate the value of assets, brands, and ideas.

This can be done through the brute force of money. Companies like Uber can offer rock-bottom prices to consumers not only because they exploit loopholes in labor laws, but because they have the funds to operate in the red for years while they strive to sideline competitors and monopolize their markets—monopoly-seeking being central to the platform economy. This is the not-so-hidden secret behind the get-big-fast strategy that fuels so-called unicorns (privately owned start-ups valued above US$1 billion), and it supposes that, if it turns out the company can never live up to the expectations it generated, investors will have reaped their return on investment by the time it opens its capital on the stock market. But the artifice may just as well be hype: If the value of an asset depends on its being perceived as valuable, those who manage to generate that impression will inevitably see it rise. A well-oiled propaganda machine and a founder who sounds convinced that an outlandish promise can be fulfilled are capable of inflating even the most misbegotten investments, from the comical (the now legendary Fyre Festival) to the tragic (the OceanGate commercial submersible, which imploded on a trip to the wreck of the *Titanic*).

It is at this point that finance and the influencer economy intersect. Not only in the sense that influencers are great instruments for manipulating opinion, but also in that their activity shares with financial markets the exact same principle: managing public perception as a mechanism for generating value. Given how this practice has become central not only to the economy but to social life as a whole, it seems perfectly fitting that one of the most defining figures of our time should be Donald Trump: a self-declared billionaire whose main source of income in this century was playing the role of a billionaire on a reality show, leveraging the notoriety this brought him into a series of licensing deals. And given the centrality of the political entrepreneur to the rise of the far right, and the fact that the most literal intersection of finance and the influencer economy is the recent trend of hiring digital content producers to promote cryptocurrencies, creating small bubbles for the benefit of early investors, it is no wonder that we should see everything come full circle in the image of two presidents elected on the back of an ecosystem of political entrepreneurs being caught engaged in a practice that the stock market knows only too well by the name of "pump and dump."

When public perception and money are so intertwined, nothing matters more than authenticity: When everyone is faking it, what is real is worth the most. The problem, of course, is that faking the real thing has never been easier. In a hyperconnected global society, with billions of producers and consumers of information, there is no shortage of ways to advertise without appearing to do so, seeding content that appears "organic" and "spontaneous" in order to generate engagement that is effectively both. The proliferation of instruments to manipulate the metrics of social networks, such as click farms and robot or cyborg accounts; the multiplication of fake news sources; the hiring of influencers for undeclared publicity; the creation of multiplatform communication ecosystems that form a closed circuit where parallel worlds are gradually constructed; not to mention the development of increasingly realistic artificial intelligence products: Everything indicates that we are living through a golden age of fraud.[33] And if in the past a good con man would always plant one or two accomplices among the public to help them attract victims, on the internet one can have as many accomplices as one's budget will allow. From Brexit to Milei and beyond, the history of the rightward shift in world politics in recent years is inseparable from the fact that contemporary democracies lack the antibodies to cope with this transformation.

AND YE SHALL KNOW THE TRUTH AND THE TRUTH SHALL MAKE YOU FREE[34]

But we should also be attentive to what else this picture is showing us. The centrality of the political entrepreneur to the far right testifies to a number of material shifts that are reshaping work, class, and the figure of the entrepreneur itself.

Underemployment, precarization, wage stagnation, the concentration of wealth and the growing disconnect between wage income, and the guarantee of a good life all increasingly conspire to make the prospect of finding a shortcut the only plausible way out of their predicament for many people. As the link between economic security and traditional forms of human capital investment—most notably a university education—is severed, meritocracy as synonymous with "making it through hard work" appears to be an imaginary that our age is in the process of killing, replacing it with the search for a lucky break. Where there is no linear path from effort to success, magical solutions grow in appeal, and graft gives way to grift.[35] It is not that the hustle disappears—how could it, after all?—but rather that, with ever less to fall back on, everything becomes hustle, and every hustle potentially has an angle. Perhaps we will one day come to see the transition from Fordism to post-Fordism as the last gasp of the Protestant ethic, at least in its old, cumulative form.[36]

The quest for magical solutions can take several forms, from dalliances with illegality to the gambling epidemic triggered by online betting. At the turn of the century, anthropologists John and Jean Comaroff described pyramid schemes as "casino capitalism for people who lack the fiscal or cultural capital to . . . gamble in more conventional markets": Dow Jones for the poor (or the lumpen elite). Today, things have been sadly much simplified by the fact that everyone can carry a casino in their pocket.[37] But a key place in which people now look for a portal that will whisk them away from a gridlocked existence is in the possibilities for the manipulation of public perception afforded by social media. That digital political entrepreneurs are so central to the contemporary far right is not just a political but also an economic fact: If many people ended up looking for a career in far-right agitation, it is also because of how attractive the influencer economy has become as perhaps the most accessible gamble with the highest prospect of potential gains.[38] This is a structural reason for the ease with which the extremist virus continues to travel and mutate. It explains, for instance, the surprisingly smooth convergence of "far right" and "far-out" that took place during the COVID-19 pandemic, as an entire online ecosystem of health influencers, many of whom had been hit hard by lockdown, emerged to spread disinformation about the disease, attack vaccines and push "alternative treatments," finding natural allies in denialist leaders like Bolsonaro and Trump.[39]

There is probably no better illustration of how the figure of the entrepreneur has been affected by these changes than the transformation of the coaching industry: Whereas the coach was originally a figure that trained and inspired people to attain success in their own businesses, increasingly what online coaches coach people to do is to become online coaches themselves.[40] In this extreme form of the new configuration of labor, the divorce between finance and production is elevated to the point of parody, a pyramid scheme at the bottom of which no productive activity in the strict sense ever takes place: It is hype all the way down. Even with the all-powerful Silicon Valley, it is increasingly hard to tell which outlandish new technological promises are to be taken seriously and which exist only to attract attention, investment, and lower-hanging fruit like government contracts.

As "faking it till you make it" becomes the dominant way of making it, an element of deceitfulness, trickery, and cunning becomes ever more explicitly encoded in the very idea of entrepreneurship. Not that it was not always there: The nineteenth-century's robber barons represented better than anyone else the intimate connection between the entrepreneur and the frontier, literal as well as figurative, as a gray zone between legality and illegality, morality and immorality, where righteousness is settled after the fact by an action's capacity to persist unchallenged. (Tech and resource extraction being today's clearest equivalents of the frontiers of the Modern Age, it is no surprise that the captains of both industries should have discovered an affinity with the far right.) The difference is that, whereas lack of an entrepreneurial spirit could once be construed as a moral failing, said spirit is now widely acknowledged to involve a considerable degree of ruthlessness when it comes to cutting corners and bending rules—and the absence of that particular sort of fiber, as a shortcoming in itself.

This, in turn, creates another element of identification across classes. From the *viração*[41] of Brazilian motorcycle couriers—a state of constant activity endlessly moving across the boundaries of formal and informal, legal and illegal work—to multimillion-dollar tax evasion, not to mention all the hustling and scamming taking place in between, it is widely understood that, like natural selection, the struggle for survival in the market is beyond good and evil.[42] Legal and moral constraints thus appear as arbitrary limitations on the freedom to compete, and being subject to them as a sign of weakness: To win, one must be ready to break the law, and the prize for winning is a position where the rules that apply to others become optional. Once again, this is where the modern and the pre-modern, the cutting edge and the archaic converge: The top of the food chain of contemporary entrepreneurship does not differ much from the position of the patriarch or the old plantation owner in its ability to stand above the law.

The fact that it has been inflated by individuals interested in personal gain does not make the global far right any less real. On the contrary, its reality must be understood precisely as the product of a feedback between a real demand and the supply political entrepreneurs provide.

Neither one nor the other was fully given before the process began: Grassroots and agitators produced them together out of contexts of crisis. It was its very mining that created this vein, and the agitators became who they were by observing which discourses produced which reactions, at the same time as the rank and file adopted their ideas and pushed them to raise the tone. It would be a mistake to see the radicalization of so many public figures and politicians as merely a symptom of a general shift of the population to the right; the symptom, in this case, is also the cause.

That far-right political entrepreneurs are opportunistic does not mean that their engagement with the ideas they espouse is merely cynical or instrumental. It is true that their commitment to public morality, rectitude, and truthfulness is elastic at the best of times; but the often-denounced hypocrisy of such "upstanding citizens" is, at bottom, a sincere commitment to something else. Like many of their followers, they believe in a society where everyone "knows their place": where women are demure and stay at home, Black people use the service entrance in buildings, boys are boys, girls are girls, and no one complains about whatever little they have. They believe in this not because of the intrinsic value of these principles but because of the distribution of power and personal advantages that follow from them. Above all, they believe in their right to occupy the position that these values assign to them in class, gender, and race hierarchies: that of someone entitled to give free rein to their will, at the very least in their private life. This is the place, simultaneously real and imaginary, that they fear losing, feel they have lost, and long to attain.

We fail to fully understand the appeal of figures like Trump, Bolsonaro, Farage, Milei, or even Musk if we perceive them solely from the point of view of fiscal, managerial, law-and-order discipline and miss the permissiveness with which they also beckon: the promise that those who "deserve it" will be left alone to pursue their goals as they see fit, while those who do not will face the letter of the law and the rigors of a life with ever-fewer protections—thus becoming less likely competitors for the scraps at the bottom or the bounty at the top. This explains why the supposed "contradictions" in their behavior—the extravagant private lives, the blatant use of office for commercial interests and vendettas, the pay-to-play politics, the admissions to evading taxes or breaking laws, the open support for actors that elude the state's presently existing regulatory functions—do not appear to harm their image. These are not simple inconsistencies but subtext; they are out in the open for a reason other than their mere enjoyment. "You would do it too," the subtext says, "and you *should* be able to do it, and the fact that *I* can do it is precisely what makes me worthy of admiration."

Every time they claim that "red tape" is what forces businessmen to cut corners, that too many taxes are the cause of fraud, that abortion is a crime but sexual abuse in the family is a private matter, every time they embody the unfettered jouissance of a subject supposed to be free, these leaders are communicating something to their followers. It is an acknowledgment that people should be allowed to "do what it takes" to get by; that the reward for "making it" should be nearly unlimited freedom; and that even those who fail to get there should still find that they will always be entitled to a sphere, however small, in which to exercise their power without limits and have someone to look down upon.

THREE SCENES FROM DAILY LIFE

In the run-up to an anti-austerity demonstration scheduled for March 26, 2011, posters go up in the occupied campuses around Bloomsbury, Central London, with the scathing slogan "Jobs are shit, growth is shit, all I want is revenge." At the time, "revenge" would probably suggest, to those involved in a then-febrile student movement, a few very concrete culprits. These included David Cameron's Conservative government, which had hiked tuition fees alongside a number of welfare cuts; their junior coalition partners, the Liberal Democrats, who had campaigned on a promise not to support the hike only to betray it a few months into the new administration; and those who had contributed to and profited from the 2008 financial meltdown—who, instead of being punished, were being set for even greater gains by austerity measures that transferred the costs of the crisis to the population.

With hindsight, that slogan reads as an incredibly prescient harbinger of the politics of the following fifteen years. As the desire for revenge became ever more central as a motive force, its objects, on the other hand, became both more varied and less precise. More varied, too, are those who express the feeling—including, of late, the self-styled white supremacist influencer Nick Fuentes, who responded to taunts from his own followers that he was not a true incel by saying, "All I want is revenge against my enemies and a total Aryan victory."

Our second scene takes place in the same year as the first, but far from Central London: in Paripe, a poor suburb of Salvador, in the Brazilian Northeast. It was registered for posterity by a TV show that is one of the most popular in its genre, a sort of infotainment that specializes in violent crime and, by fomenting fear and endorsing law-and-order discourses, plays a major role in the affective infrastructure that shapes Bolsonarista subjectivity. On this occasion, however, they are looking for the lighter side of the story: A journalist speaks to a crowd of local residents who are protesting because they had bought tickets for a presentation by a famous clown duo only to discover that the unscrupulous promoter had hired two impostors for the job. The result is a viral video celebrated to this day.

Even though the rogue impresario had to be whisked away to the police station for protection, people are clearly delighted to tell their stories and perform for the camera. About halfway through the video, the mob hit upon a chant whose curious grammatical contortion makes it instantly memorable: "We want my money! We want my money!" Silly accident though it is, the sentence becomes more profound as one hears it repeated. Intoned in a single voice, the pronoun at the start gives it the outward form of a collective demand

and the semblance of a shared struggle. But that expectation is negated by the predicate, which turns the collectivity into a transient aggregate of discrete individuals, without a higher sense of purpose or an identity beyond their immediate goal, its power merely a vehicle for private interests instead of the expression of a desire for commonality.

The third scene does not have a specific time stamp. You can see it every rush hour in large cities like São Paulo and Rio de Janeiro if you happen to be at a busy station when an empty train arrives. As it slows down and stops, commuters will huddle around the doors; when these slide open, they stampede in, trying to catch an empty seat before someone else does. Nothing could be more natural, of course. For people who have worked all day and often have long trips home ahead of them, being able to sit down offers both the opportunity for some much welcome rest and a slightly more sheltered position in hot, overcrowded cars. What is striking about the scene is, rather, one small detail: the subtle grin you will notice in the faces of inrushing commuters, as if there is something almost joyous in the daily ritual of scrambling for a place in overcapacity public transport. How to interpret this smile? Is it just the anticipated relief of finding a spot, or something else—the pleasure to be found in the gamification of everyday inconvenience, the tiny quantum of enjoyment one can extract from a situation that ought to, and sometimes does, spark anger and revolt?

Although none of these three scenes directly concerns the far right, we can extrapolate from them some observations on the affective disposition of far-right support and the material conditions underlying it. On the one hand, the blind fury and resentment, the feeling of having it hard while others appear to have it all, which inspires a desire for revenge so strong that it borders on self-harm. One would be willing to lose if it meant seeing others lose harder, and one would prefer to see things end faster than give up on the life one has—a form of *endmaxxing*, perhaps, in the parlance of our days. But this passion, and the sense of historical mission that banding together against a common enemy can inspire, is tempered at the other end by the petty calculation of private interest—not only the rewards one expects from defeating the enemy but the material gains to be made along the way, in that gray zone in which furthering the movement and furthering oneself become indistinct. Even as one discovers, in online forums and mobilizations, the potentials of community and of social bonds, it is as if, deep down, it were impossible to believe that anything but the law of the jungle could be the rule, and that commitment to a collective project, even when sincere, could not but be at least in part about individual advantage. Ultimately, the project is not about a radical reconfiguration of the world but simply about a different distribution of its spoils, and so the freedom that it seeks can only be the defense of its participants' freedom to pursue their own good against those who they see as hindering them.

A fundamental ambivalence, then, between collectivity and atomization, in which the former simultaneously offers some respite from the overbearing prevalence of the latter and a continuation of it by other means. This ambivalence is at its clearest when projected outward, in the hatred directed toward social movements and the left—whose political commitment far-right supporters find it hard to construe as anything other than a mask for self-interest, even as they experience strong feelings of commitment and devotion in themselves. (For the right, politics is simultaneously something that cannot at all be trusted and in which a lot of faith is placed.) Behind this ambivalence, the naturalization of competition and the conditions that force us into it, reproduced on a daily basis in such ordinary acts as catching a train; the resignation to perhaps never seeing those conditions change; and the search for marginal compensations and little joys in situations that, though hard to bear, do not appear to be preventable.

CHAPTER 4

ALL POWER TO THE TROLLS: THE COLONIZATION OF POLITICS BY THE ATTENTION ECONOMY

January 7, 2020, saw the sudden end of the resistible rise of Roberto Alvim, the washed-up theater director that Jair Bolsonaro had appointed as secretary for culture—an area that the new government openly despised and in which it could find few allies. Alvim's resignation, forced by the scandal surrounding an official video that couched a speech on the "new national art" in none-too-subtle nods to National Socialism and lines lifted directly from Joseph Goebbels, was one of many indications of the extent to which parts of the Brazilian government were attentive to, and inspired by, what was then still known as the North American alt-right. From their communication techniques to knowing nods, such as the cries of "Deus vult!," the White Power hand sign, and the obsession with the Crusades, it was clear that the model to be followed, especially for a small team of young, internet-savvy advisers clustered around the presidential office, was the heterogeneous constellation of groups and public figures that first came to prominence in the context of Trump's 2016 presidential campaign. But whereas in the United States this had been more of a marriage of convenience between a candidate happy to trade loyal online campaigning for dog whistles and a radical fringe that saw him as a potential vehicle for its more outré ideas, in Brazil it was something simultaneously less organic and much closer to the throne. Although an actual alt-right did not exist outside a small network of terminally online influencers, this network included two of Bolsonaro's sons and a few key aides and interlocutors, all of whom very obviously looked up to their northern counterparts and craved their recognition. Emulating and establishing contact were, for them, at once a display of cosmopolitan credentials, a form of brand differentiation in relation to the rest of the Brazilian right, and a way of claiming a place in a global movement. Even though their impact on policy and negotiations with other political forces was limited, they had great control over Bolsonaro's digital networks and could thus shape the way the far right communicated as a whole. In that limited sense, we could perhaps say that Brazil had the first alt-right government in the world.[1]

Although it is unclear to what extent these operators subscribed to the more extreme beliefs they occasionally tried on for size, one area in which they very obviously identified with their US equivalents was the latter's instinctive mastery of communication in the age of social media, clickbait, and the attention economy. Before many others, they had understood the opportunities afforded by an information ecosystem in which anyone can publish anything at almost no cost; in which many fail to distinguish suspect sources from reliable ones; in which the thirst for clicks favors sensationalist and often false headlines, and fact-checking never travels far and always arrives late; in which extreme content is pushed by engagement-seeking algorithms; and in which a pusillanimous interpretation of the journalistic duty to "hear both sides" contributes to bestowing truth value on narratives with no basis in fact, turning outright lies into "differences of opinion."[2] What is more, one thing they understood earlier (and better) than anyone else was the advantages of occupying the position of one of the central figures in contemporary culture: the troll.

Although the etymology of the term is dubious, the troll is so ubiquitous and easy to spot that the concept has migrated offline. Its origins as a cultural phenomenon lie in an ethos that puts iconoclastic, no-holds-barred humor—the *lulz*, in old internet parlance—above considerations of taste, morality, political usefulness, or even the well-being of others. This carefree attitude toward the possible effects of one's actions is something largely facilitated by the emotional dissociation characteristic of online life, in which the uninhibiting effect of technological mediation often makes us act in ways that we would refrain from in face-to-face interactions. This is compounded by the fact that, on social media, our comments, likes, and shares often contribute only a tiny fraction of a full-scale pile-on, thus creating a distance between our small, maybe relatively mild individual acts and the devastating aggregate effect that thousands of such acts put together may have.

As psychologists Paul Bloom and Matthew Jordan suggested back in 2015, referencing Derek Parfit's well-known thought experiment, regardless of whether we are reacting to a perceived injustice or merely seeking entertainment, perhaps we should acknowledge that we are all potential "harmless torturers" now, a situation which we know can very easily turn against ourselves.[3] Rather than putting a check on ironic distancing and cold detachment, however, this constant threat only reinforces them; as Richard Seymour writes, detachment "is a survival strategy in a world where one can expect to be abused."[4]

What Whitney Phillips has called the "mask of trolling" adds a further layer of dissociation to the one we experience on a daily basis, creating an affective barrier that allows the troll to minimize the consequences of what they do and maintain the innocence of their intentions—which are not intended to cause any harm, but "just fun."[5] Behind this mechanism lies an asymmetry Phillips explains through reference to Gregory Bateson's theory of play.[6] If play assumes the tacit understanding among participants that the actions that take place within the frame of a game must be interpreted in a nonliteral way, the troll is someone who privately knows that he is playing but depends on the other taking it seriously for the success of their game. There is no reciprocity, or at least not with all involved: The troll does not play with the other but at the other's expense, for their own amusement and that of an audience able to grasp what is going on and enjoy the spectacle. Their communication is therefore always double or bifurcated, communicating with two different publics at once. What other trolls know to be a joke must be taken seriously by "normies";

conversely, the farther a troll can take the game of confusing the normies about the seriousness of their actions, the more they will be taken seriously by their peers.

Therein lies the key to understanding a strategy that has, by now, been broadly adopted by the far right.[7] This double communication and the fact that the troll reserves the right to decide when they are serious and when they are not are the basis of a technique for introducing "controversial" ideas into the public debate in an ironic, humorous way, or with a certain critical distance—always maintaining the doubt as to how much of it is a joke and how much is for real. Thus, while the "internal" audience recognizes the speaker as one of its own and understands the message as serious, but its dissemination as a big joke at the expense of the other, far-right agitators will test the limits of their "external" audience, without ever failing to have an escape route. If at any point it appears they have overstepped the mark, they can always take a step back and claim they were misunderstood, that it was all a prank, and turn the tables on the accusers, making the episode into a case of persecution, a struggle for free speech, or an attack on a "woke" culture in which "nobody can take a joke anymore." This is what celebrities and politicians who have built careers as critics of "political correctness" do; it is also what the likes of Trump and Bolsonaro have done repeatedly over the years in regard to their veiled (and not so veiled) threats of a coup.

Two other elements are key to this game. The first is deceptively simple: getting the enemy to work for you. The far right is extremely adept at taking advantage of its opponents' indignation. Since algorithms are (mostly) blind to content and see no higher value than engagement metrics, any engagement is good, regardless of whether it is positive or negative. Each successful act of trolling leaves a swell of outrage in its wake, and with that swell, a long tail of thousands who will further distribute the "controversial" material, boosting its circulation, drawing attention to its source, and thus enhancing the financial and political viability of both. (Everyone should know it by now, but some ways of minimizing that effect are sharing only screengrabs, sharing only privately, or sharing the content while hiding the source.) What is more, knee-jerk, deeply felt reactions can be extremely helpful when it comes to painting a caricature of the adversary as humorless moralists, oversensitive and emotional, or mugs who fell into a trap—as uncool, as the establishment, as elitists, as enemies of free speech, or as the thought police.

The second element is the intermediate, labile layer that exists between "internal" and "external" public—as the whole point is precisely to get more people to move from the latter to the former. Here it is worth taking a minute to ponder Peter Thiel's surprisingly insightful remark during Trump's first run for president about the difference between those who took him "literally but not seriously" (the liberal establishment) and those who took him "seriously but not literally" (his followers).[8] On one level, the sentence describes the difference between those who are "in the know" and those who are not. While the second group wrings their hands over the literal content of statements, the first does not concern itself too much with what is said as long as the feeling is right: "He may not do exactly what he says he will do, but he will do things in that general vicinity, and that is good, because it is what needs to be done." On another level, the distinction allows for a degree of disavowal: "When he says he will get rid of all unwanted migrants, he cannot mean my neighbors, because they are welcome, integrated members of the community." Finally, if we consider the algorithmically mediated selective exposure that is the basis of most people's informational diet nowadays, another degree of separation becomes visible: Since people are more likely to receive some messages than others, they might be led to believe that a candidate is serious about the things they care the most about, and metaphorical or unserious about things that do not directly concern them. All of this makes it easier to dismiss violent or extreme rhetoric as humorous exaggeration.

There is probably no better example of how far this strategy of incremental normalization can go than Nayib Bukele, after a distinguished career of incendiary statements, ironically dubbing himself "the coolest dictator in the world" on social media—and then changing the Salvadoran constitution so that he could run for reelection.[9] Still, sometimes the provocateur will be caught making a provocation so outrageous that they will not be able to walk it back. This is what happened to far-right enfant terrible Milo Yiannopoulos when he had to resign from his post as Breitbart editor for statements minimizing pedophilia, to the Ron DeSantis aide fired for sharing Nazi imagery in the midst of a Republican primary, and to Bolsonaro's very own Roberto Alvim.[10] In these cases, the subject is expelled from the debate and shunned by their peers because, through their lack of skill, they end up revealing the hand of their fellow players. Alvim did not fall for "being" a Nazi; it is perfectly possible that Nazism was, for him, a mask like any other. Nor did he fall for quoting or being inspired by Nazism; other members of the same government had done similar things without losing prestige. Nor was it just because he was caught; the Nazi quote was trolling and, as such, always intended to arouse laughter among friends and fury among foes. The secretary for culture fell because he lacked his colleagues' craft in pushing the boundaries without losing grip. Eager to please his new bosses, he went so far that, like an idiot savant, he ended up producing an accidental masterpiece of overidentification: a speech that brought together some of the most sinister elements in Bolsonaro's ideology and explicitly compared them—in favorable terms—to Nazism.[11] Few outside critiques of the government could have been as damning.

Even when they fail, however, trolls always have their way, still managing to send a nod to their allies and to smuggle their ideas into the mainstream. It is only fair this particular type of troll should become known by the name *edgelord*, someone whose "edginess" serves to incrementally push the edge of what is acceptable. If anyone doubts the effectiveness of this tactic, it suffices to remember that figures such as Trump, Bolsonaro, and Milei were pet trolls on radio, podcasts, and TV shows for ages—and how much the dismissive claims that they were "only joking" helped normalize their candidacies. Remembering how several of today's far-right leaders began their rise also reminds us that the game does not solely depend on the troll's sovereignty over their own discourse, their ability to operate in a zone of indistinction between seriousness and play. It also relies on a political class, media, and market operators willing to allow or even encourage the agitators to continue playing. To treat the downfall of one troll as proof that it is possible to moderate them is to willfully ignore both the nature of that game and the cumulative effect of having several others playing it every day on social networks, in the media, and in office. If we want to understand why this game is so effective, it is ultimately to the entire setup of the contemporary attention economy that we have to turn.

NET RESULTS

The ubiquity of the troll is not, of course, the only way in which politics has changed with the spread of social media. I should, in fact, amend here what was said in the introduction about the 2008 financial crisis being a defining moment for everything that we are living through now and recognize the other epochal turning point that took place around the same time: the emergence of the web 2.0 and the definitive "platformization" of the internet. We cannot discuss the last fifteen years without talking about this event, and the processes it has set in motion have played a decisive role in the political sea change that took place in the period. With hindsight, we can see that 2011 was the last gasp of the techno-optimism that had surrounded the internet from its advent in the 1990s. From that point onward, it would become increasingly hard to sustain in good faith that the web is a univocal force for good, an open space for self-expression and free association, and a natural enemy of tyranny, monopoly, manipulation, and control.

By platformization, we should understand at once the rise of the platform as the characteristic business model of our times; a radical transformation in people's online experience, which has become predominantly routed through a handful of digital platforms; an extreme concentration of wealth and power in the hands of those few companies, which now have some direct or indirect control over most of the information produced and consumed in the world; and the emergence of the platform as a widely applicable, highly suggestive organizational paradigm and metaphor, in the same way that the network was ubiquitous in the web's early days. And if this process has led to a more sober—and somber—perspective on the internet, this is in no small part because of the ways in which it is seen as benefiting more extreme forms of politics, and particularly the far right.

Most analyses of the impact of social media on politics now focus on this. Thus, one will often hear about the issue of disinformation, although, as discussed in the second chapter, this will often stay at the superficial level of looking at the supply without considering the demand. Equally, there is much talk about political polarization, which we go into in the next chapter, and the mainstreaming of extreme positions, examined above via the figure of the troll. Some have pointed out an "elective affinity" between populism and social networks, which beckon with the possibility of bypassing discredited gatekeepers like legacy media and traditional parties, appear to offer a direct channel to political leaders, and make it easier for these to stand for a plurality of disparate demands, as it allows them to reach different audiences with different messages.[12] Exploited by the political entrepreneurs discussed in the previous chapter, these affordances enable the right to build a base in the absence of traditional organizations, which can then be used to "hack" institutional politics.[13] Finally, there is the well-known fact that platforms have a preference for more extreme, emotionally charged posts, and the increasingly well-documented evidence that their algorithms tend to amplify right-wing content.[14] And yet, since these are all end results of a single, ever more pervasive logic—one built on gratification mechanisms, the constant production of metrics, algorithmic recursivity, and the imperative to maximize engagement—it should be possible to suspend the question of who profits from that logic for a moment and ask, more generally, about the ways in which it has changed how all of us, regardless of political affiliation or opinion, relate to politics.

That social media can modulate the behavior of even those who are critical of it is, in a sense, contained in the very idea of a "platform." Originally referring to a built structure or surface, higher than the area around it, on which people and things can rest, the word has been metaphorically extended to denote "something that acts like a ground, is *analogous* to a ground, but is not a ground"—a "pseudo-ground," an artificial "ground-effect produced at . . . a detached, abstracted, differentiated level."[15] Taking the metaphor at face value thus reveals a topology that is absolutely essential to how digital platforms work, in the technical as well as in the social sense: What appears on the surface as a horizontal space of participation and collaboration among equals—a ground—is supplemented by the vertical depth of its own institution. A platform is *instituted* as a ground, that is, *by someone, for certain ends, according to certain rules*. Elon Musk's capricious interventions in favor of right-wing content on X are, in that respect, not a break with a supposed norm of neutrality but merely the rendering explicit of neutrality as a fiction; since Trump's return to power, tech moguls have been increasingly willing to come forward and tear that veil further apart.

But to speak of a hidden depth behind the superficial flatness of platforms is equally to say that the relation between these dimensions is necessarily one of *opacity*: that what users experience at the level of their interactions is conditioned, in ways that are never entirely accessible to them, by decisions made elsewhere regarding structure and rules of functioning. What presents itself on the surface as the free interplay of unmediated expressions of individuality is, in fact, a highly complex system of mediation that conditions what interactions are possible (and likely) and what information people are exposed to (and how), and thus progressively shapes users as individuals.[16] The more one believes that illusion of immediacy, the more likely one is to be misled by disinformation and radicalized; this is why a basic understanding of how platforms function and the ways in which they can manipulate (and be manipulated) has become a key part of media literacy.

Importantly, however, the effects that social media have on subjectivation cannot be simply dispelled by that knowledge. Awareness cannot change the fact that we do not ultimately control this regime of visibility, though it may lead us to be more deliberate about it (actively seeking other sources, better curating filters, being more cautious with fact-checking, and so forth). Awareness that participation in digital platforms produces us as a certain kind of subject does not stop us from becoming such subjects—and the cynical detachment that consciousness affords us may in fact help us become even more so. Finally, we may realize that, in putting all other forms of media to work according to its logic, thereby reshaping the public sphere in its image, what social media has done is above all to *definitively subsume politics under the attention economy*; yet this does not in and of itself make us any more capable of changing that state of affairs.

THE OBJECT IS TO CHANGE THE SOUL

It would always be possible to claim that politics has, at heart, long been an attention market, even before the eighteenth-century emergence of the public sphere as we know it; thus, for example, in Shakespeare's play, Mark Antony exploits the presence of Julius Caesar's freshly slain corpse to turn the tide against those who conspired to kill him. It is clear, however, that a significant transformation came about with the explosion of mass media from the nineteenth century onward, from which point it can be said that "our collective attention [became] inevitably structured by agenda-setting mechanisms governing the selection of themes serving as the attractors around which our daily conversation and social debates orbit."[17] Social media thus arrived to societies that were already highly information-rich, and as Herbert Simon, one of the pioneers of thinking about attention in economic ways, pointed out back in 1969,

> in an information-rich world, the wealth of information means a dearth of something else: a scarcity of

> whatever it is that information consumes. What information consumes is rather obvious: it consumes the attention of its recipients. Hence a wealth of information creates a poverty of attention and a need to allocate that attention efficiently among the overabundance of information sources that might consume it.[18]

What follows from this is a situation in which ever more areas become dependent on the capture and management of attention, "a prerequisite for doing profitable business as well as for winning elections and shaping society,"[19] or simply for staying afloat in the labor market: "[I]n a whole range of professions, jobs (and therefore salaries) flow along paths of visibility, sometimes to the extent that it replaces monetary exchange."[20] It could be said, then, that digital platforms have democratized visibility in an age in which it has become of the essence to most, diluting the power of established gatekeepers by making "mass self-communication" potentially available to all.[21] They have done so, however, at the cost of placing this democratization—and the data it churns on a daily basis—under highly concentrated, monopolistic control, wresting for themselves an enormous power over the workings of the attention economy and claiming the capacity to extract rent from their users' efforts to attract notoriety. What is more, by augmenting exponentially the amount of information available, they have made the allocation problem even more acute. It is indeed *because* ever more people have channels through which to express themselves that one is compelled to become ever more subject to the demands of the attention economy—and of the channels through which it primarily plays out.

Perhaps the most important thing about social media is precisely the fact that it tacitly structures its users' subjective experience of the public sphere *as a market*—by providing them with engagement metrics and training them through positive reinforcement into an intuitive grasp of the rules of the game. If Foucault was correct in saying that "the multiplication of the 'enterprise' form within the social body is what is at stake in neo-liberal [*sic*] policy," then we should see digital platforms as the most effective and widespread means for taking that multiplication all the way down to its most basic unit, the individual.[22] More than anything else, they completed the work begun in the late 1970s of making the logic of self-entrepreneurship fully internalized. They do so through the entrenchment of something we could call *brand subjectivation*; for, from guileless boomer holiday photo dumps to carefully controlled influencer timelines, online self-expression is always already an exercise in self-curation, the construction of one's digital presence as an idealized other, consciously created and managed to project a certain image of oneself to an open and potentially unlimited audience. This practice, in which the vast majority of us are engaged as performers and public on a daily basis, institutes a kind of systematic dissociation as second nature. We are true to ourselves on social media to the extent that we select, out of the daily stream of inner and outer events in our lives, the ones that best represent us to others, showing them who we believe they would most like us—that is, give us the most attention—for being. In so doing, as Rob Horning remarked, platforms normalize "what amounts to a post-authentic sense of self that won't recoil at the self-branding, lateral surveillance, opportunism and self-promotion" that the attention economy requires—which is why awareness that this is what they do to us can lead to cynical detachment and further embracing of inauthenticity just as easily as to critical distance and refusal.[23]

Of course, some level of performance has always been a part of interpersonal interactions; as Erving Goffman noted in his classic on the topic, "stage craft and stage management . . . occur everywhere in social life."[24] What is different about social media is, firstly, the fact that performance, instead of being interaction specific, takes the form of continuous self-narration in front of an audience always sensed as present, even though we do not know exactly who is watching at any given time and whose attention we are trying to grab. Secondly, to the extent that our digital presence is potentially much more visible—in reach, continuity, and archivability—than any particular interaction, or even one's offline existence as a whole, it can become more defining of who one "really is" than anything else. This is all the more so as, thirdly, social media ends up filling a void left by the decline of job stability, close-knit communities, and regular participation in offline political organizing spaces, meaning that, for many of us, a huge part of social life increasingly happens online. Last, but certainly not least, what makes digital platforms unique is the fact that they offer a constant stream of measurable feedback through which individuals can adjust their behavior according to the responses they receive from others.

This is, in fact, at once the mechanism through which attention becomes quantified and what gets us hooked: the gratification devices that platforms place at our disposal in the form of likes, shares, replies, views, new friends or followers, and the refresh button.[25] At a very basic level, digital platforms make us experience the attention economy as a gratification market, and although there is always the expectation that online attention can be converted into offline gains—relationships, career opportunities, etc.—it is as competitors in this primary market that we are all initially interpellated to manage our personal brands. Even more than in other kinds of markets, the rewards it offers are variable and unpredictable, which is a big part of what keeps us coming back in search of different results every time—hence all the comparisons between social media addiction and gambling.[26] On the other hand, the constant availability of metrics about ourselves and others helps us get a sense of how much attention is being received by whom and for what, aiding us in the effort to spot patterns that we can try to exploit in our favor. Through this combination of elusive compensation and just enough information that we can make inferences as to how to find more, social media progressively drills its rules into us and makes us adapt our behavior to its incentive structure.

Years before the platformization of the internet, and at the height of enthusiasm regarding the knowledge economy's supposedly natural propensity for collaboration, Italian economist Enzo Rullani already pointed out that proprietary logic and competition had not disappeared in the so-called immaterial economy but only become "subordinate to the law of diffusion."[27] Through its gratification mechanisms, social media has not just made this reality palpable to the vast multitude of its users; it has taught them the basics of how to navigate it. In order to successfully surf the various waves of attention that sweep across platforms, their contributions need a "speed differential" (being an early adopter, being among the first to provide a "take" or perspective on an emerging topic); a superior "mastery of context" (the real or simulated knowledge, personal experience, inside information, curation, presentation skills, etc. that can make them stand out); and a "network of alliances and of cooperation" (a web of relations, cultivated over time in more or less conscious ways, which raises their profile and increases their chances of viral success).[28] Gradually, through trial and error or deliberate study, users can also learn the power of strong affective charges (which generate the most engagement), explicit appeals for audience participation (which attract traffic and establish fidelity), self-narratives that invite identification (typically about facing or overcoming hardship of some kind), and—for extra authenticity—carefully curated moments of intimacy and "letting the guard down."

THANK YOU FOR THE FEEDBACK

There is no question that the struggle for attention is politically important in an attention economy. Likewise, it is undeniable that digital platforms have redistributed visibility, made it easier for marginalized voices to find an audience, and assisted the formation of counterpublics, including those of the far right. From the Arab Spring to the

George Floyd protests and beyond, they have also proven themselves useful for synchronizing the emotions of large numbers of people and coordinating large-scale actions, a power that different actors can, of course, harness for very different ends. The issue is, however, how they constitute us as political agents, how this conditions what we do, and how that contributes to deepening the takeover of politics by the attention economy that began with the rise of mass media.

Our complicity in this takeover is, as we have seen, not without cause. If social media occupies a space left vacant by the decline of job security, community, and political organizations, it is only natural that our lives should become ever more tilted toward the online.[29] By the same token, it is also inevitable that what happens on it should capture our attention more than what happens elsewhere, dictating our sense of urgency and significance, and making platforms appear as the key site of struggle by default. (As terminally online people will often wryly note, many vital issues seemingly cease to exist the minute one logs off.) This creates something of a self-reinforcing loop, in which the shortage of offline organizing leads to an overvaluing of online activity, which then drains resources—including attention, time, and effort—that could be put toward the former. Participation in "discourse" thus becomes tendentially synonymous with doing politics, with a series of problematic consequences: Metrics are treated as a proxy for collective power, often with no clear plan as to how one could be turned into the other; tactics that generate engagement are mistaken for strategy, subordinating movement building to gaining visibility and long-term thinking to short-term stunts; and media clout gets tangled up with leadership, as individuals who command more attention acquire a capacity to speak for and set the agenda of movements that is often at best loosely bound by any sort of accountability.

If one of the internet's founding utopias was a world without gatekeeping hierarchies, the results are definitively mixed. On the one hand, it has certainly undermined the credibility of previously solid systems of legitimation like journalism, science, and academia, with one of the effects being the cognitive disorientation discussed in chapter 2.[30] On the other, it has created a new class of gatekeepers whose main claim to authority is occupying a position in the attention economy that enables them to bestow visibility on issues, ideas, and other voices. Since our age of algorithmically curated selective exposure has accelerated the fragmentation of the public sphere into a plethora of different publics, the new hierarchy is both highly concentrated at the top—where we find platforms themselves, as the market's powerful shadowy arbitrators—and fractally distributed across layers and niches, all the way down to local hubs with very specific zones of influence.

This is where the question of incentives becomes important. Behind the addictive psychological rewards provided by likes and shares, social media offers the prospect of recognition, influence, and the material gains that may follow from that; it thus also lures us with the possibility of enhancing our capacity to act politically, of augmenting our power to shape the processes around us. Inevitably, this promotes a blurring of the boundaries between collective and individual interests, however sincere one's commitment might be. To draw attention to something is inevitably also to draw it to oneself; being politically active online is a path to raising one's profile, and since that can increase the impact of our political activity, there is a sense in which it can be said to serve a higher goal. This is how platforms devalue less visible forms of participation and silently place us under the pull of what activist anthropologist Leila Saraiva has called "politics in the selfie mode,"[31] a practice in which political involvement always involves some privately appropriable surplus and "[w]inning the fight and gaining from the fight" become hard to dissociate.[32] Online, we are all enjoined to become political entrepreneurs, even if the extent to which each person heeds that call will vary.

Understood in those terms, the attention economy is by its very nature a tool for what Olúfémi Táíwò has discussed as "elite capture": It enables and incentivizes individuals to privately capitalize on collective processes, at the very least in attentional terms, while also picking them out as representatives.[33] This power can, of course, be used in good ways, and more diverse representation is no doubt a good thing. But that predicament also makes it easier for a few to "steer resources and institutions that could serve the many towards their narrower interests and aims," and fosters political calculations "reliant on fantasies about the exchange rate between the attention economy and the material economy."[34] It is thus that access to the dominant regime of visibility comes to stand in for material redistribution, and the capacity to redress injustices by giving perpetrators a dose of negative notoriety becomes compensation for the fact that the power to address the structural causes of those injustices is lacking (and we probably cannot build it through online activism alone). At its most extreme, the kind of elite capture made possible by the attention economy can become so all-consuming that metrics become an end in themselves and the political content of one's "content" becomes indifferent. This is what explains the not-too-uncommon phenomenon of people who, having lost credit with their original audience, switch allegiances in search of a new public. As Naomi Klein writes of Naomi Wolf's cozying up to the far right: "What is Wolf getting out of her alliance with Bannon and from her new life in the Mirror World? Everything. She is getting everything she once had and lost—attention, respect, money, power. Just through a warped mirror."[35]

Social media does not just structure our experience of the public sphere as a market of gratification and attention. Since both those goods are scarce, it also pits us as competitors against one another—even when, politically speaking, we might be generally on the same side. The most ordinary ways in which competitiveness manifests itself are mostly harmless. Thus, as we saw above, posters will all try to use speed differentials, mastery of context, and a network of alliances to stand out when a new topic captures collective attention, which may generate some jealousy and suspicions of plagiarism among them, but not much more. Sometimes, however, a hasty or overblown take will carry more serious consequences, increasing misinformation or triggering a pile-on against an innocent target. But the competitive aspect of the attention economy can also account for a number of pathologies that will be instantly familiar to anyone who has spent enough time online. One is what we might call the *hermeneutics of ill will*, a tendency to read texts with the least charitable attitude toward both meaning and intent, scrutinizing them for lacks that can be construed as deliberately silencing other perspectives or reducing them to straw men that can be easily made into objects of outrage or ridicule.[36] If this behavior is so characteristically common, it is because the incentives for it are obvious: It pulls the focus to oneself while simultaneously questioning the visibility that a direct or indirect competitor enjoys. It is part of a broader propensity for bombast over nuance and divisiveness over balance; in attentional terms, it is often better to walk back an exaggerated statement than to generate less engagement with a more reasonable take. The same logic lies behind social media's regularly lamented penchant for what Freud called "narcissism of small differences," whereby relatively minor disagreements and differences in emphasis can be magnified into major oppositions and either-or choices. These situations, we should note, are often beneficial to both sides of the spat, and these will continue to pick at the scab for as long as it attracts an audience and builds up their profile. Whether strategic clarity, cooperative capacity and the ecology as a whole are similarly served is a different matter.

There is no difference between these processes as they take place among people who would be seen as broadly sharing the same politics and the larger pattern of societal polarization that has kept commentators busy for the last ten years or so. They are both examples of what Gregory Bateson named *schismogenesis*, a process whereby two sides in a dispute increasingly define themselves in opposition to one another, which we will discuss at greater length in the next chapter. And if these dynamics seem to be everywhere nowadays, it is because we are living in the world created by those two epochal events of the late aughts, the financial crisis and platformization. Their acceleration, in particular, is inseparable from how pervasive the logic of algorithmic recursivity has become—that is, the fact that algorithms continuously take data regarding users' interactions as input to shape subsequent interactions and, through the combination of variable compensations and metrics, train individuals to act in the same way.

Quantified feedback molds individual behavior by letting users know what gets the best response from their audience, and thus where the best opportunities for gratification lie. This guides them toward specialization: shaping their digital self according to those identified strengths and offering variations on the same things that got them rewards in the past, in a self-reinforcing drive toward brand consolidation. (In a show of self-reflexivity, people will sometimes describe their own posts as being "very on brand.") But the algorithm is at the same time responding to what the individual interacts with: procuring similar content, spotlighting potential new interlocutors, strengthening some interests and ties at the expense of others, in an equally circular way. If we put those two recursions together and see them taking place across a huge number of people at the same time, what we have is not a series of algorithmically enabled individuations happening side by side but processes of coevolution that produce individuals and their niches simultaneously. That is how platforms facilitate the formation of in-groups. Each one of us may belong to more than one in-group at any given time, provided they are not too incompatible; their borders will always be more or less fuzzy and potentially expansive, and the vast majority of nonmembers will simply be outsiders, not enemies. If an in-group starts to define itself by opposition to an out-group, however, the same recursive process that bolsters internal ties will tend to reinforce that demarcation, and if the movement is reciprocated, schismogenesis will ensue.

The effects of that are felt at the intergroup and the intragroup level. Between groups, relationships of the kind Letícia Cesarino has labeled "inverse mimesis" develop, which means that one side will tend to project what it finds most abject or undesirable onto the other, while simultaneously imitating what the other does with inverted signs.[37] Allowed to run unchecked, that dynamic means the out-group is pathologized, its motives perceived as either irrational or dishonest, making it ever harder to identify points of contact or shared concerns. Of course, just because schismogenic processes tend to make us see other people as the enemy, it does not mean that some people are not really the enemy, and that their views do not represent an actual threat. The problem, however, is that we can also be misled into perceiving any deviation from whatever we understand as our (increasingly rigid) norm as implying belonging to the out-group, overestimating adhesion to the ideas that we oppose and eliding distinctions—such as that between occasional far-right voters and fully convinced far-right supporters—that it may be politically useful to uphold. Inverse mimesis also accounts for the propensity to offhandedly dismiss concerns that might have a grain of legitimacy about them and to take up an uncritical defense of whatever the other attacks. By doing this, the left has handed issues like the critique of Big Pharma entirely over to anti-vaxxers and put itself on the side of an abstract "democracy" when actually existing democracy has obviously failed vast swathes of people—thus playing into its portrayal as an out-of-touch elite and surrendering to the far right the claim to being the only ones confronting the status quo.[38]

Within the in-group, the attentive policing of boundaries, the continuous surveillance of public performance, and the risk of being punished for any deviation from the markers of collective belonging become a constant presence. Managing a personal brand amid the unstable moods of the 24/7 churn of content is a fundamentally uncertain activity. As Naomi Klein puts it, "a digital doppelganger can deliver everything our culture trains us to want: fame, adulation, riches. But it's a precarious kind of wish fulfillment, one that can be blown up with a single bad take or post."[39] The shadow of digital social death—a massive viral pile-on, exclusion from the in-group—is always lurking, though so is the potential for a "rebirth" on the other side, when one is embraced into a former out-group as a valuable dissident come in from the cold. The danger is all the greater given that platforms are public spaces—even if only in the same sense that shopping malls are public spaces—that we largely experience as private, as most of our usual interactions are relatively circumscribed. This creates the risk of what danah boyd calls "collapsing contexts," when a message intended for a relatively small public ends up amplified into the screens of thousands of strangers.[40] The viciousness with which people can turn against one another, even—or especially—within their in-group, can thus be understood in the same light as Theodor Adorno's remarks on the functionality of prejudice. If, as Luc Boltanski and Eve Chiapello once wrote, exclusion from networks is tantamount to death in a networked world, the fear of so-called cancellation is the digital double of the ambient dread of being relegated to the ranks of surplus populations by economic transformation, existential risks like pandemics and extreme weather events, and the consequent shift in the biopolitical/necropolitical border between protected and expendable life.[41] In both cases, anxiety can smoothly slip into preventive violence, through which the "fear of [becoming] superfluous" is allayed by "proving to [oneself] and others that it is the other fellow who can be dispensed with."[42]

At the same time as its schismogenic dynamics tend to make identities more rigid, social media acts as an accelerator of attention and mood. Combined with the pervasiveness of financial speculation in our lives, which places marginal short-term gains above long-term planning, and an otherwise already highly mediatized environment capable of eliciting and measuring responses in real time, this gives contemporary politics its distinctively mercurial, hyperactive character: Excessive connectivity makes for an oversensitive, permanently excitable body politic. Topics, incidents, and personalities become the object of intense focus for a few days, surges of outrage demand immediate answers, heroes and villains are made overnight—and then people move on, and there will often not be enough of them left behind to ensure that anything concrete comes out of the initial frenzy. In the majority of cases, intensity of feeling does not translate into any commitment beyond participation in "discourse." Conversely, issues that go on for too long without there seeming to be anything that can be done—or that anyone in power wants to do—about them, like climate change or the genocide in Gaza, will lead to a certain anesthesia. For governments already habituated to low levels of legitimacy, that excitability can present sudden threats, in the rare occasions in which an episode crosses a certain threshold of intensity and spills out onto the streets, but it also gives them incentives to play politics as a waiting game. Sometimes, especially if it means punching down on usual scapegoats like migrants, they will react to the latest outburst with symbolic gestures or hastily put together measures. If more substantive action is implied, however, they can bide their time to see if it will turn into a sustained challenge or merely fizzle out and have something else take its place.

Anton Jäger has branded this "politicization without clear political consequences" as "hyperpolitics," noting that it is "an abidingly 'low' form of politics—low-cost, low-entry, low-duration, and all too often, low-value."[43] While he is correct in contrasting it with the "post-politics" of the 1990s and early 2000s, we should recall that there was a moment in which the shifting weather patterns of opinion constituted the terrain in which spin doctors—that quintessential archetype of the post-political era—flourished. At the time, those fluctuations seemed amenable to a voter-as-consumer approach based on offers of more efficient managerial solutions and the courting of microconstituencies whose marginal electoral impact might be enough to carry an election. What has changed since then is, first, that platformization has made those changes in humor less dependent on mass media and more likely to occur "organically," produced by platform users themselves; second, that a situation in which gatekeeping is distributed and everyone can respond to everyone else in real time all the time is vastly more volatile; and, third, that the baseline public mood has significantly soured, as the promises of an earlier period were replaced with rising insecurity and a growing number of people have come to expect change from radical overhauls, not piecemeal tinkering. As we know, however, this has not ushered in a new age of ambitious long-term thinking—to put it mildly. Whereas post-politics was all about tactics because the strategy was beyond debate, governance in the time of hyperpolitics is largely about the proactive management of short-term attention: replacing thought-out policy with red meat announcements, measuring consequence in terms of ratings rather than of lasting impact, keeping supporters and opponents busy with proclamations that may or may not turn into anything durable, rejecting expertise and evidence in favor of things that *feel* like change is happening.[44] Instead of management in lieu of politics, politics in lieu of government. This, of course, is especially well suited to a contemporary far right that makes no pretense of governing for everyone but is rather concerned with maintaining a loyal, engaged social base, while the actual business of administration is farmed out to vested interests that are given the license to make the state compatible with their short-term gains—and long-term strategies—rather than subjecting themselves to any consistent plan.[45]

The far right's success in exploiting the subsumption of politics by the attention economy, not least through its strategic use of the position of the troll, has led to much talk about the possibility of countering it through emulation. Can the tendencies and techniques that have served it so well be put to different ends? There is certainly something to be said about that; let us remember that probably the only redeeming moment of Kamala Harris's doomed presidential campaign was when it managed to rattle its MAGA opponents by saddling them with the label *weird*.

At the same time, it is important to recognize the fundamental ways in which this terrain of struggle may ultimately be more compatible with the right than with any emancipatory project. Whereas the former can count on the sympathy of capital and the state, and therefore has a lower bar to clear in terms of building leverage—for which an intensely online base that can be mobilized and demobilized by political entrepreneurs may suffice—the latter is constrained to assemble a capacity to act so much larger and more sustained that it cannot forgo offline organizing. Besides, emancipation supposes a degree of control by the base over their leaders—a capacity to not only react with more or less approval but to give and recall mandates, establish red lines, and condition the content of their actions—that is hard to obtain, and even harder to sustain, soley through social media.[46]

There is no question, of course, of abandoning digital platforms to the right altogether, although exactly what that means when those platforms side with it ever more explicitly remains to be seen. But it is important to consider this struggle at all its different levels: the fight to increase digital literacy among the majority of the population; the fight to expand social control over platforms; the fight to build other types of platforms with different architectures and ownership structures; and, finally, the fight to dismantle the concentration of power that major platforms currently wield over the internet and our lives. It is also important to understand not only the ways in which the far right is winning the battle offline—through spaces such as churches and martial arts clubs—but also the limitations of treating digital platforms as the primary spaces for political activity. It is therefore necessary to reframe the use of these platforms as part of broader strategies and to be more self-reflective about how our participation in them may end up reinforcing trends and powers that work against us in the long run.

OF MMA, ICE, AND MEN

In its long, hallowed history of hosting festivities of all kinds, the White House had never seen anything quite like the event held on June 14, 2026, to mark Donald Trump's eightieth birthday: an Ultimate Fighting Championship showcase in a specially built arena designed for some thousand people. The occasion crowned a long-running relationship between UFC CEO Dana White and the US president, who received fights organized by the mixed martial arts (MMA) promotion company in his Atlantic City casinos years before it became the global brand it is today. But it was also evidence of a deeper enmeshing of the MAGA and the MMA worlds, with intense traffic between leading figures and media channels on both sides and a strong shared cultural identity built around the celebration of virility, traditional gender values, US chauvinism, and an idiosyncratic understanding of freedom. This, finally, is but the gaudy, big-money, "only in America" version of a process that has been occurring in more silent ways all over the world in the last decade, through which fitness and martial arts has become on- and offline spaces of radicalization and recruitment of (mostly) young men to the far right.

Brazilian jiu-jitsu, it should be remembered, played a key part in the birth of MMA and UFC. Interdisciplinary, no-holds-barred challenges were popularized in the 1990s by the Gracies, a family of California-based transplants, to promote the fighting style that patriarch Hélio Gracie had begun developing in Rio de Janeiro in the 1920s. That provided the basic format for the competition whose first edition took place in 1993, with elder son Rorion as one of its organizers. The dominance exercised in the first years of MMA by his younger brother, Royce, did wonders to enhance the profile of Gracie jiu-jitsu, not just internationally but in its country of origin. The number of adepts exploded around the turn of the century, spawning in its hometown of Rio a youth subculture that would become something of a minor moral panic for a couple of years: the *pitboys.*[1]

Rather than an allusion to fighting pits, the name was a portmanteau of "pitbull" and "playboy," referencing both the Rio slang for upper-class young men and the dog breed that they favored and resembled in their ferocity. Avid gymgoers and enthusiastic practitioners of martial arts, usually jiu-jitsu, pitboys were famous for going around in gangs and getting into fights. They were also, very noticeably, the result of an important social and urbanistic shift: the first generation to have grown up in the gated communities and self-contained apartment blocks that became increasingly normal from the 1980s onward as a response to mounting concerns around security. This was especially the case in the newly developed, lower upper middle–class parts of the city. Raised in an intensely homophilic environment, this was a fraction of the elite that had sequestered itself from the friction with other classes that the streets made unavoidable, reinforcing its sense of the outside world as a threat or inconvenience to be shut out, and of themselves as not bound to it by any sense of civic duty or shared belonging. Despite all the clamor in the media, pitboys could generally expect from the law the same treatment they received from the private security at their places of residence: a slap on the wrist and a pat on the head because they came, after all, from good families. It is curious that this story is seldom remembered as part of the far right's genealogy in Brazil, not only because it foreshadows a type of masculinity that would later become strongly correlated with Bolsonarismo, but because it is the exact same demographic that would produce, twenty years later, some of Bolsonaro's most ardent supporters—not least Bolsonaro's three elder sons themselves, who, though by all accounts not pitboys as such, grew up in that very social milieu.

If gym, martial arts, and gun enthusiasts represent the brawn side of far-right masculinity, it is certainly to the internet that it owes its brain—or brain rot, as the case may be. Few figures could represent the coming together of those two sides as well as media entrepreneur turned militia leader Gavin McInnes. As a founder of *Vice* magazine, he was at the helm of one of the main cultural arbiters of the early 2000s, helping set the tone for hipster culture and what would become retrospectively known as "indie sleaze": a hard-partying, irony-drenched ethos that embraced the end of history's loss of greater meaning instead of internalizing it as self-effacement and dysphoria, as much of the 1990s had done. It is not that this attitude, which peaked somewhere between the 2008 financial crisis and the first millennials turning thirty, was not by and large progressive on issues like race, drug use, and gay rights. (Gender was a more complicated matter: Female sexual freedom was celebrated, but sexism was rampant.) Yet it was also suffused with a sense that nothing mattered much, that one should not take oneself too seriously, and that a deep understanding of social codes regarding what could be said and how granted the right to playfully transgress those codes on occasion. One could sometimes be a troll precisely because one knew the game, in a sort of ironic mimicry of the uneducated, maladroit political incorrectness of those who existed outside the hipster bubble. Nihilism, instead of tortured, was recreational. It was thus that, perusing the "Dos and Don'ts" section of *Vice*, one would be treated to a series of pictures of regular folk captioned with typically nasty remarks about their looks and background—only to be reminded every now and then that gay Black teens were the coolest people on earth.[2]

With the financial crisis and the onset of platformization, that cultural moment would split in two opposing directions. One, facing the suddenly dire prospects of the post-subprime era for young people, identified with other disadvantaged groups and became politicized, acquiring a newfound seriousness along the way. (Perhaps the earnestness associated with 2010s online activism had something to do with the fact that, after 2008, most millennials had little more by way of marketable skills and sources of self-esteem than a command of social codes and of the critical tools with which to analyze them—and social media was the arena par excellence in which those could be exercised.) The other path, trodden by a predominantly male cohort, doubled down on the irony while becoming ever more serious about it; whereas the cooler end of this particular spectrum may have been making a name among the *Vice* and Twitter crowds, thousands of others were filling anonymous forums like 4chan's /pol/ discussion board, short for "politically incorrect."[3] Casual transgression coagulated into a permanent countercultural rebellion against what was perceived as the dominant mores of liberal tolerance, multiculturalism, and the promotion of minorities; tongue-in-cheek nihilism became a full-blown passion for destruction, and gained very specific targets. McInnes's founding of the Proud Boys militia in 2016, eight years after being cast out of *Vice* for "creative differences," was at once the beginning of a new chapter and the perfect epilogue for this transformation.

The shift seemed to accompany the intensification of "depressive hedonia"[4]—to borrow Mark Fisher's turn of phrase—that came about with the popularization of digital platforms and smartphones. As more and more people became "too wired to concentrate,"[5] existing in a state of "continuous partial attention,"[6] the constant, empty-feeling search for little dopamine hits turned into an increasingly dominant feature of everyday life. Consumed or produced, the odd act of transgressive mockery became part of that pursuit, a small jolt of guilty pleasure to ease the chronic boredom of living under overstimulation. In time, however, desensitization would kick in: For some, tolerance would require increased dosage, the guilt would disappear from the pleasure, and the habit would go from indulgence to staple, becoming integral to identity and sense of belonging.

The schismogenic dynamics described in the previous chapter go some way toward explaining this irony-to-seriousness pipeline, a phenomenon often noticed online. But there is something that invites reflection in the nature of irony itself, which, as Richard Seymour suggests, is perhaps better understood as a sign of ambivalence than as detachment.[7] At a more superficial level, the detachment may be there to conceal a passionate commitment that is best not openly confessed, as is the case with the fully conscious right-wing edgelord. But deeper down, it is not the content of any actual commitment but the passion with which it is held that the ironist is afraid to admit: In an uncaring world, caring for or about anything is potentially a display of weakness to be seized and preyed upon. This is the sense in which detachment can be understood as a "survival strategy."[8] What it disguises is, ultimately, attachment itself or, rather, the anxiety that feeling attached to something generates: The ironist must enact detachment so as not to be caught caring. And care, finally, is at the heart of why so many (white, hetero-, cissexual) men have gravitated toward the far right over the last decade. As feminist, anti-racist, LGBTQI+ and other struggles intensified, they were being asked to care—to "check their privileges," to "decenter" themselves, to put themselves in the place of others—precisely at a time when conditions of life seemed to become more inhospitable, on- as well as offline. The intensification of those struggles is, of course, not an unfortunate coincidence but a direct consequence of the very same crisis of reproduction these men were caught up in. They experienced their situation as a zero-sum game in which they were *being made the victims of other people claiming the position of victim.*[9] Their response was to put their well-being first and reclaim their right to indifference, to being unmoved by the suffering of others, to the carefree enjoyment of the dividends afforded by their position—and the far right was there to reassure them in their choice.[10]

The need to gear up for a world of ever more cutthroat competition is a recurrent message within the so-called "manosphere": "Be successful or be invisible," as professional kickboxer turned influencer turned alleged human trafficker Andrew Tate puts it in a video. This discourse hits especially hard a mass of young men who sense even the most elementary markers of what until recently constituted adult manhood (a steady job, becoming a breadwinner, just moving out of their parents' home) receding beyond their grasp—and, with that, their prospects of sexual or romantic satisfaction. It also intersects in strange ways with the pervasive meritocratic discourse of entrepreneurialism.

In some, the discourse inspires a peculiar, inward-turned variant of the Protestant work ethic: an ascetic program of self-improvement comprising everything from protein diets and workout routines to semen retention challenges. This particular form of human capital development is very much inspired by figures like Tate, not just in its focus on physique but in what it projects as a path toward success: joining the ranks of manosphere coaches, a dream for which many are willing to spend hefty sums paying for online courses and tutorials offered by more established names. Among the "involuntary celibates," however, the imperative to "put in the work" runs up against the idea of a natural sexual order, a perverse twist on the tendency, noted by Quinn Slobodian in late strains of neoliberal thought, to turn to biology as a way of "quantifying the potential and capacity of members of groups to . . . perform historically and in the future."[11] The result is, of course, suffering—but a suffering expressed in the mode of detachment. As Justin Gilmore writes:

> On the one hand, incels imagine that market-like competition is how people naturally interact. On the other, incel ideology is defined by the argument that sexual competition is biologically encoded, meaning that fair market competition is impossible. This internalized contradiction has led to a peculiar emotional status that is observable in incel communities: an aggressive indifference to suffering, including their own.[12]

Both alternatives are entirely premised on a dark vision of the sexual market: Relationships are always one-sided, self-interested, and instrumental; women cannot be trusted; only power and cool dispassion can make you safe. To that, the first option responds with the fake-it-till-you-make-it performance of a strong, confident hypermasculinity that strives for absolute self-mastery and seeks to forgo all forms of attachment—expecting, as the return on that investment, the callous, unaccountable enjoyment afforded to those who arrive at the top of the food chain. The incel, seeing the possibility of earning that position as blocked in advance by nature, finds in his own suffering a source of perverse enjoyment, an exemption from concern with others, and a reason to inflict—imaginary or real, symbolic or physical—pain. In one case as in the other, uncaring appears as the logical game-theoretical response to a world in which one cannot trust others to care; indifference is indeed *aggressive*, not only in that it is exaggerated but also in that it is preemptive.[13] In either case, it seems evident that, for many of the men who fall under the spell of these ideas, the root of indifference is the fear of being vulnerable, the root of detachment the fear of attachment, the root of uncaring the fear of not being cared for. "Taking the red pill" is the solution to a crisis in which, under pressure for both failing to meet traditional expectations and being told to question the advantages of their position, they double down on the instincts that dominant male socialization has drilled into them: to suppress their feelings of weakness by repressing vulnerability.

Me ne frego ("I couldn't care less," in polite translation) was a Fascist motto born out of a story of Great War heroism popularized by Gabriele D'Annunzio and then taken up by the *squadristi* that acted as shock troops for Mussolini.[14] In the latter's gloss, it stood for "the education to combat, the acceptance of the risks which combat implies, and a new way of life for Italy."[15] We could say that the motto lives on among the men attracted to the contemporary far right, but its original sense of readiness to die for a cause, Crusader fantasies notwithstanding, has been replaced with something rather more pedestrian. Instead of haughty disregard for personal well-being, today's reclamation of indifference expresses a belligerent will to prioritize oneself, to place one's comfort before all else. "I couldn't care less" thus might translate as either "I do not care because my position means I need not" or "I do not care because I feel I cannot afford to."

This might seem at first to outline the two subjective positions that correspond to the far right's vision of masculinity as a two-tiered hierarchy: Betas cannot care; alphas do not need to. But, whereas those at the top still complain about being put upon by a culture that will not let men be men, the idea that the only true enjoyment is the alpha's is a fantasy that probably only those who feel entirely shut out from the privileges of manhood, like incels, entertain. Most are likely to find themselves somewhere in the middle: not really hoping for *jouissance* at the levels of obscenity writ large in the Epstein files, only to be "left alone" to enjoy whatever perks they can access without having to worry about "doing the work." The relationship between the two meanings of "I couldn't care less" thus becomes complementary, even circular. Whether it really is because of more constraining material conditions or simply because one is not prepared to respond to it, the demand to care comes across as excessive ("I cannot afford to"); and, because it is experienced as excessive, one is justified in falling back upon one's privilege, whether this be on a grand scale, alpha-style, or only in the very circumscribed sphere that may be no larger than the household or an online forum ("I need not").

If we take Claude Lévi-Strauss's point that binary oppositions are the building blocks of myth (and ultimately of human thought in general), it is striking that the manosphere's narrative does not include a name for this "somewhere in the middle" where most men actually are.[16] True, it seems at first that its mythical space is not exactly bipartite, as it recognizes a third figure: the cuck. The cuck is a man who does not cover his ears to the demand that he should care; he is (almost) literally a victim of the call of the sirens. This makes him stuck waiting for rewards in a game that he can only lose, both to women (who just want to use him) and to alphas (because, as the saying goes, "nice guys finish last"). But "cuck" is not really the middle term between alpha and beta; it is one end of a second axis that is orthogonal to the first. Its opposite is "red-pilled"; that is, the one who heeded the call of the manosphere and covered his ears—or opened his eyes—to the Matrix. If we want to find a name for the figure who occupies that third space, we have to look outside manosphere discourse. We can encounter it, for example, in the Brazilian *tiozão* (literally "big uncle"), a word often deployed in relation to Bolsonaro and his supporters. (That this is an uncle, not a father or son, is a detail with which someone like Lévi-Strauss would no doubt have a field day.)[17] What it designates is the type of masculinity that Bolsonaro represents: unreconstructed but dull, old-fashioned yet friendly, uncool and somewhat silly—all dad jokes and sexist clichés, off-color humor and Sunday barbecues.

The *tiozão* is distinct from a character like Trump, who, though never quite the formidable, lantern-jawed Chad that incels imagine as the ultimate recipient of female desire, personified an ideal long before becoming president. Rich, famous, (mostly) successful, with a reputation for sexual conquests that would acquire more sinister connotations over time, even—or perhaps especially—as an older, unattractive man, he could still be an object of aspiration to the extent that he acts as a reminder of what power and money can buy when nature falters. An alpha among alphas, obsessed with projecting strength to the point of comedy, Trump's need to associate himself with winners goes as far as seeking a photo op with Zohran Mamdani even after the then newly elected New York mayor had called him a fascist.[18] Although Trump's prickliness with the press suggests that his enormous self-confidence may in part be an act, he does not seem to doubt that we believe him. Bolsonaro, in turn, embodies something more down home and prosaic. Even if his rise to the presidency made him a major player, he retained the air of an everyman done good, a boomer-next-door whom luck and a sense of opportunity had lifted from relative obscurity. His image never shed that aura, and with that, the brittleness of someone who expects sooner or later to be found out; but that also made him highly relatable. Whereas Trump's reaction to being shot was pumping his fist and stoking the crowd, the former Brazilian president often falls back on weakness when he feels threatened, making a regular spectacle of himself in the hospital ever since his 2018 campaign stabbing. Finally, when he led crowds at rallies into chants about his immunity to sexual impotency, he appeared to be in on the joke, knowing full well that everyone would find the claim highly implausible.

Here, then, are the two possibilities of identification that far-right leaders offer, two extremes of what typically appears as a "composite": "King Kong and the suburban barber," ego ideal and one of us.[19] The fact that both take on an hyperbolic character today is symptomatic of the size of the double danger—from material conditions and different forms of contestation—that "hegemonic masculinity" perceives itself to be under.[20] As Klaus Theweleit points out in his classic study of writings by members of the paramilitary Freikorps that foreshadowed the Nazis, the rigidification of male identity responds to a fear of being overwhelmed, of losing control, of a chaos imaginarily associated with the feminine.[21] The anxiety to establish oneself as sovereign and active is always reactive; its exaggerated violence is, at an unconscious level, defensive. Situations of crisis tend to stimulate "hypermasculinity," a term that Anna M. Agathangelou and L. H. M. Ling have retooled from Ashis Nandy to denote a "reactionary stance" that "arises when agents of hegemonic masculinity feel threatened or undermined, thereby needing to inflate, exaggerate, or otherwise distort their traditional masculinity."[22] This is evident, for instance, in what Cara Daggett has dubbed "petro-masculinity," which experiences the "affront" of global warming and environmental regulations as an emasculatory danger "on par with [those] posed by feminists and queer movements," responding with an "attachment to the righteousness of fossil fuel lifestyles" that reasserts "white masculine power on an unruly planet . . . perceived to be increasingly in need of violent, authoritarian order."[23]

If the need to assert invulnerability is born from the dread of feeling vulnerable, it should come as no surprise that the striving toward a hardened, detached, self-reliant personality secretly harbors the search for that which it ostensibly refuses: connection and care. For many young men bereft of much by way of community or meaningful offline relationships, the contacts they make with like-minded individuals in gyms, on social media, and in online forums offer sources of affirmation and belonging that are otherwise hard to find, and thus some shelter from a world that feels cold, unfeeling, and cruel. In a perverse twist, what they find in these spaces meets some of the needs that they had joined in order to free themselves from—but this is only more likely to enhance their emotional dependence on the surrogate father figures of influencers and to reinforce their trust in the comfort of homosociality. That overblown displays of strength conceal a sense of weakness does not make them any less dangerous.

Looking at all these phenomena through the lens of a reactive, overcompensatory hypermasculinity allows us to see the reclamation of the right to indifference as a spectrum that goes from the simplest, everyday forms of not caring to support for and participation in its most extreme manifestation—violence. Not just the misogynistic violence of incels but the casual ferocity of gangs of MMA practitioners, the organized brutality of paramilitary militias, the spectacularized, indiscriminate use of force by ICE, and the cartoonish, almost parodic "lethalitymaxxing" glee with which the Trump administration has dealt with its foreign military adventures: all symptoms of the same crises and ways of repeating the same refrain, *Can't care, won't care, don't have to.*

CHAPTER 5

EVERY SIDE HAS TWO SIDES: ON THE IDEA OF POLITICAL POLARIZATION

"Political polarization" has become such a catchall explanation in the last decade that one would be excused for wondering if it really explains anything, and if so, what. On the one hand, it undeniably appears to grasp something true about our time. From social networks to electoral politics, everywhere we see processes of the kind Gregory Bateson described as schismogenic, in which groups respond to each other's actions with reactions that gradually consolidate not only their respective identities but also their mutual opposition and understanding of each other as the only possible alternatives in a bipartite space.[1] At the same time, it is precisely because such processes are everywhere nowadays that the term can be misleading. After all, there is no guarantee that we are always talking about the same thing—that it is the same causes or dynamics that are at play or the same poles with the same relationship between them. The risk of confusion is all the greater because, in a polarized environment, realities perceived from different perspectives are expected to diverge to the point of being virtually incompatible, and because accusing an opponent of extremism or claiming to be positioned outside what one identifies as two extremes are natural strategic moves within a chessboard crisscrossed by one or more such oppositions.

To take the Brazilian case, what if the diagnosis actually confuses two (perhaps even three) different polarizations, and what if this confusion is in itself advantageous to some of those who are responsible for the polarized scenario? To unpack this, it would be necessary to recover the context in which the discourse on polarization emerged, distinguishing among different assumptions, genealogies, and consequences. Understanding the way in which these different strands intersect would allow us to untangle them and help us to finally address the problem that the diagnosis implies: What to do in the face of a polarized scenario? The answers are applicable not only to Brazil but to any place that can presently be said to be in such a predicament—which, if what we hear is true, may very well be most places.

POLARIZATION ENTERS THE SCENE

In Brazil, the discourse on polarization began to consolidate in 2014, registering a debate then current in US political science that, in turn, referred back to an analysis originally advanced in the 1980s. In 1984, Keith Poole and Howard

Rosenthal had remarked that elections in the United States were becoming contests between "two opposing coalitions, liberal and conservative, each with relatively extreme positions."[2] Increasingly, this meant that the middle-of-the-road voter, whom the authors saw not as "a member of a silent majority desiring some radical social change, but a moderate individual seeking to avoid the wild swings in policy engendered by our political system," was in the process of becoming unrepresented in institutional politics.[3] In 2006, when the same authors teamed up with Nolan McCarty to write the book *Polarized America*, they offered three criteria for identifying polarization: the reduction of politics to two camps; the progressive disappearance of intermediate positions; and the sorting of these camps according to the two main parties in the North American political system, Democrat and Republican.[4] In addition to describing a deepening of the trend observed in the early 1980s, the book suggested a circular relationship between polarization and inequality, which had declined together between 1913 and 1957 and begun to rise again after 1975.

Why this conversation would make a comeback during Barack Obama's 2009–16 administration was obvious. Despite being a staunch centrist with an innate penchant for compromise, the then-president had encountered a Republican opposition in Congress that was unwilling to negotiate on anything; and, in the Tea Party, a grassroots movement—with abundant corporate funding—that demanded ever more right-wing positions from its representatives. It was then that the noun *polarization* gained an important qualifier: *asymmetrical*. It was not just that the gap between liberals/Democrats and conservatives/

Republicans was growing, as a comprehensive 2014 study pointed out.[5] It was growing markedly because of the radicalization of the conservative camp, which left liberals with the burden of seeking compromise. As two researchers who could not be accused of leftist sympathies summarized it at the time, "Let's just say it: the Republicans are the problem."[6]

It was in this context that the North American debate arrived in Brazil. Its importation was linked to the realization that, in the wake of the June 2013 protests, a process begun a few years earlier was starting to bear fruit: A new, more radical and organized right wing was emerging in the country. In a 2014 interview, philosopher Paulo Arantes drew attention to the formation of a political camp "that is no longer interested in governing"—at least not for everyone—and could therefore "afford the luxury of having clear and non-negotiable positions."

> The talk of a polarised Brazil is just talk, it is just theatre. In the United States, Democrats and liberals are characterised by moderation, like the official left in Brazil, which is moderate. The other side is not moderate. Therefore, the polarisation is asymmetrical.[7]

To be sure, this asymmetry was not a matter of consensus in the United States, and some commentators wished to apportion blame equally between the two camps.[8] The very dissent on this issue can be understood as a symptom and an instrument of polarization at the same time. Symptom, in that the more a person identifies with one end of the spectrum, the more they will tend to construct that identity in a totalizing way, communicating primarily among equals, obtaining information from a limited set of sources, perceiving the political space as bipartite, and viewing the opposite side monolithically. This will make anything that deviates from their own norm seem "radical," and the mere presence of the other—women, Black people, transgender people, etc.—in public debate or in a shared space of appearance liable to being experienced as offensive. Yet disagreement around the existence and symmetry of polarization can also be an instrument, since blaming opponents for extremism provides the accuser with a pretext for their own radicalization.

In any case, none among those who accepted that a process of gradual polarization was underway failed to connect it to another process begun in the 1980s, which by 1991 had received the definitive name of *culture wars*.[9] No surprise, then, that this term would enter circulation in the Brazilian debate around the same time polarization came into fashion, in an article whose title announced its understanding of the big novelty of the post-2013 period: the arrival of "culture wars in Brazil."[10] The text did not mention the debate on the asymmetrical nature of the polarizing dynamic but recognized that the initiative, until then, had belonged to one of the sides in the dispute. Although there was "no unanimity about what might have started the culture wars," it claimed, "it seems clear that it was the conservatives who reorganized political discourse in these terms, and that the progressives still need to adapt to the new terrain of discursive contestation."[11]

This suspension of judgment regarding the origins and causes of the transformation made the latter appear as a mysterious phenomenon, something that had happened to politics rather than was a product of it. "The relationship between moral and political discourse is not new. . . . Before, however, moral discourse was instrumentalized by political discourse, and now the opposite seems to be the case."[12] The same tendency to make the "culture wars" into an epochal change that came "from without," supplanting politics and rendering it obsolete, would figure a few years later in an analysis of Jeremy Corbyn's final defeat as Labour leader. "So long as the main focus of electoral politics was on economic questions," wrote Yascha Mounk in 2019, "the leaders of the Labour Party could . . . hold this broad coalition together." "But in the past decades," he concluded, "partisan alignment has shifted away from matters of economic policy toward what one might call questions of culture, such as immigration and, of course, Brexit."[13]

THE CONTINUATION OF POLITICS BY OTHER MEANS

To what extent can this appearance of an unfathomable reversal in the relationship between morality (or culture) and politics be sustained? It is true that conservatism began to reorganize itself as a political force in the United States in the 1960s, responding to processes such as the sexual revolution, the Civil Rights Movement, feminism, and the counterculture. But it is also true that this was never simply a matter of mores. Neither for the New Left, which sought to think about power relations beyond institutions and saw the political in areas that were until then conceived as personal; nor for conservatives, who sought to politicize those issues by creating what Ernesto Laclau and Chantal Mouffe would later call "chains of equivalence" between, for example, the implementation of social benefits for Black single mothers and the loss of opportunities for white blue-collar workers.[14] Ultimately, the blueprint for contemporary right-wing populism is to be found not so much in 1930s Europe as in the "Southern strategy" of Kevin Phillips, the Richard Nixon adviser who mobilized the resentment of white voters in the US South to build a social base that remains Republican to this day. "'Based in university enclaves," as Michael Kazin writes, "New Leftists included few who comprehended the tangled emotions of envy and indignation that shaped response of less privileged whites to ghetto rebellions and anti-war demonstrations."[15]

In the 1970s, as the welfare state went into crisis and the transition to the post-Fordist regime of accumulation produced massive deindustrialization and mass precarity across the Global North, the deterioration of living conditions in general, and those of the "white working class" in particular, made the ground even more fertile for such operations. In the United States, the 1980s witnessed the marriage between conservative evangelicals in defense of family values and Ronald Reagan's Republican Party; while one side sought political influence, the other was looking to build a popular base for its program of neoliberal reforms. Stuart Hall identified a similar tendency in the Thatcherite project, although the greater secularization of British society meant that it was predominantly expressed in terms of public safety, race, and immigration.[16] But the convergence between the economic freedom agenda and the defense of traditional values was not simply arbitrary either. As Melinda Cooper has shown, the family is of interest to neoliberalism as an institution that can fill the void left as the state moves out of areas like education, health, and welfare, simultaneously providing individuals with a tenuous safety net and instilling them with the values needed to survive in a world in which they must bear all risk.[17] Moreover, as Wendy Brown has argued, Hayek himself already saw an intrinsic value in tradition insofar as, like the market, it was a spontaneous order that resisted demands for social justice from different groups, which, if heard, would imply a limitation on free competition.[18]

This, then, is where the origin of both asymmetrical polarization and the culture wars is to be found: The latter was at once an instrument and a consequence of the former. In other words, the culture wars have never been a substitute for political struggle, although many people would no doubt like to think of it that way. Morality was the field in which political contestation was continued by other means, just as institutional politics became the terrain where cultural issues began to be contested.

FROM PROGRESSIVE NEOLIBERALISM TO "GLOBALISM"

This does not, however, tell the whole story. If it is the case that morality and culture did not replace politics, we must also recognize that they were *the form that politics took once the dispute over the economy as an instrument for organizing different projects of society was removed from political debate.* This is what happened in the 1990s, when neoliberal hegemony became consolidated in the so-called Third Way and formerly social democratic parties accepted offshoring, financial deregulation, and growing inequality as irreversible facts and limited themselves to managing their risks and excesses in the hope of giving them a "human face." Insofar as it represented a capitulation to the economic credo of Ronald Reagan, Margaret Thatcher, and Augusto Pinochet, the election of figures such as Bill Clinton, Tony Blair, and Gerhard Schröder also marked the emergence of an internal variant of the neoliberal project.

In Nancy Fraser's description, what these governments offered was a *progressive neoliberalism*—neoliberal in its distributive politics, but progressive in its politics of recognition—as opposed to a *conservative neoliberalism*, whose distributive politics were equally "expropriative and plutocratic" but which did not provide the same possibilities of "meritocratic" advancement for members of historically underrepresented groups.[19] In lieu of traditional values, progressive neoliberalism promoted multiculturalism, gender equality, sexual diversity, a "post-racial" world, and a market-mediated environmentalism. For it too, then, the impression that politics was in the process of being substituted by culture and mores was instrumental: By polarizing against the alliance between neoliberalism and conservatism in the realm of values, it concealed the fact that the comprehensive reorganization of society by market forces remained out of discussion. On this point, there truly was no alternative. In the 1990s and early 2000s, authors such as Chantal Mouffe and Jacques Rancière would stamp this centrist consensus, which safeguarded economic policy, reduced politics to management, and made morality and culture terrains in which different calibrations of the same thing confronted one another, with the name "post-politics."

If, on the one hand, this strategy provided the old social democratic parties with a coalition of minoritarian social movements and an urban middle class with liberal attitudes, it had, on the other, the effect of leaving large sectors of their old base to their own devices—and to the siren song of the far right. The fact that both sides of the partisan spectrum now presented politics essentially as a contest over cultural values, and that the former champions of the working class had embraced the ideal of a supposedly cosmopolitan globalization, made things easier for those who told the losers in this process, "You are losing because *they*—women, Blacks, foreigners, gays—are winning." Naturally, the far right was much abetted in this project by a press that never hesitated to encourage moral and antimigrant panics, as well as by "moderate" politicians always willing to recycle extremist themes in exchange for votes or attention.

The repetition of the idea that disadvantaged groups exist in direct competition with one another, and that the gains of some can only come as a loss to others, lends an air of evidence to this fallacious discourse. But this is not simply a "lie told a thousand times" until it becomes true: In a world where it seems impossible to imagine economic conditions different from the existing ones, where failure is an exclusively personal responsibility, and where the profits of the richest are for all practical purposes untouchable, the bottom of the social pyramid is effectively engaged in a struggle of all against all for most of the time. Given that changing the rules of the game appears to be out of the question, what remains is a zero-sum confrontation resignified as a clash of "cultures" or moral values.

It was from this festering petri dish that the bogeyman of "globalism" was born. Through it, the far right could blame progressive neoliberalism not just for the global crisis that took place under its watch but equally for the ravages of the three preceding decades, which could now be retrospectively constructed as a single, continuous liberal project. In this version of reality, the "globalists" are not, or not primarily, the banks and corporations that drove and benefited from those transformations. Rather, and in a none-too-subtle rehash of certain old anti-Semitic tropes, they are the cosmopolitan urbanites, the intellectual elite, academia, the mainstream media, the parties that gave a pluralist veneer to unregulated capitalism, and the minorities whose interests they supposedly protect. The degree of asymmetry implied by this formulation can be measured by the fact that it makes both of the main variants of neoliberalism, as well as any proposals for overcoming them, equally qualifiable as "left wing." "Globalism" is thus more about making the left responsible for the failures of globalization by retooling preexisting conspiracy theories about global government and Cold War paranoias than it is about a retreat into nation-state; the far right's nationalism continues to be highly selective when it comes to the internationalism of capital, and it is certainly very compatible with financial and labor deregulation. Apart from a renewed emphasis on national interest and defense in the face of global instability, and a rather haphazard use of economic protectionism—for those countries who can actually afford to do so—the contemporary far right does not seek to break with the hegemonic ideas and policies of the last four decades but only to offer a supposed majority (the "native population," the "heirs of Judeo-Christian values," the "upstanding citizens") a competitive advantage over others.[20]

THE IDES OF JUNE

No sooner had it entered the Brazilian debate than the trope of polarization crossed paths with a rather different conversation. In June 2013, the global wave of protests that, since the 2011 Arab Spring, had constituted society's delayed reaction to the 2008 crisis arrived in Brazil. Alongside this wave, a novel discourse had developed that, under the name of *centrist consensus* or *post-politics*, decried what it perceived as the *false* polarization between conservative and progressive neoliberalism that the timid reaction to the financial debacle had exposed a few years earlier. By transforming the banks' private debts into sovereign debt, shifting the burden of the crisis onto the population in the form of cuts in public services and the loss of rights, governments of the right and center left had proved that they defended the interests of the market above all else. Progressive or conservative, they were, in the end, all neoliberal; as the Spanish streets chanted, *They do not represent us.*

The fact that in Brazil the protests occurred before the crisis (or its aftershocks) really broke does not substantially alter that analysis. What matters in the comparison was that, like its center-left counterparts around the world after the 2008 meltdown, the Workers' Party (PT) had had a historic opportunity to adopt a program of structural reforms yet had not only retreated but doubled down on its strategy of conciliation. Caught unawares by the eruption of a formless but potent anti-systemic sentiment, the party's reaction was to isolate this emerging energy rather than attempt to direct or interact with it, dismissing it and siding with its repression. With one hand, it negotiated the restabilization of the political system with the forces to its right; with the other, it blackmailed the left, accusing anything short of unconditional support of playing into the hands of the opposition. The aim of this operation to shut down the space that had opened up was clear: to bring post-2013 reality back within the political coordinates that the June protests had shuffled, forcing a return to a situation in which the only existing polarization, and therefore the only possible choice, was between PT and the traditional right-wing opposition. Successful in its immediate objective of reelecting Dilma Rousseff, this strategy contained two errors that would cost the party dearly: It further associated PT with the establishment, and it left the road open for the far right to present itself as the legitimate repository of anti-systemic desires.

Although both of them spoke of "polarization," the two analyses that intersected at that time differed considerably. What preoccupied North American political scientists was an exacerbation of the two-party system that led the two major blocs to diverge ever more in terms of identity and policies, eliminating centrist positions among both politicians and voters. What was lamented was the loss of reasonableness, of cooperation across the aisle, of a middle of the road conceived as a social reservoir of prudence and pragmatism. While it is not difficult to agree that openness to dialogue in the name of the common good is a virtue, what this discourse never seems to question is that, at any given moment, ideal solutions will be found around the center of the political spectrum. Behind this belief lies an idea of the "center" that operates in a double register: on the one hand, as the middle ground of the political spectrum as it actually exists in a given period; on the other, as an absolute point of equilibrium between left and right assumed to be both a space of disinterested, nonpartisan, and hence more perfect, calculation of costs and benefits, and the normal choice for most people regardless of social position, culture, tradition, and moment in history. In the end, what the discourse derived from US political science bemoans in polarization is precisely that it moves the actually existing political spectrum away from this ideal center, bringing out irrational ideas and clouding the search for what all sensible people are supposed to want.[21] The critique of polarization thus ends up being the centrist complaint against the end of what is perceived as "normal" politics—which is, in the end, not too distinguishable from the supposedly neutral administration of things and interests proper to post-politics.

Yet the critique of post-politics that burst onto the streets in 2011 challenged the very idea of normal politics. From this perspective, what centrists do is model their conception of the middle ground on the limits of their own political imagination, erroneously attributing to the contingent limits of the historical formation in which they live (what seems reasonable here and now) an absolute and necessary character (what is reasonable as such). What the second discourse denounced was that the false polarization between progressive and conservative neoliberalism amounted to a tacit agreement to exclude from the outset any questioning of the concentration of political and economic power that had been mounting since the 1980s, giving it an air of inevitability and placing it outside the realm of a dispute between alternative social projects. The artificiality of this false equilibrium became evident in 2008, when the crisis exposed its arbitrary nature, and yet no mainstream political force had the courage to question it.[22] According to this analysis, the problem is not the existence of polarizations per se but the fact that a false opposition can hide a real antagonism, such as that between the 1 percent who benefited from the crisis and the 99 percent who lost out. While in the 1980s Poole and Rosenthal had explicitly rejected the hypothesis of a "silent majority desiring some radical social change," this analysis suggested instead that inequality had since been pushed to such a point that, if such a majority did not yet exist, the conditions were in place to constitute it, and that doing so implied creating another polarization between "us" and "them" that would facilitate the formation of a new social consensus.[23]

It is no surprise that the reception of this discussion in the Brazilian context would, from the outset, be inseparable from something we might call the "third force hypothesis": the idea that only a new mobilization that cut across the polarization between the PT and the opposition, as had been the case in 2013, would be capable of unblocking the impasse into which the country had since been thrown.[24] For some, the "third force" could only come from below, from the same tangled mass from which the June 2013 upheaval had emerged. Unable to conjure it with their own limited forces, those who held fast to this conjecture would only come close to proving it with the (left-leaning) high school students' movement of 2016 and the (right-leaning) lorry drivers' strike of 2018. In any case, what they saw as the main enemy was the attack on the advances that PT had made in the previous decade, which had already begun in Rousseff's tumultuous second term but would gain pace under Michel Temer's caretaker government; this was why they opposed both Rousseff *and* her impeachment.

Others, mistrusting the prospects of social mobilization, gambled on the possibility of building a third position from the top down and saw the 2014 presidential candidacy of Luiz Inácio Lula da Silva's former environment minister, Marina Silva, who at the time had severed ties with PT, as the ideal vehicle for this. When Silva's campaign succumbed under the weight of her own contradictions and her former party's vicious negative propaganda, they began to see the anticorruption agenda that had gained momentum with Operation Car Wash scandal as a possible shortcut. Realizing that they could not compete on the streets with the fresh-faced organizations of the new right that dominated the anticorruption and pro-impeachment protests, some even placed their chips on Operation Car Wash itself, naïvely identified as the only independent force capable of intervening in this scenario. Once this final gamble had failed, all that remained was for them to turn the PT/anti-PT polarization into the great strategic enemy instead of a tactical obstacle. More than austerity policies or the rise of the far right, they saw polarization itself as what had to be fought, regardless of whether strengthening those policies or abetting the rise of the far right was part of the price to pay. This was how a small but very vocal fringe of the non-PT left ended up declaring neutrality in the second round between Jair Bolsonaro and PT's Fernando Haddad in 2018, even going as far as establishing an equivalence between the two alternatives.

Confusing the two discourses on polarization was part of PT's strategy to close the space available to its left from the outset; the fact that the right rallied around the campaign for Rousseff's impeachment from 2015 onward only reinforced this operation. In the face of an opposition that had decided to ignore the tacit agreements that underpinned the political system and bring the government down—with the collaboration of a sizable portion of that government's own parliamentary base—PT supporters denounced those who criticized the polarization as washing their hands of a situation in which there were effectively only two sides. The term *isentão* (from *isento*, or exempt) was coined to disparage those who took this stance. How could the polarization between the party and the opposition be false, when one side had clearly entered into an asymmetrical spiral of radicalization against the other? The irony is that, from a certain point onward, this operation would be supported by part of the so-called *isentão* camp. For the latter, who were seeking to carve out a new political space for themselves, the equivocity of the term *radicalization* served to build bridges with sectors for whom PT's problem was not moderation but "radicalism," and whose understanding of politics was closer to neoliberal centrism. Whether it was to excommunicate it from the left or to make it more palatable to the center, both sides were eager to associate a discourse stemming from the critique of post-politics, which wagered on the potential for a project of democratic radicalization, with a centrist appeal for restraint and common sense.

There is, however, nothing necessary about this confusion. It is perfectly possible to say that Rousseff's impeachment was the expression of an asymmetrical polarization between an opposition moving further to the right and a PT increasingly stationed at the center, and that *precisely for this reason* this polarization distorted and falsified the real antagonism between the economic elite, which was preparing to pass on the costs of the economic crisis in full to the poorest, and a working class whose interests were not actually being defended by any major political force at the time. It is also perfectly possible to claim that this polarization functioned as an obstacle to the search for better solutions without assuming that these solutions were necessarily the middle of the road between the existing "extremes." All it takes is to consider that the opposing forces within the political system did not adequately represent the existing conflict of interests in society, or that finding a point of equilibrium between them was unfeasible—either because it led to undesirable effects in the medium term or because it presupposed conditions of possibility that were no longer given.

TWO SIDES ON THE ONE HAND, NONE ON THE OTHER

The interest that the idea of polarization has aroused obviously derives from its possible practical consequences. Particularly for the left, its background is the question of what to do in the face of a rising far right: to move to the center in order to build alliances? Or to fight radicalization with an equally radical stance? This is where it is necessary to be clear what polarization is at stake, who occupies its poles, whether it is symmetrical or asymmetrical, and where its center is.

In Brazil today, no one—least of all Bolsonaristas themselves—has any doubt that the far right occupies one of the extremes. Regarding the opposite side, versions might vary. One of them places the left as a whole, and the Workers' Party in particular, at the opposite end, and demonstrates this thesis by establishing equivalences between phenomena such as Bolsonaro's very real coup machinations after he lost the 2022 election and over-the-top outbursts from PT supporters on social media.[25] The far right, for its part, agrees that its adversary is the left. The problem is that, for them, "the left" is such an infinitely elastic label that it can accommodate everything from anti-capitalists to insufficiently conservative neoliberals, and potentially includes anyone who comes to be seen as an enemy.

There are clearly two distinct operations of polarization at work here. In the second, patently asymmetrical, one pole takes extreme positions to draw the center of the debate in its direction and shift all responsibility for negotiating compromises to the other side. The far right is able to do so because it openly does not seek to govern for all; its plan is to lock in a sufficiently large and radicalized social base that will allow it to retain its electoral clout, confident that, when push comes to shove, self-professed centrists will always choose it over the left. (This wager worked when Bolsonaro won in 2018, and if it did not quite do so when Lula beat him in 2022, it is largely because part of the right feared being overrun by an even more powerful far right.)

The first polarization is, so to speak, against the polarizers: a rhetorical operation in which, making use of a false symmetry, some actors present the two poles as equally extreme in order to situate themselves against both as the only non-radical alternative. They do not do so, however, in the name of options that the existing polarization would be leaving unrepresented, as was the case with the Spanish *indignados*, but rather to position themselves as pragmatic and commonsense spokespeople for a lost middle ground.

But what is that middle ground today? To answer this, it is necessary to begin by looking at what was at the center of the Brazilian political spectrum from the mid-1990s until 2015: a combination of the "three pillars" of neoliberal macroeconomic policy (floating exchange rates, fiscal and inflation targets) with distributive and recognition policies that became more or less ambitious according to the economic conditions and the perviousness of those in power to social pressure. In other words, a neoliberalism that became more progressive or conservative depending on the occasion. The first question to be asked is: What happened to make this cease to be the center? It is true that, in her first term as president, Rousseff eschewed the rigors of the macroeconomic tripod with highly inefficient and income-concentrating fiscal incentives for big business, but by the time she was ousted, she had already made a U-turn toward orthodoxy and embraced the austerity that her reelection campaign had fervently attacked. Rousseff did not fall because she promised radical measures but because the Brazilian elite saw in the conjunction of an economic crisis and an utterly demoralized PT a historic opportunity to unilaterally "renegotiate," without hardly any resistance from the left, social movements, or the working class, the "social contract of the redemocratization process" that had resulted, in 1988, in a constitution with some strong social democratic tendencies.[26] Although it stirred its supporters with rhetorical flourishes, at no point did PT propose anything that went beyond what had been admissible until then; *it was the right that displaced the center of the spectrum.*[27] The latter's miscalculation was that, instead of restabilizing the system by casting out PT, the maneuver ended up boosting the far right; without viable candidates of their own, several self-proclaimed liberals did not hesitate to covertly or overtly support Bolsonaro. This is why, in the mouths of some, the narrative that blames the left for the rise of Bolsonarismo ends up sounding like a bad-faith attempt to outsource responsibility for one's own decisions—the half complaint, half blackmail of those who demand, "Do not make us support the far right again."

What were the material conditions that made the old center possible, especially its more progressive inflection under PT? Any answer must necessarily consider three points: the all-round tacit agreement regarding post-democratization institutional stability, which included a generous degree of tolerance with corruption; the existence of a large left-wing party with high levels of popularity; and the win-win situation produced by the early 2000s commodity boom, which allowed for the promotion of redistributive policies without eating into capital's rising profits. After 2015, none of these conditions were present. The ease with which the Brazilian ruling class embarked on the twin adventures of Rousseff's impeachment and Bolsonaro's election demonstrates a very fragile commitment to institutions, negotiation, and power sharing. The effort made throughout the Bolsonaro administration to draw a line between its "good side" (the ultraliberal agenda) and its "bad" (the blatant antidemocratic tendencies) showed that the country's elite could cope very well with more extreme solutions, although it would probably prefer not to have to deal with intermediaries as volatile and unreliable. As for PT, it would be hard to fault anyone for believing, after Lula was imprisoned in April 2018, that it was destined for a swift decline. The party faced a historical nadir in the 2015–21 period, and the absence of its founder and leader served to underscore the absolute dearth of figures who could even come close to taking his place. After Lula was released from prison, PT could rely on his charisma and votes to win in 2022, as it will try to do again in 2026; but not only is the octogenarian now nearing the end of his glorious career, he is also up against a much more right-wing Congress and a lot less goodwill from the establishment. This, finally, is also due to the fact that the economic room for maneuver has shrunk, and nothing at the moment suggests the prospect of favorable international winds even remotely like those encountered in the early 2000s. Besides, in Brazil, as in several other places, the economic debate has undergone its own process of asymmetric polarization and is now populated by caricature textbook liberals for whom measures that were once commonplace or are applied in other parts of the world are not only considered "socialist" but treated as the first step in a totalitarian escalation whose inevitable end point is Venezuela.

Thus, if by *center* we understand a kind of arithmetic average of the available political positions and their relative weights, it should be clear that today the center in Brazil is further to the right than it has been at any time since the end of the military dictatorship in the 1980s. (Something like this can, again be generalized to several other countries.) It is clear that, in the short term, the left must seek alliances that allow it to mitigate the damage that Bolsonaro's government has caused to institutions and the population, especially the least protected. However, the notion of an abstract "search for the center," without any defined content, not only ignores the fact that the center has moved but forgets two elementary truths: Negotiating is something that is done around concrete points and within defined nonnegotiable limits; and no one negotiates with those who have nothing to negotiate with. In the absence of electoral strength and/or social hegemony, the left has no trump card (no pun intended) to force the right into dialogue, and the latter will naturally lean toward those who have it—which, under present circumstances, will inevitably push it toward the far right. Without touching on this fundamental point, the abstract defense of centrism ends up being little more than a nostalgia for a pact that is no longer possible, an inability to think politics beyond the electoral game, or a resignation to the current horizon of possibilities—one that can, at most, make the left into the junior managing partner of a state of affairs whose social and environmental costs tend to grow.

NARCISSISM OF THE WILL

There remains the other option: to "radicalize." But what does that mean? Perhaps we can begin by clarifying what it does not mean. Here we find the small grain of truth in the account that claims that escalating polarization should be blamed on the radicalization of the left.[28]

It is true that the Brazilian left underwent a process of radicalization in the years between 2013 and 2018. Not unlike what occurred in other places, however, that radicalization did not take place in the realm of proposals or actions but mostly in that of *identities*. There are several reasons for this, among which are the hypertrophy of online activism and the platform-enabled schismogenic dynamics discussed in the previous chapter. It should be made clear, however, that the critique of identitarianism made here does not refer exclusively, or even preferentially, to those struggles that are often pejoratively lumped together as "identitarian" (feminist, antiracist, for gender and sexual diversity, and so forth). A certain self-appointed "anti-identitarian" left, with its ham-fisted and one-dimensional defense of "universalism," "Enlightenment values," and other such clichés, is certainly as much prone to stereotyped behavior as are any of the groups it likes to contest. In the sense in which I use the term here, *identitarianism* refers to an excessive attachment to one's identity, whatever that may be, and the exaggerated, repetitive performance of a closed repertoire of attitudes that function as its markers: words, terms of abuse, slogans, references, aesthetic preferences, and so on. While this performance takes place in the public space, it is made mostly for the benefit of an audience of peers and thus serves the purpose of signaling belonging and of securing one's standing within an in-group more than of communicating with outsiders. Stimulated by the hypervisibility of an increasingly mediatized social life, including the fear of social death generated by lateral surveillance, identitarianism values the abstract assertion of principles more than it does the development of the capacity to apply these principles to the world, and the exemplarity of personal conduct over the power to intervene effectively in the course of events. Indeed, insofar as effectiveness depends on the capacity for dialogue with those who are different, and the construction of an activist identity implies constantly demarcating the differences that set it apart, the overvaluation of performance tends to restrict the power of political intervention, a restriction that, perversely, is often experienced as proof of one's own superiority. According to this logic, the problem is not that we cannot move others but that others are not already like us.

This crystallization of the left as an ensemble of identity traits is inseparable from two of the dynamics discussed above. On the one hand, it is a response to the polarization promoted by the right: The more identity is reinforced on one side, the more it tends to be affirmed on the other, with all that this implies (tribalism, greater confirmation bias, susceptibility to misinformation, etc.). On the other hand, this shift to the realm of culture and values has, since the 1990s, been a response to the need to give cohesion to the idea of the left in the absence of a long-term vision effectively differentiated from the market economy and neoliberal globalization. "Left" thus became the identity of those who recognize the rights of minorities, believe in the secular state, and understand their mission as one of controlling the excesses of the market and of conservatives. Contrary to the story often told by the anti-identitarian left, it was not because it began to concern itself with the "particular" (race, gender, and other oppressions) that the left renounced the "universal" (an alternative project of society); it was when it ceased to articulate its own idea of totality that it filled the vacuum with particular causes. This shows that the consolidation of the left as an identity and the tendency to move toward the center are not contradictory but can in fact very easily complement each other. As the center of the debate shifts to the right (the consensus on tightening migration controls, for instance), it is perfectly conceivable that a strengthening of one's own identity ("I stand with migrants") could be accompanied by merely attenuating positions (*humanizing* the tightening of controls). A symmetrical schismogenesis in the field of identities (matching more with more) is entirely compatible with a complementary schismogenesis in the field of effective actions (matching more with less).

The use of identity as a substitute for substantive politics became more pronounced in Brazil after the 2014 elections, and especially after the process that led to Rousseff's impeachment. While willing to negotiate anything to retain the presidency, the PT leadership mobilized the memory of the dictatorship and the struggle for democracy to revive a historical base that had drifted away in disillusionment. The move was successful in galvanizing traditional supporters and even bringing some critical sectors back in line.[29] Whether it worked in a broader sense is questionable: Precisely at the time when economic turmoil and corruption were making more people sensitive to the right's depiction of the left as a dangerous foreign body infecting the nation, the party was calling on people to take to the streets dressed in red to defend their right to be left wing, thus reinforcing the impression of them as a group set apart from the rest of society. The contrast was all the starker since the far right had by then managed to appropriate the national colors—which, differently from other places, were not necessarily politically coded before becoming the signifier of a generic, nonaffiliated citizenry during the 2013 protests, taking on an ever more definite identity in the following years.

Here we find the grain of truth in that conception of the center of the political spectrum as an oasis of common sense and pragmatism. For those who fully invest themselves in a political identity, the latter becomes central to their sense of themselves and their own value.[30] But most people are driven by desires, interests, values, and opinions that are not necessarily constant or coherent; *it is only those with a sharply defined political identity who make consistency with their own identity a central factor in their decisions.*[31] This does not mean that the "center" will always correspond to the same kind of middle-of-the-road politics imagined by the likes of Poole and Rosenthal, nor that it will always have the best solutions, but that the choices made by those for whom identity is not a primary source of motivation will tend to be less consistent and, therefore, more flexible. In a situation in which there is a struggle to define the middle ground, emphasizing one's own identity risks making it appear exclusive, alienating those who have not yet picked a side and bringing grist to the mill of a polarizing operation in the opposite direction.

That the choices made by those with weak political identifications are flexible does not mean they are necessarily more rational. As Richard Seymour puts it, people like bread-and-butter issues, but they do not necessarily *love* them, and that they might be moved by passions that can hurt them in the long run is something that hardly needs arguing in a time when the far right is on the rise.[32] Yet we should be careful not to overstate the irrationality of far-right support. As I have been arguing throughout, it offers prospects of compensation that are at once psychological and material, even if conditional and comparatively short term (the maintenance of racial and gender hierarchies can be perceived as useful from the point of view of economic competition, for example, just as doubling down on a commitment to fossil fuels can be seen as a safeguard to existing ways of life). It is not simply a matter of fighting passion with passion, therefore, but of building different compositions of interests and desires. Although the left likes to conceive of adhesion as conversion (the individual takes on a complete package of convictions) and commitment as selflessness and sacrifice (a duty that takes precedence over all interests), sudden, complete conversion is rare, and pure selflessness hard to sustain in the face of material constraints. Most people are less motivated by feeling that certain values are morally correct than by seeing the potential these values have to reorganize their lives in ways that at once offer answers to their problems and feel desirable. This is a special challenge in a time when hanging everything on promises of future material abundance is no longer viable.[33] The point is, then, to at once articulate a plausible vision of a good life in a differently organized world that is materially rather different from what people imagine now; transform expectations and interests in such a way that this vision seems desirable; offer an idea of the steps through which it could start being built right now, without requiring sacrifices much greater than people are already making; and create the spaces through which the work of building it can be experienced in the present not only as work but also as a source of joy.

Like "seeking dialogue with the center," "radicalizing" in the abstract does not mean much either; in the absence of any content, it is likely to end up being little more than a radicalization of identity. But expecting people to convert to ever-stricter identities or to adopt ever less tangible ideals is a recipe for isolation. What matters is not becoming more radical in performance or in the assertion of generic principles but in concrete ideas. In other words, what matters is developing the ability to construct alternatives that, without fear of giving radical answers to the problems people face, do not fail to communicate with their everyday experience and that appear not only more sensible and desirable than what they have but actually achievable under existing conditions.

REALISM OF THE POSSIBLE, REALISM OF THE REAL

Many of those who lament the polarization of contemporary society do so in order to claim the role of spokespeople for a realism they see as sadly lost; yet most voices calling themselves "realist" today repeat dogmas of a reality that no longer exists. While this decade began under the shadow of an Intergovernmental Panel on Climate Control report stressing the need for a drastic reduction in carbon emissions by 2030 if the global temperature were to stay below the 1.5 degrees Celsius (2.7 Fahrenheit) target, 2025 saw another all-time record in emissions, and it is now apparent that whatever progress made thus far in renewables has only added to the energy matrix rather than replaced fossil fuels.[34] It *should* be impossible to continue to speak of economic growth as the cure to all ills without taking any of this into account, but apparently it is not. In any case, since the 2008 crisis, there is no safe prospect on the global horizon of a new cycle of growth that could create jobs and reduce inequality; on the contrary, existing trends point to a low-growth, low-productivity capitalism based on rent extraction and structural un- or underemployment.

It is instructive to compare the current frenzy around artificial intelligence with that which surrounded the so-called New Economy in the 1990s to notice how things have changed. While the early days of the internet inspired excitement with the promise of constant productivity gains and stable growth, our latest speculative bubble is presented as an unpredictable and inescapable disruptive force that will "leave behind" those who do not participate in it but that is conspicuously devoid of any promise that everyone will benefit. (If anything, given all the jobs estimated to be lost, quite the opposite.) Even the boosters and apologists are no longer announcing a "tide that lifts all boats"; now it is just a matter of clambering into the lifeboats before one drowns, while the superyachts of billionaires safely sail on by. And yet, what passes for realism in politics continues to react to the illness by prescribing the same medicine that caused it in the first place: Crises caused by deregulation are met with more deregulation, the market's inability to deal with climate change is met with the search for new "market solutions," income stagnation and rising inequality are met with more precarity and cuts to public services, revenue shortfalls are met with fiscal restraint and tax cuts for the rich. If a growing number of people are open to positions that were until recently considered "extreme," whether on the right or on the left, it is primarily because the "center" is no longer able to convince them that it has answers to this scenario or can deliver on its pledges. That is why the middle ground between conservative neoliberalism and progressive neoliberalism has lost its aura of being a natural equilibrium point.

That this "realism" is out of sync with reality does not mean that its "solutions" cannot work. They will work in their own way, for a shrinking portion of the world's population. To seek compromise in these conditions is worse than innocuous: To continue to pretend that things can go back to the way they were is to waste time we no longer have and to make sure we will soon live in a world where extreme weather events, heightened social conflict, and repression without precedent will be the norm. Any liberals who really care about liberties other than economic ones would do well to understand this very soon. As for the left, if it wants to be of any use in the future, it will have to propose realistic answers to the problems posed by this new reality, above all that of promoting a transition to a postcarbon, postgrowth, postwork economy in a climate that will be less much less predictable in every sense. But this will also involve redefining what "realistic" and "possible" mean.

It probably speaks well of the right that political science has baptized the idea that politics is about transforming the limits of the possible with the name of a libertarian ideologue, not of a revolutionary leader. As Joseph Overton saw it, at any given time, there will be a finite number of policies that the majority of the population finds acceptable; since what politicians of any stripe wish above all is to remain electable, this limited range of options delimits what they will consider politically viable. This, the so-called Overton window, is what vulgar realists evoke when they claim people are "naturally" conservative or, faced with a successful asymmetrical polarization on the opposite side, they begin to abandon their convictions and move toward the center. The difference between Overton and them is that he understood this window in dynamic terms, and the correct relationship to it as active instead of passive: Making ideas previously considered absurd become mainstream was, for him, the way to force the political system, driven by the instinct for survival, to adopt them. Moving the window—that is, transforming the limit of the possible, and hence what people believe and want—is the very point of politics. And this is exactly what we have seen time and again in the last decade, except it was for the most part done by the right: Attitudes, statements, and policies that were unthinkable until not long ago have been normalized at a staggering pace.

In order to bring the possible up to speed with the reality of what is necessary, however, the left will need more than an attractive vision of an alternative future and plausible ideas on how to achieve it. It needs to constitute a social force for change, which supposes making itself present in the lives of people, listening to and acknowledging them, supporting spaces where they can experience their own power, composing interests and desires, and thus offering answers that are situated not only in the future but in the here and now. For that, finally, it will need radicalism that is different from the intransigent assertion of an identity. Thinking politics relationally—in terms of poles, ranges, thresholds, points of equilibrium, windows—teaches us that the relationship between a desire and its outcome is always indirect and must go through a series of mediations: with the desires and interests of others, with existing power relations, with institutions, and so on. Precisely for that reason, not everything is possible at any given time. To do politics, it is not enough to want things: It is necessary to calculate the mediations that lead to them. To do *transformative* politics, however, it is not enough to just calculate the mediations either. It is always necessary to calculate them upward, to raise their tempo and tension, to bring them to their limit, so as to open up possibilities that were not there before. No one is radical intransitively, in abstract terms; radicalism of this kind is merely aesthetic, an end in itself, the performance of an identity. To be politically radical is to be radical in relation to a concrete situation. It is not a matter of demarcating a position in abstraction from any context but of discovering here and now what is the most transformative position capable of winning the most support and producing the most effects—so that, at a future moment, bigger and better goals are possible.

CHAPTER 6

FROM TRANCE TO VERTIGO: IMAGES OF POLITICAL DEFEAT IN BRAZILIAN CINEMA (AND BEYOND)

Glauber Rocha's *Terra em transe* [Entranced earth] came out in 1967 to immediate controversy. Initially banned by the military regime, it met with a conflicted response from the Brazilian intelligentsia upon its return from Cannes, where it had garnered two awards. "The film touches on an unpleasant truth in an unpleasant way," critic Maurício Gomes Leite summarized at a specially dedicated debate at the Museum of Image and Sound in Rio de Janeiro.[1] The source of that unpleasantness lay in how the film dealt with both the recent past and a future already bubbling under the surface. In March of the following year, the murder of a student by the military police would light the spark for the Brazilian 1968, a series of demonstrations and strikes that would last until October. By December, the hardening of the regime put an end to any hope of bringing it down through peaceful means; a growing number of people started seeing the prospect of armed struggle, which the film ambiguously contemplated, as inevitable. Even more uncomfortable, however, was what *Terra em transe* had to say about the recent past. Despite being set in the imaginary South American country of Eldorado, the film was immediately available to viewers at the time as a roman à clef about the João Goulart presidency that the 1964 coup had cut short, along with the dream of a "Brazilian revolution" that it had inspired.[2] More than that, it zoomed in on the crisis in which the coup had thrown the left: the shock at how easily it had been swept aside, the sudden realization of its own fragility, and the painful process of picking through its illusions and self-delusions, mistakes and inadequacies, in the cold hard light of a new conjuncture.

On the fiftieth anniversary of 1968, Brazil would find itself in comparable circumstances. After thirteen years of left-leaning governments by the Workers' Party (PT), the country elected a former army captain who openly reclaimed the heritage of the regime that lasted from 1964 to 1985, including the torture of political dissidents. That situation had been precipitated by a unique confluence of factors, including a severe economic crisis, a corruption scandal engulfing most major political parties, an erosion of trust in all branches of government, and an electoral collapse of the country's center right, which allowed the far right to ride the wave of public discontent. More importantly, in a sequence of events many would not hesitate to describe as a coup, the country had seen the impeachment of Dilma Rousseff, the country's first female president and a former guerrilla, and the jailing of Luiz Inácio Lula da Silva, the country's first working-class president and hitherto frontrunner in the polls. No tanks on the streets this time: Rousseff was ousted by her erstwhile coalition partners in a trial that maintained all the trappings of due process despite being based on very shaky grounds, while Lula was convicted according to the law, albeit in a uniquely expeditious manner and based on inconclusive evidence. (Four years later, of course, the conviction would be overturned by the Supreme Court in light of a leak that revealed extensive collusion between the prosecutors and Judge Sergio Moro, who after 2018 had gone on to become Bolsonaro's minister of justice.) The whole thing unfolded without sharp breaks with constitutional normality, relying instead on the capacity of some political forces to "turn institutions on and off" at will, according to their interests and those of their allies in the Brazilian ruling class.[3] While this episode of Brazilian history is yet to be given fictional treatment in film, a host of documentaries—Lula Buarque de Hollanda's *O muro* [The wall] (2017), Maria Augusta Ramos's *O processo* [The process] (2018), *Excelentíssimos* [Lower house] (2018), Boca Migotto's *Já vimos esse filme* [We've seen that film before] (2018), and Petra Costa's *Democracia em vertigem* [The edge of democracy] (2019)—attempted to portray it.[4]

Looking at the filmography from both moments, particularly *Terra em transe* and *Democracia em vertigem*, allows us to investigate the images of political defeat that these films project and, through them, to read the left's response to these two historical junctures. To speak of "defeat" obviously says something about the choice of material: films whose directors position themselves on the losing side of their stories, and therefore also on the left in some broad sense. What is of interest here, however, is more than just overt political identification. Beyond their self-understanding as belonging on the left, these directors have in common a certain social position as members of the country's cultural elite and its middle or upper class. Particularly in a country as riven by inequalities as Brazil, this position is bound to come into some tension with their chosen political identity, given how it shapes and limits their perspective on reality, not to mention the conflicts of interest and allegiance it potentially creates. That being the case, the experience of defeat is bound to illuminate those tensions in interesting ways. Therefore, when I speak of "images of political defeat," what I have in mind is both the way in which those films attempt to pin down the causal mechanisms leading to those historical setbacks and the way in which their narratives implicate—or fail to implicate—the narrators themselves, or those who share their social position. In other words, what makes these films interesting is both the stories that they tell and what those stories have to say about those who tell them—that is, what they reveal about the situation in which they were produced, directly and indirectly, through presences as well as absences, what they show as well as what they fail to show.

THE GAPS OF DEMOCRACY

A dominant trait in the films that have tried to tackle the events of the 2015–18 period is a tendency to focus on the "palace coup" aspect of Rousseff's overthrow.[5] There is, of course, a lot to explore there: the salacious tale of a vice president leading the plot against his superior, the grotesque spectacle of notoriously corrupt politicians posing as champions of public morality, the at-once erratic and very targeted interventions of the judiciary, the numerous plot twists and cliff-hangers as individuals and factions changed sides and strategy. This approach could also be justified for the way it mimics the very nature of the impeachment procedure, which exposed the political process in Brasília as little more than a competition among self-serving political elites with their backs turned to the population at large. Upon seeing the machinations surrounding Rousseff's fall on the screen, it is hard not to recall a famous passage in Aristides Lobo's account of the proclamation of the Brazilian Republic on November 15, 1889, which to this day rings like a curse in many ears: "The population observed [the scene] in astonishment, dumbfounded, stupefied, without a clue as to what it meant. Many seriously believed they were watching a parade."[6]

Yet this choice also has its problems if it is not taken self-reflexively. One might be critical of the result of the impeachment as a breach of representative democracy—which it was—but not be sufficiently critical of the quality of the democracy that it interrupted. One might question existing mechanisms of representation but fail to question the limits of political representation or of one's own capacity to faithfully represent social reality by looking solely at the political forces clashing with one another in Congress and in the streets. The risk, in the end, is that one will end up reproducing the exclusions of the political system even as one denounces that system as exclusive, for the simple reason that one shares the same blind spots. By turning the outside world into a mere backdrop for palace intrigues, rather than seeking the stories that lurk there, one ensures that what is made invisible will continue to be so, and that what was silenced in the moment will also pass into history as silence—that is, will not pass into history at all. The cost of not looking into the gaps and cracks surrounding the drama unfolding in Brasília is an ultimate blindness to the structural conditions that created the opportunities in which the dramatis personae acted as well as to the relative indifference with which the population at large, outside of the groups mobilized for and against PT, reacted to the entire process.

This blindness becomes evident in the way *Democracia em vertigem*, which has the broadest historical scope among this crop of films, deals with two of the most important elements for understanding recent Brazilian history. These are the wave of protests begun in June 2013 and the economic crisis begun in 2014. The former is widely regarded as the great point of inflection between PT's apogee and downfall, a thesis to which the film subscribes by calling it "the seismic shift" after which "something in our social fabric started to change, giving birth to the deep division that would rip us apart."[7] Yet this only makes it all the more curious that the film has literally nothing else to say on the subject. Even the way in which it is introduced—"until came the seismic shift"—suggests an inscrutable enigma, a natural phenomenon that defies all intelligibility or interpretation. June 2013 thus ostensibly names a gap in the director's knowledge, but it is one that she does not seem compelled to investigate or fill, even as she acknowledges its centrality. The same thing happens with the economic crisis. The film prefaces a reference to it with footage of a presidential address in which Rousseff communicated her decision to bring down interest rates against the wishes of the financial sector. The voice-over is quietly admiring of her political courage, but once the announcement is over, all it has to say is "Contrary to expectations, the economy starts to slow down." Once again, a gap is recognized but not thematized: Something happened, we have no idea how or why; it is no use asking, next topic.

What those two gaps hide, evidently, are elements that could implicate PT in its own demise. After all, if everything was going so well before 2013, why did millions of people suddenly take to the streets all over the country following the heavy-handed repression of a protest against a bus fare hike in São Paulo? And if the economy moved in the opposite direction from the one that the government had projected, what might Rousseff and her advisers have gotten wrong?

Not that any of these films let PT and its leaders off the hook entirely. In the case of *Democracia em vertigem*, its distinctive framing device of interweaving the story of postdictatorship Brazil with that of the director's parents—upper-class former guerrillas and early-day PT supporters—means that the whole story is told from the point of view of a section of the party's historical social base that became estranged from it over the years.[8] In one of the film's finest sequences, a montage of TV ads from Lula's presidential campaigns between 1989 and 2002 shows the evolution of his discourse toward an increasingly conciliatory tone. And yet, when we try to grasp what, in the film's account, were the causes that led to PT's fall from grace, we are faced with a curious, perhaps symptomatic, irony. For most of the explanatory brunt seems to fall on the very same reason that the party's opponents would name for wanting its overthrow: corruption. Ultimately, the film suggests, PT's fatal error was the decision to buy into a system that had always run on corruption instead of trying to change it; apart from being a moral failing in its own right, that was what gave its adversaries the ammunition needed to bring it down. None of that would have been necessary if the party had been willing to push for political reform, and it still may not have had the same outcome if the party had not abandoned its long-held demand for media reform: Despite all the advantages it had gained under PT, Brazil's highly concentrated corporate media openly agitated for the impeachment.

This is the analysis laid out in the only moments in which *Democracia em vertigem* and *O processo* attempt a sustained critique of PT's blunders. Curiously, it is voiced in both films by the same person, former Lula and Rousseff aide Gilberto Carvalho.[9] That may be a coincidence, but it is hardly a surprise; as the government's top social movement liaison and one of Lula's oldest associates, Carvalho played for a long time the part of official critical consciousness of government and party. Yet that is exactly what makes his position, and hence his critique, ambiguous. For if his function consisted in mediating between social movements and the state apparatus, it also involved acting as proof that the government was listening—even, or especially, when that failed to yield any practical results. "Talking the talk" was part of his very job description as the person who brought grievances and criticisms from the party's base to the leadership but who was also counted upon by the latter to mollify the former. It is only fair, then, that when we see him expound on PT's limitations, we should ask ourselves in what capacity he is speaking. Is that a genuine recognition that announces a change of course, or is it just another appeal for patience, an ultimately empty gesture to renew the party loyalists' broken faith?

What Carvalho "really" means is, of course, beside the point; the problem is that neither film even poses the question. This seems to derive not from a lapse in sincerity but from a lack of critical distance. It is not that the directors are simply toeing the party line but rather that they inhabit the same perspective—that is, they share the same blind spots. This is why, when they come up against the gaps in that discourse, they stare at them but literally cannot see anything that demands (or can receive) an explanation; they see nothing that is being left unsaid. Hence the striking result that, in both cases, the sharpest criticisms of PT we see on the screen come not from marginalized sectors or even left-wing dissidents—both of which are largely absent from the narrative—but from the party's "official" self-critique.

This position is still preferable to others within the left that are even less sober and repentant and sometimes still resist to even admit PT's involvement in corruption. Yet once we begin to examine the gaps in this discourse, it becomes apparent that there is something convenient about an account that places corruption at the center. Firstly, corruption allows the party's policies to go unexamined. It is as if everything else was uniformly good and progressive apart from the leadership's connivance with practices that were already endemic anyway. This precludes one from seeing, for example, that the 2013 protests were already pointing to the limits of the development model that Lula and Rousseff had pursued—in which quantitative improvement in economic prospects was not being matched by a change in the quality of life (access to public services, institutional accountability, safety, urban mobility) and increasingly fed off exclusion and exploitation (precarization, property speculation, encroachment of the extractive frontier on the environment and Indigenous land). Secondly, given that PT's achievements are thus taken at face value, with no question as to their costs or consequences, it is possible to read the party's integration into the status quo as the evil that had to be done to achieve a greater good. After all, that had always been the way things worked, "until came the seismic shift." This, finally, obscures the ways in which the success of the route PT had found—a win-win deal through which the rich got much richer so that the poor could get a little less poor—effectively sowed the seeds for its disgrace by strengthening the sectors that would get rid of the party once the crisis gifted them the chance for an attack on the working class.[10] The party can then be portrayed as a passive victim of elite revanchism, brought down "above all for what it did right, for going against the greatest interests of capital," as Carvalho claims in *O processo.*

It is this truncated, weirdly depoliticized analysis that facilitates an analogy between the present and 1964, which *O processo* and *Democracia em vertigem* toy with and *Já vimos esse filme* directly deploys. This parallel was naturally ubiquitous at the time of the impeachment, but it is highly misleading. João Goulart was ousted less than twenty days after announcing an ambitious program of structural reforms; Rousseff, by contrast, fell not because she had gone on the offensive but because she had nowhere else to retreat to. Apart from the slowdown in Chinese demand for primary commodities, the unraveling of the economy under her administration was caused not by social spending but by a disastrous, wealth-concentrating policy of loans and fiscal incentives for companies that pocketed the money and refused to invest.[11] After campaigning as the only anti-austerity candidate, she committed to a harsh program of fiscal adjustment, at once alienating her supporters and failing to convince financial markets that she had the political muscle to see it through. When she came down, it was not by the hand of forces external to her government but by that of her own coalition partners and PT's erstwhile allies among Brazilian capital. The analogy therefore functions like a distorted, flattering mirror that soothes the left's conscience and exempts it from further examination: From the fact that what was done to it was class struggle, it licenses itself to deduce that so was what it did. Tellingly, the two images that dominated PT iconography after Lula's imprisonment are his and Rousseff's mugshots from the 1970s. It is as if the only way to deal with the recent trauma was to erase it altogether, replacing it with an earlier, more distant one that was less ambiguous and uncomfortable.

In the end, these films say as much about the perspective from which they speak as they do about the reality they speak of. This does not make them invalid, of course, but it means their analysis is clearly circumscribed.[12] It is worth noting that in Lula's three failed presidential runs since 1989, the bulk of PT's vote came from the educated middle and upper class; only in 2002 did the party conquer the poor. Over its years in power, many of PT's original supporters would drift away, disenchanted with the party's alliances and involvement in corruption. That critique of realpolitik was, however, more ethical than political, and more concerned with symbolism than with the costs and consequences of actual policies. When the crisis and corruption scandals wiped out much of Rousseff's working-class support and the threat of impeachment became imminent, it was that historical base that rallied in the party's defense. That was when those estranged sectors returned to the fold, and it is from their perspective that that these films were made.

Because these sectors had not developed a *political* critique of the externalities of PT's realpolitik—attacks on the Indigenous and the environment, militarization of the *favelas* and mass incarceration, the growth of the primary sector at the expense of the rest of the economy—nor paid attention to the groups affected by them, their defense of the party would also take on a mostly ethical form. PT was worth supporting, the argument went, because it had worked to improve the lives of millions. Little consideration was given to the various ways in which that could have been done, the different strategic horizons that each of those implied, the implications of the path effectively chosen, or even the fact that the conditions that had made those advances possible—the commodity boom of the early 2000s—had ceased to exist. To some extent, the response to realpolitik simply changed signs: Previously rejected on ethical grounds as a means that contaminated the ends, it was now retrospectively validated by the Brazilian elite's willingness to rip up the rulebook in order to bring the party down. Not only a comparatively lesser evil, this particular realpolitik was one that had at least been done for a greater good. What is more, it appeared in hindsight as having been unavoidable. For if even with all the concessions and compromises the backlash had been so vicious, was this not proof that nothing else could have been done?

"THE ABYSS IS THERE, OPEN"

Although it was also the best among them, *Terra em transe* was but one of several Cinema Novo (New Cinema) films that tried to make sense of the situation after the 1964 coup. Like Nelson Pereira dos Santos's *El justicero* (1967) and *Fome de amor* [Hunger for love] (1968), it touches upon middle-class ambivalence toward a political commitment they hesitate to assume or—as in Gustavo Dahl's *O bravo guerreiro* [The brave warrior] (1969), Cacá Diegues' *Os herdeiros* [The heirs] (1970), and Joaquim Pedro de Andrade's *Os inconfidentes* [The conspirators] (1972)—eventually betray. Whereas early Cinema Novo had wished to jolt its eminently urban audience into action by conveying the brute shock of extreme poverty in the country's rural Northeast, the films now moved to the big cities in the Southeast and trained their eye on the intelligentsia, that is, on their own audience.[13] The tonic thus goes from being a denunciation of underdevelopment *to* the public to being an indictment *of the public itself*, which was all the more vicious given that the directors could not be entirely sure that they were exempt from it themselves.[14]

On at least two levels, however, *Terra em transe* cut deeper than the two films that initiated this trend, Paulo César Saraceni's *O desafio* [The challenge] (1965) and Arnaldo Jabor's documentary *A opinião pública* [Public opinion] (1967). First, in its autopsy of the illusions of the pre-coup period, particularly the limits of Goulart's populism, the Communist Party's naïve wager on an alliance with the "progressive national bourgeoisie," and the left's deluded conviction that, when push came to shove, the people would be on their side. Second, in the masochistic courage with which it dwelled on the discomfort of defeat. *A opinião pública* was a relentless exposé of middle-class idiocy that, while legitimately interested in what its subjects had to say, distanced itself from them. *O desafio* still allowed viewers to feel sorry for its protagonist and, by identifying with him, to pity and absolve themselves. *Terra em transe* offered no such respite, no position from which its audience could escape the film's all-encompassing critique. Its finger firmly pointed at them—and therefore also itself—it asked the question in the back of everybody's mind: What if the blame for the defeat lay neither with the "forces of reaction" nor with "the people," but with the self-styled "revolutionaries," that is, with the left itself?

The film's dissection of populism is embodied in the character of Vieira, a provincial politician who wavers between his commitment to the poor and his compromises with landowning elites, deciding in favor of the former only when it is too late and the conservative leader Díaz has already set his coup in motion. But it is also materialized in a number of audiovisual metaphors representing the idea that, even under populism, the people still lack a *voice*: At Vieira's rallies, supporters move their mouths without making a sound, blank placards held aloft. What is exposed here is the solidarity between a system of cognitive representation (*Darstellung*) in which the people can only appear as inert and silent and a system of political representation (*Vertretung*) in which they can only participate through the mediation of a leader.[15] On the one hand, the populist leader's position depends on people remaining in a position in which "they cannot represent themselves, they must be represented"; on the other, as no one expects the people to be capable of speaking or acting for themselves, populism appears as their only access to political life.[16] Present only as an absence, included only as represented, silent unless someone else speaks on their behalf, the people are thus transformed into a variable whose potentially explosive force can be managed according to circumstantial interests. For that force to express itself directly would be a threat not only to the leader—whose primary political capital consists in being the one who can manage it—but to the whole system of representation that reduces the people to muteness and passivity.

It is one of Vieira's rallies that provides the film's most memorable sequence, dramatizing the limits of populist representation through a traumatic *double presentation* of the people. Jerônimo, a trade unionist, is cajoled to speak: "Don't be afraid, son. You are the people." The soundtrack goes silent and the camera closes in on his face. But the people's word, which we have waited so long to hear, is timid, conciliatory, resigned to the subalternity of those who "don't know a thing" and prefer to "wait for the president's orders." This is the people presenting themselves as their own representation. The film's protagonist sidles up behind him and covers his mouth, staring into the camera. The fourth wall is broken, representation is interrupted, and he addresses us directly: "Do you see what the people are like? Idiotic. Illiterate. Depoliticized. Can you imagine Jerônimo in power?" At this point, however, the camera starts following a man who snakes his way through the crowd and, arriving at the center of the frame, announces himself: "If you gentlemen excuse me, Mr. Jerônimo does our politics, but Mr. Jerônimo isn't the people." A group of peasants silently cram into the screen. "I am the people, with seven children and no place to live!" Yet the game of representation cannot tolerate that rupture in its surface: The "real" people underneath populist politics is a threat, a shock demanding that one take sides; it is unrepresentable. To cries of "Extremist! Extremist!," the man is shot.

The sequence condenses a number of political questions. How to criticize populist paternalism without assuming a paternalistic stance oneself? How to introduce into the symbolic order that which it excludes without making oneself into its representative? Was compromise with the order the only possible way, as the coup suggested, or should the coup instead be read as evidence that compromise was no longer possible? Through an admirable narrative short circuit, the scene not only exposes the exclusion on which political representation is founded but puts the limits of *cognitive* representation—its characters', the audience's, the film's own—into question. Was the way in which the left had been blindsided by events not a sign that they too had made the people into a cipher, an empty screen onto which their own words, ideas, and desires were projected? Was this not possible because they too participated in a politics that could only speak *for* or *about* the people, but never *with*? Was this not evidence of the chasm that separated them from the people as it existed outside of the political and cognitive representations that fixed and neutralized it? Did this not show that, whereas the left had conceived themselves as a true revolutionary force fighting alongside the people, they had been no more than an elite fraction all along—an isolated and ineffectual one at that?

This is precisely the kind of question that appears to be missing from the films that deal with the events of the last ten years. In these, the problem is always much more "out there" than "right here." Even *Democracia em vertigem*, on the surface the most self-reflexive of the bunch, is surprisingly oblivious to this problem: cognizant of the exclusive access afforded by the director's family connections but blissfully unencumbered by questions regarding what that says about the country, the perspective the director occupies, or the blind spots she might have. In *Terra em transe*, on the other hand, these problems are inescapable and very much what defines the protagonist, poet and journalist Paulo Martins.

It was one of Rocha's masterstrokes to place at the center of the film a character so flawed and unlikable, eliminating any distance viewers might put between themselves and the story. To identify with Martins is to identify mostly with his failings, with the suspicion that they are our own, with the "unpleasant truth" that he reveals about us.

The core of this truth lies in the character's split nature, expressed in a number of unreconciled dualities. An heir who does not want to accept his inheritance, Martins exists within the political space defined by the two figures that mark its extremes: Díaz, of whom he is an erstwhile protégé, and Vieira, with whom he has an ambivalent alliance. A narcissist who dreams of losing himself in a collective project, he oscillates between the extremes of poetry and politics, reckless individualism and commitment, the vapid socialite Silvia and the passionate militant Sara, his bourgeois class origin and a thirst for justice that is more meta physical than political. Throughout the film, he hesitates between an identity that he has rejected but not fully left behind and one he cannot quite come to terms with.

This leads him, at first, to overidentify. An idealist turned political hack, he keenly defends the constraints of realpolitik against those whose interests he believes to represent, personally repressing a group of disgruntled peasants. His investment in the people is shot through with a haughty, paternalistic conviction that they are not ready to be the subjects of their own fate; what troubles him is less the fact that he spanked a peasant leader than the latter's lack of reaction. ("They're a weak bunch, always," he laments to Sara. "Weak and fearful.") Disgusted, he renounces politics altogether and goes back to Silvia and a dissolute bourgeois life, a "beautiful soul" that cannot countenance his own complicity in the imperfections of the world. When Sara convinces him to return, disgust has soured into a nihilistic desire for rupture, moved at least as much by contempt for his peers as by the hope of reparation for the downtrodden. Revolution for him is not an attempt to organize the transition to a new order but a violent spasm to be incited from above, as if only that "trance of mystics" (as he puts it) could jolt the people out of their passivity.

In the meantime, however, his friends among the "progressive bourgeoisie" have started to take sides. In a scene that formally and narratively echoes the rally sequence, Díaz addresses media magnate Julio Fuentes while speaking directly to the camera: "Listen, imbecile, class struggle is real. Which is your class? Come on, say it." Finally, once the coup is consummated, Martins's nihilism is channeled into a solitary gesture of defiance that costs him his life. This was enough for some critics in 1967 to accuse the film of flirting with armed voluntarism. (Ironically, one of the journalists who made that accusation would take part in the kidnapping of the US ambassador only two years later.) But that misses the gesture's desperate, empty (non) performativity; as Rocha put it in an interview, "[t]he Revolution does not explode when [Martins] wants it to, and he takes a quixotic stance."[17] It also misses the darker truth that this meaninglessness suggests: that perhaps there was no room for Martins in those circumstances because Díaz and Vieira truly exhausted the field of possible politics.

Terra em transe did not claim to have an answer for the questions it raised—but it did not allow people to avoid them either. Not having answers was, in fact, part of the point. Commenting on the polemic that greeted the film, Rocha would say that *Terra em transe* had been "criticized for not providing a synthesis": "But if I had provided a synthesis, I would have made an anti-Marxist, idealistic, anti-dialectical film."[18] He added: "I did not intend to solve problems on a theoretical level, to make a utopian film, to give political advice."[19] "If I made a film about the trance of Latin America and gave it a finished form, I would be going against the film's very praxis. A film of rupture, of crisis, must be as poor as its theme, the two things must be integrated."[20] Rather than flatter or soothe anyone's conscience, the point was rather to force the left to face its collective predicament—to acknowledge that, as Martins tells Sara at one point, "the abyss is there, open, and we're all marching toward it."

FROM TRANCE TO VERTIGO

What do these stories about Brazil have to say about the crossroads in which the left finds itself in many countries now?

Compared with the unforgiving soul-searching of *Terra em transe*, the documentaries dealing with the fall of PT cannot but feel a little too cozy, too willing to let the left off lightly. Combined with the evasion from the present toward imagery and analogies from the past, this suggests that the process of learning from defeat is largely hindered by a melancholic attachment to the victories and possibilities of a recent but bygone past. Whereas the shock of 1964 inspired in the likes of Rocha a radical disidentification with the hegemonic left and the urge to thoroughly revise earlier beliefs, the successive defeats from 2016 to 2022 (and the many legislative upsets that followed Lula's return to power) often appear to have the opposite effect, confirming people in their convictions and reassuring them that they have always been "on the right side." Even more, they appear to have produced a sort of retrospective overidentification that justifies behaviors criticized in the past, rejects all reservations about them as unrealistic, and ultimately concludes that things could not be otherwise.

There is, of course, no way of knowing that things would have been different if PT had favored politicization from below instead of making deals at the top, had looked for alternatives to its dependence on the primary sector early on, had pushed for political and media reform, had leveraged the 2013 protests instead of repressing them, and so on. Nevertheless, to give the realpolitik it practiced in power the monopoly over political realism, relegating any attempt to question it to the realm of the naïve and the utopian, not only is the worst lesson one could possibly draw from defeat, it is also wrong. It is bad because, in the end, to conclude that things could only be as they were is to draw no lesson at all. It is wrong because it refuses to see that one's actions have an effect on the constraints that determine what is and is not possible: a politics that intends to be transformative must necessarily work at once *within the limits of possibility and on those limits themselves*, so as to expand them.

Nothing represents the mismatch between the pre-1968 context in which *Terra em transe* was made and the dominant reaction to the present conjuncture better than the way in which the latter misreads the former. What Rocha's film signaled was a younger generation's rejection of the politics of conciliation of the Goulart period, even if it suspended judgment on whether an alternative path was available. Today, many who turn to that time draw the opposite conclusion: While identifying with the heroism of those who fell fighting, they see no other option but trying to reconstitute PT's pact with the Brazilian elite. But since the conditions that made that pact possible are no longer in existence, and Rousseff's impeachment and ruling class accommodation of the far right proved that even a "weak reformism" will be resisted if the alternative seems viable, this conciliation cannot but occur on even less ambitious bases.[21]

One could always object that the difference between the two moments is that PT was founded by many people who lived through the experience to which that rejection of conciliation led after 1968: the armed struggle. Today's caution would thus be explained by the fact that radicalization was tried then and proved both politically and militarily unfeasible. But speaking as if an impossible armed struggle were the only meaning that "radicalization" could have is exactly where the problem lies: It ultimately guides us back to the conclusion that the only possibility is pursuing the same conciliatory tactics again, even as they too have arguably been demonstrated impracticable. By assuming that "radical" can only mean "extreme" and that only one course of action is "realistic," we put arbitrary limits on our political imagination and foreclose any questioning as to how things could have been different. This prevents us from looking for that which might be both feasible *and* radical at the same time—that is, for solutions that act within existing constraints while also working to transform them over time.

A realpolitik that does the former but not the latter not only abdicates from pursuing long-term change but offers no resistance to those that wish to further constrain it, and thus can only watch defenselessly as its room for maneuver continues to shrink. A realism that treats reality as a fixed quantity is not worth the name. As Rosa Luxemburg once put it, a revolution is like a locomotive traveling uphill: It either "drives forward full steam ahead to the most extreme point of the historical ascent, or it rolls back of its own weight again to the starting point at the bottom."[22] The Brazilian experience shows this is a piece of advice that even would-be reformers or self-professed realists should heed.

THE ENCOUNTER OF BATMAN WITH THE PEOPLE

One thing Brazilian legislators are famous for is their passion for creating holidays; a few notable ones include the National Day of the Goalkeeper, the National Day of the Telemarketing Operator, and the National Day of Mixed Martial Arts. So, in the future, it may be that one of them will look back upon the turbulent period from 2013 to 2022 and propose January 19, 2014, as the Day Things Stopped Making Sense.

That was the date when a group of activists in Rio de Janeiro called for a demonstration at a shopping center in one of the richest parts of town. This was not a normal demonstration, in fact, but a *rolezinho* (something like "day out"), capitalizing on the trend that had started at the end of the previous year in São Paulo, in which working-class youth from the peripheries would organize through social media to gather en masse in shopping malls to socialize and collectively occupy spaces in which security often eyed them with suspicion and chased them out.[1] The event in Rio, however, which only a tiny fraction of the nine thousand people who had confirmed on Facebook actually showed up for, never took place. The commercial space closed its doors in advance as a precaution, so the small number of people who gathered quickly dispersed. But it gave rise to a YouTube video that would become known as "Batman in Leblon," a Tropicalist delirium in which dental prosthetist Eron Morais de Melo, famous for attending all the many protests taking place in the city at the time wearing a full Batman costume, argues with a filmmaker known for his 1980s work—a local resident and PT supporter. The two are constantly interrupted by passersby, other demonstrators, a French TV crew, and a self-declared right-winger who shows familiarity with the conspiracy theories that at that time were still practically the monopoly of right-wing Ur-influencer Olavo de Carvalho.

The reference to the 1960s artistic movement known as Tropicália is not arbitrary. The video has many similarities with the rally sequence from *Terra em transe*, both formal—the play between a camera that chases characters and characters who come to present themselves to it—and thematic.[2] Although one is fictional and the other is not, both function as allegories of the country at a particular time—allegory being, as is often observed, the Tropicalist procedure par excellence.[3] While Rocha's film stages a carnival both literal (with samba dancers and drums) and figurative (with stock types such as the Trade Unionist, the Peasant, the Man of Letters, the Priest, and the Radical Students), the frustrated demonstration offers a carnival situation in which equally one-dimensional characters (the Batman from the Protests, the Petista Filmmaker from Leblon, the Olavista Photographer) confront one another.[4] The 1967 film makes carnival (and the Baroque, with which the popular feast has much in common) a kind of allegory of the allegory, its proliferation without synthesis functioning as a resource to represent the juxtaposition of the modern and the archaic characteristic of the fictional country of Eldorado. In turn, the 2014 video validates this choice by confirming the thesis that there is something fundamentally carnivalesque—confused, mixed up, excessive—in the very reality of Brazil. Both are characterized by the saturation of representation, in the exaggeration of features (one-dimensionality, schematism) as well as in the elimination of any possibility of identification that would allow for a privileged point of view. (In the film, this saturation goes as far as to include in the diegesis people who are documenting the scene—a role played in the YouTube video by the French journalists and other people with cameras.) In both cases, we are dealing with a question of masks: the people and those who "do the politics of the people," the activism that hides behind masks, the things the masks represent and hide (symbol of imperialism and empty revolt, as the filmmaker denounces? A right-wing destabilization plot, as he also suggests? Or a left-wing false flag operation, as the Olavista retorts?). Which is to say that, in both cases, what is at stake is ultimately the problem of representation in its double sense, political and cognitive.

When Rocha was filming his sequence in the 1960s, the urgent question was, Who are the real people? What is under discussion at the start of the long hangover from the 2013 protests that "Batman in Leblon" documents is, above all, Who is the real left? Symptomatically, the "people" are not in the video: The *rolezinho*, which in São Paulo had been a spontaneous movement of peripheral youth, in Rio was promoted by activist networks that had come out of the demonstrations six months earlier, which failed in this instance to attract any public other than themselves. But the dispute inevitably involves references to this absent entity. The masked activist claims to speak on behalf of those who are being left behind by PT's developmentalism; the filmmaker's progressive credentials are based on the memory of the 1980s struggle for redemocratization and on his support for a government "in which the country has advanced, [in which] there are jobs." Both lay claim to being "the left" to the extent that they suppose to speak on behalf of someone who is not there. Ironically, the moment when the filmmaker is seen in agreement with the Olavista, also a local resident, is when they both reply to the French journalist, who asks if the protesters are right to say that there is social discrimination in access to the city, with the answer that this discourse sows "hatred among brothers." To foment a "civil war," according to her; to create division where none exists, according to him—who backs up his statement with the argument that he, who earns "a lot of money," drinks in the bars of the area with residents of a local housing estate.

Apart from its (in equal measures) comic and prophetic value, "Batman in Leblon" is important, first of all, because it represents, with something like Rocha's power of synthesis, the operation whereby PT's decision to close the political space to its left ended up paving the way for the far right to make itself the heir to the 2013 protests. It is remarkable that, in the 2014 video, the moment that is equivalent to 1967's "I am the people!" is not about either the left or the people, but the right. It begins with the filmmaker and the Olavista, who has just appeared, calling the activist "manipulated." When the PT supporter explains that the demonstrators are ultimately "fascists" and "right-wingers," however, his hitherto ally interrupts: "Fascists, yes, but not right-wingers. I am right wing!" It is only then that the two realize that, although they are saying the same thing, they are doing so with inverted signs. That the protests are part of a hidden and nefarious plot is not in dispute; but what for him is an attack on a good left-wing government, for her is "a plan for the totalitarian communist occupation of the country."

We are witnessing at this moment the genesis of two polarizing operations. The one coming from the far right rejects all those who are doing politics, institutionally or on the streets, and opposes them to the ordinary people who are their so-called victims. The one coming from PT asserts that theirs is the only possible left-wing position, which automatically throws everyone who criticizes the government into the right camp, whatever beliefs they may actually profess. Between the two operations, there is a third, abortive polarization that cannot take hold: Given that Petismo, with whom they would need to form a pole, rejected them, the demonstrators are left with the option to either face a "fight on two fronts" for which they have neither the discursive nor the organizational wherewithal, or group Petismo and the right together in the pole to which they are opposed, which they hesitate to do because of the risk of abetting the latter's offensive.

The far right's operation has a clear hegemonic vocation, as it is aimed at all of those who do not yet have a defined political identity—which is, at any given time, the majority. The one undertaken by PT is organized around an identity, the "true" left, whose power of interpellation depends on a prior identification: One must want to be on the left before they will want to claim the title of "real" left. The problem with this strategy is that it premised the capacity to build a majority on an association (between "supporting the government" and "being on the left") that Lulismo, with its ideology-light discourse of inclusion through consumption, had worked for a decade to weaken.[5] What is more, it chose to repel any questioning of the government at the very moment when criticism was most widespread, fatally limiting the audience it could reach. In the end, the most it could do was reestablish the party's hegemony over its own political camp. As for the young activists who had lit the fuse for the 2013 protests, even if they wanted to fight for hegemony, they were unable to draw a line of antagonism adequate to the task, and found themselves, in the end, reduced to reaffirming their identity against the two other sides, instead of trying to constitute a new identity that could communicate with more people. The result would be ever-greater isolation.

"Batman in Leblon" is important, secondly, because it draws attention to the figure of Eron Morais de Melo, whose trajectory is paradigmatic of this period. Joining the protests for the first time on the colossal June 20 march, he would go on to become a familiar presence in Rio de Janeiro activism, attending every single demonstration, even after they became less frequent and more conflictual. A working-class evangelical *batalhador* from the suburbs with no previous political experience, it was on the left that he initially found a space to express an indignation that, if somewhat confused, was nonetheless sincere.[6] In 2015, he would resurface on top of a sound system at a pro-impeachment rally, and the following year would declare his support for Bolsonaro and run for the same city council whose building he had once unsuccessfully tried to occupy. (His election bid was equally a flop.) In 2017, he publicly broke with the future president's family and distanced himself from politics for good.

It is comforting to conclude that Morais de Melo only found out who he had always been—"a fascist in a fascist costume", as I heard from one of his erstwhile comrades—, since it exempts us from asking whether his trajectory could not have led somewhere else. It is harder to assume that identities are not given but are formed recursively from the stimuli available around them; that people are not this or that, but become so. The peak of the June 2013 demonstrations attracted millions of people into politics who could have arrived at different positions if there had been enough suitable stimuli—and if the left had not ended up contributing to the environmental evolutionary pressures that increasingly selected for right-wing developmental paths. The truth is that, faced with a mass of people they did not recognize, both the institutional and the autonomous left—whose only chance of success in those circumstances lay in an unlikely partnership—panicked and gave up trying to offer the masses experiencing a political awakening some kind of orientation. Instead, the left prioritized the dispute within its own camp. As a result, the greatest pedagogic opportunity that Brazilian politics had seen in a long time was left to be exploited mostly by the right, which could also count on the sympathy of the media and the political establishment to push its message.

Brazil was a unique case in the early 2010s cycle of struggles in that, not only was it the only country in which the left (or at least a not entirely discredited left) was in power, it was also the only one where the media switched sides regarding the protests, going from initial condemnation and calls for the police to "clean up the streets" to support and a targeted attempt to redefine them as "anticorruption"—a none-too-subtle shorthand for "anti-PT." But revisiting this curious relic from those days offers lessons that are still valid, not only in Brazil but more broadly; this is the third reason why "Batman in Leblon" matters.

One such lesson is the following. In a country like Brazil, where the left can still count on the recent memory of transformative (if limited) governments, banking on identity was enough to push Lula's replacement after he was jailed, Fernando Haddad, into the second round in 2018. Haddad still lost. In the United States, meanwhile, a country where voting is not compulsory and often curtailed by state legislation, the looser, more distant memory of the Democratic Party as the party of civil rights and minorities was not enough to rally support for Kamala Harris against Donald Trump. Relying on old allegiances or vague ideas like "democracy" to fill the void left by a lack of substantive commitments is highly unlikely to cut it as an electoral strategy at a time when the far right is forging new identities and many feel democracy has failed them. It is much more likely, in fact, to play directly into the right's hands, confirming its depiction of a self-serving liberal elite and reinforcing the feelings of being lied to, ignored, and taken for granted on which it capitalizes. Even if it might work electorally on occasion, it is certainly no way to build long-term power.

But if substituting policy with identity is not a solution, neither is it to drain politics from identity, vision, or sense of purpose altogether, substituting those things with policies exploiting tiny marginal differences and promoting minor, very gradual change. Both are, in the end, only two sides of the same centrist coin. The expectation that at some point people will just become "tired of polarization" and wish for nothing more than gray, managerial technocracy rests on the mistaken assumption that the reason why so many people agree with those who say that something has to give is that they are temporarily blinded by passion, not that they are acting on things they experience every day. As Emmanuel Macron in France and Keir Starmer in the United Kingdom are in the process of proving, this recalcitrant wager on resurrecting the post-politics of the 1990s and early 2000s can be little more than a holding pattern for the far right as it continues to grow. Joe Biden's failure to elect his successor is a cautionary tale in this regard: Even the most ambitious attempt to relaunch centrism with a program of reforms—one that was more wide ranging than anyone had tried in some time—ultimately failed because its effects did not get to the majority of the population, that is, because it did not attack head-on the problem of distribution.

Another lesson concerns what governments can do in the face of movements that demand speeding up the rhythm of transformation. As we have seen, PT's choice when the 2013 protests exploded was not to try to use them as leverage against the opposition and its own coalition partners but, apart from a very brief moment early on, to dismiss, marginalize, and suppress. Fearful of something it did not control, but was not necessarily hostile, the party fell even deeper into the establishment's arms—losing popularity, further associating itself with the status quo, and making it easier for the far right to claim the legacy of that movement and present itself as the sole force for change. There is, of course, no guarantee that things would have turned out differently had another road been taken; what is clear, on the other hand, is the spectacular failure that the one taken was.

It could always be objected that, like so many of its peers around the world, PT is not actually a radical party that failed to seize an occasion but a moderate party juggling the effort to retain its political niche with the desire not to rock the boat too much. As we saw in the last chapter, however, what this story shows is that even moderation requires boldness and the discernment to recognize when it is time to up the tempo. The issue is not, as one-gear realists like to pretend, one of acknowledging that it is impossible to do everything at once and making concessions is inevitable when one is power. It is, rather, that there is no ideal quantity of concessions that will ensure a stable equilibrium or a perfect cruising speed. Not only does the balance of forces change as situations change—as PT learned the hard way when its allies turned against it the moment its popularity dropped—but this is precisely why one must constantly have an eye on changing the balance of forces in the long run: Those who do not actively work to become stronger than those to whom they make concessions today will tend to need to concede more and more in the future.

For that, one must be able to see challenges from below not only as threats to a present equilibrium but as opportunities for establishing a new equilibrium in a more advanced position. This entails replacing the expectation of blind conformity and unconditional support with the capacity to welcome and manage tensions, and ceasing to conceive of unity as homogeneity and centralization of command to view it instead in ecological terms: as a form of cooperation that does not exclude difference, divergence, and competition.

CONCLUSION

ENDGAME

On September 11, 2025, the Brazilian Supreme Court found Jair Bolsonaro and seven allies, five of whom high-ranking military officers, guilty of plotting a coup d'état to reverse the result of the 2022 elections, in which PT leader Luiz Inácio Lula da Silva won a third term against the far-right incumbent. On November 25, Bolsonaro started serving his twenty-seven-year sentence. Before that, in 2023, he had already been convicted of abuse of political power and undue use of the media by the Superior Electoral Court, becoming unelectable until 2030.

This is an outcome often held up as an example of how North American institutions should have dealt with Donald Trump, and there is all the more reason for that given that the moment the judges identified as the culmination of a plan to pervert Brazilian democracy was so clearly inspired by the US president. Even before the start of the 2022 campaign—in fact, literally since the January 6, 2021, riots in Washington, DC—it was clear that Bolso naro toyed with the prospect of having his own storming of the Capitol. Like Trump in 2016, he had been sowing the idea that any result other than a massive triumph would be a sign of fraud and potentially justify the use of force since before the election he actually won, in 2018. By doing so, he consistently communicated that, regardless of whether they took the claims of electoral interference literally or only seriously, he and his electoral base would recognize no other will expressed at the ballot box except their own.

Yet what eventually unfolded in Brasília on January 8, 2023, was, in some important respects, quite unlike the events that took place in the US capital—which, if anything, only makes Trump's case more damning. However botched and on the hoof it may have been, the attack on the Capitol was the result of a clear strategic calculation. Its goal was to use the crowd gathered at a rally to stop Joe Biden's certification as the winner, thus preventing his election from becoming a fait accompli and keeping open the possibility that Republicans might find a way to hand power back to the outgoing president. In Brazil, the wave of roadblocks and encampments in front of barracks that went on for months after Lula's triumph was an obvious trial run to test the chances of a movement along the same lines, with the important difference that the goal from the start was to drum up military backing. Although they impressed with their size and duration—abetted by funding sources that are yet to be fully identified—these mobilizations were not enough to obtain that result. As the investigation into the plot has since revealed, on December 7, 2022, Bolsonaro met with the heads of the three armed forces to present them with the plans that he and his closest collaborators had hatched. Two of the chiefs demurred, no doubt partially because of signals that the Biden administration had been sending through diplomatic channels. Without that support, the risk of failing and being caught was substantially higher; as a consequence, from that point on, no one who had anything to lose would want to break cover and be seen as explicitly supporting a coup. This included Bolsonarista members of Congress and several figures in the military, however much they might have wanted to join in. More importantly, it included Bolsonaro and his family, who, since the electoral defeat in November, had been so concerned with reducing their legal exposure that they had refrained from openly leading the troops at all—first limiting themselves to timid claim-then-deny troll tactics, then fleeing to Florida on the eve of Lula's inauguration.

All of this meant that, by the time January 8 came around, all relevant deadlines—announcement of the electoral result, certification, inauguration—had been missed, and all the main players saw the possibility of a turnaround as vanishingly remote. Thus, whereas the order for a march on the Capitol came directly from Trump, at a rally in full view of news cameras from all over the world, Bolsonaro's top brass may have underhandedly supported and incentivized the attack on Brasília, but wanted their fingerprints nowhere near it. What ensued was very revealing of the Ponzi scheme–like way in which Bolsonarismo is organized, and of the relationship between its leaders and their base.

As the top of the pyramid retreated, it was the middle layers that took the initiative. They understood the huge blow that the end of coup-mongering hopes would be to that segment of the Bolsonarista base who for months had been kept at fever pitch by the mobilizations and conspiratorial narratives of the postelection period—those for whom Lula's victory represented an imminent existential threat, making any surrender to the principle of political reality a betrayal pure and simple. Keeping this sector engaged despite the diminishing chances of success was, for these intermediate tiers, a way of preserving their own base at a time when the whole edifice might fall apart, while simultaneously establishing their credentials for future flights. This made the whole sequence leading from the roadblocks and protest camps to the January 8 events a meeting of two types of people with little to lose: the political opportunists who wished to squeeze the last gains off the good times that were seemingly coming to an end and the true believers for whom the end of their coup fantasy was the end of the world. Behind them, and split between these two categories, were the funders, drawn not from big capital, which had resigned itself to Lula's victory and in any case had too much to lose, but from the lower ranks of the upper classes in which Bolsonaro's most fervent supporters are to be found. These include small- and medium-sized family capital and the most backward sectors of agribusiness and the extractive industry—illegal loggers, gold miners, producers who are less integrated into financial and international markets—for whom the years of officially tolerated Wild West capitalism under the far right had been a golden age.

This social composition and lack of political leverage help explain why the January 8 insurgence ended up being much more symbolic than strategic. Whereas in Washington the target had been a congressional session in progress, the Brasília rioters attacked empty buildings on a Sunday; and whereas Trumpists restricted themselves to trying to coerce legislators, their Bolsonarista epigones went on a rampage against the three branches of government, in an implicit acknowledgement that no support could be found in any of them. If this was undoubtedly a coup attempt in its participants' intention, it was not so in actual fact. Short of the by then very faint hope that the military would use the disturbance as an excuse to step in, there was no plan or power analysis—and, crucially, no support for it among those with real decision-making power.

Not that these did not support *the actions*. On the contrary, many politicians had given the protesters aid or spoken in their favor beforehand in varying degrees of explicitness, and refused to condemn them even after the backlash that followed. As for the military and police forces, they not only deliberately failed to control the crowds but often guided them into buildings, helped, and cheered them on. But nobody—and certainly not for lack of want—supported *the coup*. In the end, this was as far as they were willing to go: a show of force that was not meant to be taken to the next level, as the next level would require them to take risks they were unwilling to take. And since without their mediation the base did not have the institutional means to achieve what it wanted, Bolsonarismo's greatest moment of excess was also an exercise in containment, a demonstration of social strength that doubled as a confession of political weakness.

One would be advised not to confuse the inability to enact a coup with weakness tout court, however. The 2022 election pitted those who could be described, according to several observable metrics, as the best and the worst Brazilian presidents of all time, and the best won by no more than a 1.8 percent margin. The vote also yielded what is widely regarded as the most right-wing Congress since the military regime, with the majority in both houses consisting of an alliance between hardcore Bolsonaristas and the more versatile, pay-to-play right. The latter—who, in one capacity or another, have long been the center of gravity of the country's politics—became simultaneously more powerful and more prone to taking on the colors of the far right during the Bolsonaro years. Their increased power reached a new peak in 2019 with the former president handing congressional control over a large chunk of the federal budget with little oversight as a way of shoring up support, a practice declared unlawful by the Supreme Court in 2022 but subsequently resurrected under different guises with the lenience of the Lula government, which uses it for the same purpose. But this was only the culmination of a trend of ever-growing legislative autonomy dating back to Dilma Rousseff's impeachment, a vote of no confidence in all but name, despite the fact that no such thing exists in Brazil's presidential system. This soft parliamentarist coup was a perverse consequence of the 2013 protests' cry against unaccountability, in that the crisis of the Workers' Party and the hitherto main opposition party, the Brazilian Social Democratic Party, emboldened the mass of amorphous parties-for-hire that would normally hitch their wagons to one or the other to take the reins of the situation. Alongside the general drift to the right and the extractive industry's coming of age as an independent political actor, it meant that the new Lula administration would never be in a position as strong as it enjoyed in the first decade of this century.

Most of the leaders that not too long ago were being touted as part of a "second Pink Tide" have since been ousted or failed to elect their successors. Argentina's Alberto Fernández moved to the center, failed to control inflation, and was replaced by Javier Milei in 2023. Peru's Pedro Castillo was hounded by a right-wing Congress that tried to impeach him three times in under two years, then was arrested for an attempted self-coup; his vice president, Dina Boluarte, moved to the right but was herself impeached three years later. Bolivia's Luis Arce, who returned the Movement Towards Socialism (MAS) to power a year after the 2019 coup that stopped Evo Morales from claiming an unprecedented fourth term, fell out with Morales over control of the party, presided over an economic crisis, and saw his anointed favorite come in at a distant sixth behind center-right newcomer Rodrigo Paz in the following elections. Unable to control rising gang activity and plagued by corruption allegations, Honduras's Xiomara Castro watched Donald Trump's candidate defeat another right-wing runner-up in the same week that the North American leader pardoned a former Honduran president convicted for participation in a drug-trafficking scheme almost two decades long. Chile's Gabriel Boric wasted the momentum of the 2019 protests that became known as the "social outburst" (*estallido social*): While his administration was perceived as too timid, the new constitution drafted by a left-dominated assembly was seen as too radical and was rejected. A second draft, dominated by the right, was also rejected, but the far right continued to grow by capturing the anti-systemic sentiment with which the new government lost touch, eventually fielding two strong candidates in

2025 and winning with José Antonio Kast by a large margin. Colombia's Gustavo Petro, while impressing on the international stage with radical stances on climate action, such as suspending all new gas and oil licenses, struggled domestically with an uncooperative legislative, rising public debt, and reliably poor ratings. His appointed successor lost by a small margin to a far right newcomer. Only Mexico's Claudia Sheinbaum, who has managed to build on Andrés Manuel López Obrador's welfare expansionism and economic nationalism despite slow economic growth, comes across as strong success-story material. If the reasons why the new batch have failed to match the impact of the first wave of left-leaning governments in the region may vary according to national context, it is clear what their common background is: The absence of anything like the early 2000s' commodity boom to support an expansion of redistributive policies, making their room for maneuver tighter and local elites even less willing to play along.

Lula's case is especially poignant given that the more successful predecessor he is bound to be compared to is himself. Next to the big strides of his first two terms in areas like cash transfer programs and access to higher education, his third administration is certainly a lot less remarkable. A welcome period of normalization after ten years of dysfunction—but well below the level of radicality required to challenge the conditions that caused the abnormality—it will probably be remembered for only one major achievement, a tax reform that made Brazil's hugely regressive tax system fairer. While that is certainly nothing to be scoffed at, it is hardly the kind of issue that captures the hearts and minds of the masses, or whose effects become manifest right away. More importantly, this was a victory negotiated in exchange for a "new fiscal framework" offered as a sop to finance capital. Limiting increases in public spending to 70 percent of gains in tax revenue up to 2.5 percent per year, the new rule "enforces a gradual reduction in the size of the state," threatens the constitutional floors for education and health investments in the long run, and places Lula's weak reformism "in even lower gear"—"Lulismo in slow motion," as André Singer and Fernando Rugitsky have called it.[1]

The drop in enthusiasm produced by this arrangement could be seen in the 2024 mayoral elections, in which the right grew and put forward a new line of leaders that had come up through its internet ranks—mostly notably supercoach Pablo Marçal, who at one point looked set to challenge Bolsonaro for his throne but has since been kicked out of politics for electoral crimes. From that point on, Lula's popularity kept falling, and a harsh legislative defeat in June 2025 put him at risk of becoming a lame duck with a year and a half to go. That was when the government finally adopted the approach that many to its left had advocated all along, and instead of trying to mollify the opposition with shady backroom deals, took it to task with a highly successful media campaign that accused it of defending the interests of the superrich. It was then that disaster struck—and it could not have been at a better time. Just as it had finally chosen to go on the offensive, the administration received the news that, under intense lobby from one of Bolsonaro's sons, Trump had decided to impose 50 percent tariffs on a host of Brazilian products. The move, meant to put pressure on the Supreme Court in the run-up to the coup trial, backfired badly: It brought the judges together, handed the left a sovereignist discourse that had been the right's preserve for a decade, and painted the Bolsonaro family as holding the country to ransom. With the former president's guilty verdict and the scramble to succeed him among the right, Lula was gifted a year of relatively smooth sailing ahead of the 2026 elections. At the time of writing, he is still likely to win, but set for a tight contest with Bolsonaro's oldest son, Flávio, personally chosen by his father to lead his former troops. However, if part of the problem for the far right is that there have been too many people jostling to become the elder Bolsonaro's heir, the left struggles with the opposite, and there are no evident successors to Lula on the horizon. Even if he does become Brazil's next president, it is unclear whether there will be anyone capable of defeating the far right once he is gone.

* * *

Unlike figures such as Nigel Farage, Donald Trump, and Javier Milei, Jair Bolsonaro's political career was not tied from the start to what I have been calling the contemporary far right. In many ways, he was a transplant: a curio, a relic, a folkloric representative of a nostalgia for military rule that seemed to have no proper place in the present. It took extraordinary political turmoil, a sudden economic backslide, and several years of institutional crisis to make this marginal, somewhat laughable character into the right person at the right time. It also took the work of a growing base of political entrepreneurs and grassroots supporters, including those who connected him to the talking points and preoccupations of a far right that was rising elsewhere at around the same time. As in many other places, pent-up anger at a system seemingly incapable of meeting people's needs, but impossible to change through the usual channels, combined with other symptoms of broader stagnation and decline—status anxiety, feelings of abjection and humiliation, fears of losing one's place in the world, dread about the future—and a whole constellation of emerging on- and offline counterpublics to produce a culture that the new right, with its simplistic scapegoating and promises of simple solutions, could pose as the ideal political vessel for. Finally, it took the Brazilian elite's willingness to gamble on an entirely untested alternative when it became clear that the former army captain was the only roadworthy vehicle for its interests.

Though its leading man may initially have been something of an odd fit, the Bolsonaro government would go on to be revelatory, presenting in sharper contrast some features of the contemporary far right that were not, or had not yet become, as clear in other places. Perhaps some things are possible in Brazil before they become possible everywhere else. Thus, while Trump in his first term was an object of sometimes embarrassingly fanboyish emulation for the Brazilian leader, it is the US president's emboldened second administration that has come to resemble that of his Brazilian counterpart, starting with the fact that the main criterion for ministerial selection appears to be enmity toward any sort of traditional policy in the field and the determination to dismantle one's own ministry's executive apparatus. Whereas chaos and inaction in the first act of Trump's rule often seemed to be a consequence of inexperience and political rudderlessness, it is now much more evidently a method, as it was in Brazil: the work of keeping the base engaged and the headlines busy as the wrecking job continues in the background, and ever more areas are taken over by private initiative and interest groups organized in advance for the assault. In his favorite blunt weapon, tariffs, Trump has in fact found a great tool for this kind of job: something that makes it look like big decisions are being made despite the absence of a long-term plan or much by way of discernible rationale. It is not even just always a case of allowing market forces to do their job, although it is certainly also that, especially in sectors such as health and education; in the likes of energy and tech, the government is actively intervening not against (that is, redistributively) but in the very direction in which the wind blows. "They're picking winners and losers. No doubt of that," as a more ideologically consistent free marketeer in the US right has put it.[2]

What these signs suggest is that we can find the truth about the contemporary far right not in entrepreneurial utopias, fantasies of national renewal, or dreams of returning to strict gender binaries and traditional morality, central to mobilizing and heartfelt among the foot soldiery as all of those might be. Although it is certainly essential to take the ideas that move their base seriously, we should be careful not to treat these movements one-dimensionally, as if they truly were instruments designed with the sole purpose of delivering what they promise, and avoid taking their discourse entirely at face value. Instead, we should look at them as systems composed—and serving the interests—of leaders, allies (national and international), agitators, political entrepreneurs, and grassroots activists; as well as remind ourselves of Stafford Beer's deliciously Occamian maxim that "the purpose of a system is what it does."[3] This demands, in turn, that we be extra attentive to the different things its different component parts might want as well as to what Theodor Adorno dubbed the "phoniness" of all involved, even the truest believers—that is, the fact that everyone will have motives that are not openly stated among their goals and may well hope for other results contained within the ones they explicitly pursue. The *acceleration of disintegration* is my attempt to name what is objectively common to this disparate, inconsistent set of interests, independently from national variations of political genealogy and social composition. It is also what sets it apart from the much less equivocal nation building of historical fascism. What I mean by that term is that even what might overtly present itself as struggles to locally contain the deterritorializing effects of late capitalism, be that within legal borders or imaginary boundaries like the family, is in fact better understood not as a series of attempts to stop or reverse change but as efforts to harness and direct disaggregating tendencies that have been vastly intensified by neoliberalism and, even more so, its crisis. Regardless of whether they are framed as resistance against the all-encompassing force of a phantasmatic "globalism," they are in fact traveling in the same direction toward which these tendencies point, namely, that of breakdown: of liberal democracy, universalism, and inclusivity; of equality before the law, of indivisible sovereignty, of state capacity (except for a few very well defined functions), of our living environment, of the so-called rules-based international order.

While different components of the far right may claim this is not what they are doing, and some might even genuinely believe that is the case, this is the resultant force of their partially divergent efforts, and at once the momentum that carries them along and to which they add.

Thus, for instance, while many who voted for Brexit imagined "taking back control" as a return to past imperial glories, its masterminds saw it as the path to turning the country into a low-tax, lightly regulated "Singapore-on-Thames" that would be even more exposed to foreign capital. (The double irony is that not only was this a complete misread of Singapore's history of strongly state-led development, the European Union could still block it by threatening to deny the United Kingdom privileged access to its market.) Likewise, Trump's alliance with Big Tech, while it certainly has national strategic interests in sight, also involves handing (even more) money, freedom, and sensitive information to actors whose stack and platform power are increasingly not constrained by any nation-state; a field like crypto, in which the US president has become (literally) invested, drastically reduces the state's capacity of oversight in money laundering, financial fraud, and other sorts of crime. When the religious right stacks education boards and works to get their own onto the Supreme Court, it is not simply seeking shelter from a modernity that threatens the coordinates of its world. It is following the migration of a winner-takes-all logic from the market into politics, the consequence of which is an understanding of democracy that abandons tolerance or protection for minorities in favor of the unilateral assertion of the will of the majority (that is, whoever is better at playing the system to win). Combined with the sense that some have been unduly protected for too long, this becomes democratic governance as a form of collective revenge: revanche republicanism. Similarly, when the far right makes demands on the state, these are stripped of any sense of universality and very explicitly reclaim the right of some to be favored over others. After decades of hearing that there was not enough to go around and that sacrifices had to be made, some have started organizing to ensure that they will not be the lambs. Accepted as a basic fact, the idea that the state cannot, and hence must not, offer protection to all has led to what, in retrospect, was a predictable consequence: the boundary between bio- and necropolitics, protected and unprotected life, became an object of direct political competition. Equally, when self-appointed guardians of free speech on the right do not flinch as the United States government gives border agents discretion to deny someone a visa on account of opinions expressed on social media, they are not simply being hypocritical; if anything, they are taking advantage of the fact that hypocrisy has become less necessary and been replaced with more or less open cynicism.[4] Whereas one was previously obliged to affirm the formal universalism of institutions even while profiting from the material inequalities that undermined it—the gap between ideal and reality being the stuff that claims to justice were made of—years of de-democratization and disaffection with politics have, as it were, made the quiet parts sound out loud. By making reduced legitimacy and unaccountability into the norm, while simultaneously creating a desire for rapid solutions that bound over checks and balances, they have made the notion that power can be openly wielded against certain groups or ideas much less shocking. The far right is the politics of a world that is no longer trying to pay lip service—and this, more than anything else perhaps, explains why Obama-style liberalism has become such a devalued coin.

Amid the mounting wreck, in something like an act of advance salvage, different groups and factions rush to carve for themselves whatever space their capacities will allow: to each according to what they can grab. In so doing, they are, of course, hastening the very disintegration they try to exploit. Naturally, those who can grab the most are the ones who are already the most powerful: finance, Big Tech, Big Oil, the extractive industry in general. Not by coincidence, the direction in which they lunge headlong is that of the great accelerator, climate change: Since humankind changing course would entail huge losses for them, they seek to lock in market and policy path dependencies that will safeguard their profits for decades. True, as it displaces huge masses of people, disrupts global logistical chains, and puts even more pressure on outmatched institutions, rolling environmental catastrophe will put those interests at risk by sparking geopolitical conflicts, empowering nonstate sovereign actors, and multiplying the amount of "rogue states" around the world. If we try to read some rationality into such a seemingly irrational long-term wager—which may or may not be the right thing to do—the best answer seems to be that those making it expect that, by the time the situation has degenerated to that point, their interests will be sufficiently integrated with state and nonstate security apparatuses as to make them personally and economically insulated. This, it can never be stressed enough, *is already the direction in which we are moving*, all things remaining equal. It is not that those betting on it are pursuing fantasies of "patchwork" sovereignty or following a right-wing accelerationist call to "speed up the breakdown."[5] Rather, it is the likes of Curtis Yarvin who are providing the speculative window dressing for a much more violent process already underway.[6]

This is why I have described the horizon in which the far right moves as that of a *privately managed differentially distributed state of nature* and suggested that something like an *overseer capitalism* may well turn out to be one of its ideal forms.[7] The latter term was born out of a reflection specific to the figure of Bolsonaro, with his strong-man image stemming from his origins not in the officer-class technocracy of the Brazilian dictatorship but in what is usually referred to as the regime's "basements": at once the spaces in which torture took place and the same low-ranking military and police milieu from which today's militias emerged.[8] The idea was that his political trajectory could be seen as encapsulating broader trends in the history of the relationship between economy, repression, and the state, and thus much more easily generalized. "Overseer" refers to the fact that, in plantation colonies like Brazil and the US South, policing evolved out of the need to contain a population seen as a threat because it was first enslaved and restive, then free and marginalized. The development of an internal security apparatus distinct from the colonial army is thus intimately connected to the progressive transformation of a private economic function (the overseer ensuring the good running of the landowner's workforce) into a public, political one (the taxpayer-funded policeman securing civic order). This is a process whose partial reversal we can observe today in three interconnected symptoms of disintegration: the rise of nonstate sovereign actors such as militias and cartels; the expansion of the private security sector, including surveillance and military contractors like Palantir, Blackwater, and the Wagner Group; and the intermingling of both with the state at various levels. Overseer capitalism thus hypothesizes a type of late-capitalist formation in which sectors of capital wishing to secure ideal conditions for predatory accumulation in a scenario of growing instability and surplus populations consolidate an alliance with private agents in the security sector, be those corporate, paramilitary, or even parts of the state's security apparatus become independent political and economic actors. In this arrangement, those who take on the role of managing political power do so in such a way as not to interfere with the economic and/or territorial control exercised by others. (Thus, for example, the Bolsonaro government worked to deregulate the economy and hand over more areas to private initiative, while turning a blind eye to the expansion of paramilitary militias, land grabs, illegal logging and mining, drug trafficking, and so forth, especially in the Amazon.) This is not incompatible with some sort of degraded democratic institutionality, and it is different from what we usually understand as authoritarianism in that it entails not strengthening but deliberately eroding national sovereignty, covertly ceding the legitimate monopoly of violence to economic actors that profit from its use either indirectly (through what it enables) or directly (since security has become a site of accumulation in its own right).[9] Rather than starting with a strong source of political power that then proceeds to reorganize the economy around it, it is more like a coordinated takeover and partitioning of the state by a set of different gangs with reconcilable economic interests—in which whoever has the guns and whoever takes the top spot is entitled to a share commensurate with their role in letting everyone else prosper.[10]

This helps us understand why so much of the contemporary far right resembles a Ponzi scheme that political entrepreneurs buy into in the hope of leveraging whatever audience they garner into a career, connections, and a chance to climb the ladder. It also suggests the need to revisit the Frankfurt School's old diagnosis of fascism as symptomatic of a "racket society" in which individuals, frustrated by their incapacity to obtain "compensation for their individual efforts . . . from the mere functioning of impersonal market agencies," come to realize that "acquiring and maintaining" social status depends less on skill and grind than on access to "groups which occupy and defend their strongly entrenched respective positions"—and, we might add, come to see securing such access as an integral part of what is meant by "entrepreneurship."[11] Such a revision could take in capital's present tendency toward the establishment of monopolies and the control of "choke points" for the extraction of rent,[12] the infiltration of the state by lobbies and organized crime, and, once again, the rise of far-right authoritarianism as a solution to the problem of coordinating divergent social interests among groups with very disparate powers.[13]

Yet it is obviously not only those who stand to profit directly who are behind the contemporary far right.

Through a combination of cumulative loss of status in different areas (access to goods and services, gender, race, sexual orientation) and an ever-sharper struggle for survival at the bottom, many among the poor and in a downwardly mobile middle class have come to invest higher or lower hopes in that project. Part of this has to do with the affects that this state of affairs produces, part with the expert rhetorical operation that bundled the various relatively independent processes that led to it into a single enemy, "globalism," that is all the more stirring because, being imaginary, it can be everywhere. In the background, there is the accumulated desensitization resulting from decades of ever more atomized, individualistic, punitive, each person-for-themselves conditions of life (another thing, in fact, that helps explain why the unmaking of democracy can be not only tolerated but supported). *Differentially distributed state of nature* also speaks to the psychological compensations that the far right can offer to those who may not stand to gain much from it in material terms but find in it the promise that they too will be allowed a sphere, however small, in which to exercise whatever little power they have without interference. This is where we find such aberrant "rights" as the right to cut corners and evade taxes, to drive at your chosen speed, to protect your "imperial mode of living"[14] even as the world burns, to look down on those who are below you in hierarchies of class, gender, race, and so on, to be indifferent to the pain that others suffer and that you yourself may cause, or indeed revel in its spectacularization. It is also where we find the notion of owning and using guns as the ultimate expression of liberty. Here, a noticeable difference to historical fascism shows us how far we are from its world, and how much closer to that world's disintegration. If Foucault correctly observed that the penetration of Nazism in the masses was tied to the large numbers of people that were called upon to take on "the responsibility for a number of state functions of repression, control, policing," giving them an official license to exercise some of their most sadistic and antisocial wills, the delegation of power on offer today has less to do with participation in the state apparatus—the dramatic expansion of agencies like ICE notwithstanding—than with enjoying the freedoms made possible by its withdrawal.[15]

It must be noted that, while these are things that can be said about the contemporary far right everywhere it can be found, the main reasons why it "works" will vary from place to place. The greatest issue of the years leading up to Javier Milei's victory was inflation, and while social indicators have gone down and bailouts from Trump and the International Monetary Fund have been needed, the Argentinean president has cut it down by 170 percent to levels that, while still high, provide some welcome respite. In El Salvador, the big question was crime, and Nayib Bukele's popularity rests on having been able to control it, making him an increasingly influential model in Latin America despite (or because of) human rights abuses and persistent accusations of cutting deals with the largest gangs. The United States, a declining global hegemon, can throw its weight about in ways that no one else except China can, and this no doubt brings the occasional economic advantage and satisfaction to those who hope to see it become great again. At the same time, we must wonder whether there is not a limit to how far psychological compensations can compensate for the lack of material gains. We certainly know, as we saw in chapter 2, how elastic their power can be. But is it *infinitely* elastic? Or is there a point beyond which it will break if—as is most likely—the far right is unable to improve, and in fact worsens, the living conditions of the majority of their base? Could this be what we are already witnessing with Trump's drop in popularity as the economic outlook for most people continues to decline?

True, we have been here before: Many people thought that out-of-control mortality during COVID-19 would be a "rock bottom" moment, and it was not, at least not to the expected extent. At the same time, if it was not callousness in the face of death that did it for Bolsonaro, his opposition to vaccines had a clear political cost: The moment people thought they had an alternative, blocking that alternative on ideological grounds was seen as prioritizing political football over their well-being. They will not always have to deal with crises as extreme as the pandemic, but there may be political opportunities ahead as the far right, no longer sniping from the margins but in power, shows itself incapable of solving the material problems of the majority. If that turns out to be the case, it is important to be ready and with a different set of proposed solutions in hand.

Looking at the contemporary far right from the point of view of the periphery allows us to see it as a force carried by a preexisting momentum that it seeks to accelerate. This, in turn, has an important consequence to how we conceive of the moment we are in. The twentieth century was probably guiltier than any other time of making itself into the measure of all that came before and after, finding in that the confirmation of the narratives that modernity spun about itself. From within that period, particularly the *trente glorieuses* after the Second World War, it was possible to believe that time could travel in only one direction, despite the occasional glitch or misstep, and the future could only look the same, except even more so. What our perspective today forces us to ask, instead, is if *that* was not the real interregnum, a Golden Age of the expansion of rights and material well-being made possible by a political and economic arrangement that capitalism will never be able to hit upon again. Ours is a time of *decline*, the far right tells us repeatedly, and the measures with which it promises to arrest that movement can only speed it up. But if that diagnosis seems to chime with so many people, we must also recognize that, *even as a force of acceleration*, the far right may still seem to them as a rational response: the most efficient way of getting the best deal out of the fall, the most appropriate game theory for the endgame.

To put it bluntly: *This is not a blip*; as said above, *this is the direction in which we are currently headed*. Thinking about it in this way should provide us with the sense of urgency that the situation requires, and put to bed any fantasies that, left to its own devices, the arc of history will eventually go back to bending toward justice. Rather than sticking to the illusion that a permanent backslide is impossible and that progress must eventually resume, it asks us to take seriously the possibility that present tendencies are taking us to a very different kind of future, and act accordingly.

ACKNOWLEDGMENTS

Since before the original, Portuguese-language edition of this book came out in 2022, I have had the privilege of discussing the ideas contained here with scores of researchers, activists, friends, journalists, and members of the public in Brazil, Argentina, Chile, Spain, Portugal, France, Italy, Germany, Greece, Australia, the United States, and the United Kingdom. There would be simply too many of you to thank, so I will trust that you know who you are. For the English-language edition, special thanks are due to my editor Katy O'Donnell, who was onboard from our very first chat; to Sarah Jaffe, who introduced me to Katy and persuaded me to write the section on masculinity; Jameka Williams, Anne Rumberger, and everyone at Haymarket Books.

An earlier version of chapter 1 appeared as "Of What Is Bolsonaro the Name?," *Radical Philosophy* 2, no. 9 (2021); of the excursus on affective infrastructures as "Affective Infrastructures and Political Organisation," *Dialogues in Human Geography* 13, no. 1 (2023); of chapter 2 as "Are We in Denial about Denial?," *Public Books*, November 25, 2020; of chapter 3 as "Pequenos fascismos, grandes negócios", *Piauí* 181 (2021); of chapter 5 as "Todo lado tem dois lados: Sobre a ideia de polarização," *Serrote* 34 (2020); and of chapter 6 as "From Trance to Vertigo: Images of Political Defeat in Brazilian Cinema," *South Atlantic Quarterly* 119, no. 3 (2020).

NOTES

INTRODUCTION

1 That book was Rodrigo Nunes, *Neither Vertical nor Horizontal: A Theory of Political Organization* (Verso Books, 2021).

2 The alternative label of "right-wing populism" strikes me as simply swapping one ill-defined term (*populism*) for another (*fascism*), and, through the very equivalence it suggests (there are right- and left-wing versions of the same thing, and they are both bad), as underestimating the asymmetry between what the far right and the left are effectively proposing today. Other names, such as *authoritarian neoliberalism* and, more recently, Richard Seymour's *disaster nationalism* (understood as indicative of a "prefascist" situation), pick out aspects of the phenomena in question that are undoubtedly important, but either fail to account for the discontinuities between them and what came before or build a generalization out of some national contexts that does not apply to others. (I return to this point in chapter 1.) See Richard Seymour, *Disaster Nationalism: The Downfall of Liberal Civilization* (Verso Books, 2024). In general, I have found more agnostic options—such as "postfascism" and "late fascism," which seek to indicate both continuities and discontinuities between historical fascism and contemporary manifestations, as well as between "fascist" and "nonfascist" periods—to be the most productive in grouping together such disparate processes without the risk of reductionism. See Enzo Traverso, *The New Faces of Fascism: Populism and the Far Right* (Verso Books, 2019); and Alberto Toscano, *Late Fascism* (Verso Books, 2023).

3 On this point, see Toscano, *Late Fascism*, 1–4; Ernesto Laclau makes an even more eloquent exposition of the limits of this approach in relation to that other problematic concept, "populism," in Ernesto Laclau, *On Populist Reason* (Verso Books, 2005), 5ff.

4 Gilles Deleuze and Félix Guattari, *A Thousand Plateaus* (University of Minnesota Press. 1987), 215.

5 See Paul Virilio, *L'insécurité du territoire* (Galilée, 1976); around the same time, Foucault employed the expression to talk specifically about Nazism in Michel Foucault, *"Society Must Be Defended": Lectures at the Collège de France, 1975–76*, ed. Mauro Bertani, Alessandro Fontana, and François Ewald, trans. David Macey (Picador, 2003), 260. Vladimir Safatle has recently recovered it to talk about the Brazilian case and beyond; see Vladimir Safatle, "Beyond the Necropolitics Principle: Suicidal State and Authoritarian Neoliberalism," *Crisis and Critique* 7, no. 3 (2020): 361–75.

6 Roberto Esposito, *Bios: Biopolitics and Philosophy* (University of Minnesota Press. 2008), 117.

7 Brian Massumi, *A User's Guide to Capitalism and Schizophrenia* (MIT Press, 1992), 117.

8 See Ruth Wilson Gilmore, "In the Shadow of the Shadow State," in *Abolition Geography: Essays Towards Liberation*, ed. Brenna Bhandar and Alberto Toscano (Verso Books, 2022), 179–92, EPUB.

9 As Quinn Slobodian puts it, we ought to see today's far right more as a "mutant strain" of neoliberalism than as a rejection of it. Quinn Slobodian, *Hayek's Bastards: Race, Gold, IQ, and the Capitalism of the Far Right* (Zone Books, 2025), 18, 69. See also William Callison and Zachary Manfredi, eds., *Mutant Neoliberalism: Market Rule and Political Ruptures* (Fordham University Press, 2019); Melinda Cooper, "The Alt-Right: Neoliberalism, Libertarianism and the Fascist Temptation," *Theory, Culture & Society* 38, no. 6 (2021): 29–50.

10 The championing of welfare chauvinism by (non-majoritarian) sectors of the contemporary far right is a case in point: The project is never really to rebuild the state capacity that was taken apart by neoliberalism but to restrict access as a way of making what is left of it work for the (typically white) native population. For a study of how political practice does not reflect the discourse of even the more outwardly protectionist sections of the far right, see Gabriela Greilinger and Cas Mudde, "Talking Left, Voting Right: An Assessment of Far-Right Voting on Socio-Economic Issues in the European Parliament," ETUI Policy Brief 5 (2024), www.etui.org.

11 Another appeal of the trope of fascism as inherently suicidal is probably that it provides some kind of answer to the problem of "deprogramming," that is, of undoing fascist contagion: Once

people have been converted or "red pilled" by the far right, how to pull them back? Projecting a future moment when fascism necessarily collapses into itself somehow obviates the question, since that would mean there is a point beyond which subjective adhesion, at least of the public sort, becomes impossible.

12 The sentence is actually by Žižek, who appears to mean it as a paraphrase of Benjamin's position in such texts as "On the Concept of History" and "Theories of German Fascism." See Slavoj Žižek, "Slavoj Žižek on the Charlie Hebdo Massacre: Are the Worst Really Full of Passionate Intensity?," *New Statesman*, January 10, 2015, www.newstatesman.com/world/2015/01/slavoj-i-ek-charlie-hebdo-massacre-are-worst-really-full-passionate-intensity.

13 Toscano, *Late Fascism*, 113; 33–7.

14 Angelo Tasca, *The Rise of Italian Fascism, 1918–1922* (Routledge, 2010), 82ff. I thank Matteo Polleri for drawing my attention to this formulation.

15 This is why cases such as Marine Le Pen's Rassemblement National and Giorgia Meloni's Fratelli d'Italia, for whom that legacy possesses a greater weight, have a marginal role in my analysis—even though they have not only profited from the rise of younger political forces but also moved closer to them in both content and style. The same goes for the Israeli far right, which is not so much a new presence in that country's politics as simply a natural (if not inevitable) consequence of much of its operational logic. In my choice of scope, I am therefore closer to definitions such as "far right 2.0" or "post-internet far right," although I prefer the neutral term *contemporary* to avoid sounding as if these phenomena are restricted to or entirely determined by web. See Steven Forti, *Extrema derecha 2.0: Qué es y cómo combatirla* (Siglo Veintiuno, 2021); 12 Rules for What, *Post-Internet Far Right: Fascism in the Age of the Internet* (Dog Section Press, 2021).

16 Revisiting the same debate on the relationship between the rise of fascism and the existence of challenges to capitalism touched upon above, Andreas Malm and the Zetkin Collective arrive at the same conclusion: "Fascisation happens because of the *extreme political weakness* of labour, as it approaches or falls below pre–First International levels. It is not the unnerving presence but the total absence of both revolutionary and steadily reformist working-class politics that now sets the slide in motion." Andreas Malm and the Zetkin Collective, *White Skin, Black Fuel: On the Danger of Fossil Fascism* (Verso, 2021), 316 (e-book).

17 I take the expression "the end of mediation" from Michael Hardt, *The Subversive Seventies* (Oxford University Press, 2023). Hardt uses this as a "native concept" employed by movements in the 1970s and does not draw explicit parallels with the present apart from describing it as "a theory of neoliberalism avant la lettre." Hardt, *The Subversive Seventies*, 210. I believe it is not a coincidence that this diagnosis is making a comeback: Like the 1970s, ours is a time that combines economic stagnation, geopolitical instability, and a ruling class offensive to ensure that the cost of these crises will fall disproportionately upon the poor.

18 Will Davies, "The New Neoliberalism," *New Left Review*, no. 101 (2016): 121–34; Nancy Fraser, *The Old Is Dying and the New Cannot Be Born: From Progressive Neoliberalism to Trump and Beyond* (Verso Books, 2019).

19 See Wolfgang Streeck, *Buying Time: The Delayed Crisis of Democratic Capitalism* (Verso Books, 2014).

20 Robert Brenner, "What Is Good for Goldman Sachs Is Good for America: The Origins of the Present Crisis," Los Angeles: Center for Social Theory and Comparative History, UCLA (April 18, 2009), 2–3. This appears as the prologue to the Spanish edition of Robert Brenner, *The Economics of Global Turbulence: The Advanced Capitalist Economies from Long Boom to Long Downturn, 1945–2005* (Verso Books, 2006), published in 2009 by Akal.

21 The figure is based on data provided by the foreclosure listing firm RealtyTrac. See Susanna Kim, "2010 Had Record 2.9 Million Foreclosures," *ABC News*, January 12, 2011, https://abcnews.com/Business/2010-record-29-million-foreclosures/story?id=12602271.

22 In any case, as Melinda Cooper has recently pointed out, "we misunderstand the scope of neoliberal fiscal policy if we assume austerity to be its sole setting." Rather than a dismantling of fiscal and monetary capacities, the "last four decades of counterrevolution" promoted their "intensification . . . in the service of a dual mandate": austerity for anything that might "empower labor or lift the social wage", public spending and tax incentives for wealth creation and asset valorization. Melinda Cooper, *Counterrevolution: Extravagance and Austerity in Public Finance* (Zone Books, 2024), 17–23.

23 See Frédéric Lordon, *Willing Slaves of Capital: Spinoza and Marx on Desire*, trans. Gabriel Ash (Verso Books, 2014).

24 Jodi Dean, *Democracy and Other Neoliberal Fantasies: Communicative Capitalism and Left Politics* (Duke University Press, 2009).

THE POINT OF VIEW OF THE PERIPHERY

1 Among these, most of whom would be collectively grouped under the label *dependency theory*, we could mention Raúl Prebisch (Argentina), Celso Furtado, Ruy Mauro Marini, Vânia Bambirra, Theotonio dos Santos, and Fernando Henrique Cardoso (Brazil), Enzo Faletto (Chile), Samir Amin (Egypt), and Andre Gunder Frank (Germany, but long based in Latin America). Their work intersected with and influenced the world-systems approach that Immanuel Wallerstein and others would develop at around the same time.

2 Francisco de Oliveira, *Crítica à razão dualista / O ornitorrinco* (Boitempo, 2003), 60, 32. All translations from other languages are the author's, unless otherwise noted.

3 De Oliveira, *Crítica à razão dualista*, 55–60.

4 For an introduction to the Brazilian debate, including a list of the international authors who used Brazil as an example that it is in dialogue with—among which are Douglas Coupland, Ulrich Beck, and Michael Lind—see Alex Hochuli, "The Brazilianization of the World," *American Affairs* 5, no. 2 (2021): 93–115.

5 Paulo Arantes, "A fratura brasileira do mundo: Visões do laboratório brasileiro da mundialização," *Zero à Esquerda* (Conrad, 2004), 30.

6 Arantes, "A fratura brasileira do mundo," 58.

7 Thiago Canettieri, *A condição periférica* (Consequência, 2020), 152 (italics in the original).

8 See Mike Davis, *Planet of Slums: Urban Involution and the Informal Working Class* (Verso Books, 2006).

9 Subset of Theoretical Practice, "Working Through Political Organization: Current Results of the Subset of Theoretical Practice (2021–2022)," *Crisis and Critique* 9, no. 2 (2022).

CHAPTER 1

1 Reginaldo Prandi, "Adeptos fiéis a Bolsonaro são 15% da população adulta, indica Datafolha," *Folha de São Paulo*, July 2, 2020, www1.folha.uol.com.br/poder/2020/07/adeptos-fieis-a-bolsonaro-sao-15-da-populacao-adulta-indica-datafolha.shtml. Bolsonaro's popularity remained fairly constant apart from a dip in 2021, even though rejection of his administration had a first peak at the height of the pandemic, when Brazil had over one thousand deaths a day between early June and August, and then rose more

or less constantly from early 2021 to the 2022 presidential campaign, when he was the most rejected candidate. What changed in the meantime was the social profile of his support, with losses incurred among the upper class being recouped by gains made among the poor.

2 A June 2025 survey showed for the first time the number of self-declared Bolsonaro supporters to be as high as that of PT supporters (35 percent). Júlia Barbon, "Datafolha: Petistas recuam, Bolsonaristas avançam, e grupos empatam pela primeira vez," *Folha de São Paulo*, June 18, 2025, www1.folha.uol.com.br/poder/2025/06/datafolha-petistas-recuam-bolsonaristas-avancam-e-grupos-empatam-pela-primeira-vez.shtml.

3 Ernesto Laclau, *On Populist Reason* (Verso Books, 2005), 101ff.

4 See Gabriel Feltran, "The Revolution We Are Living," *HAU: Journal of Ethnographic Theory* 10, no. 1 (2020): 12.

5 See Eder Sader, *Quando novos personagens entraram em cena: Experiências e lutas dos trabalhadores da Grande São Paulo*, 1970–1980 (Paz e Terra, 1988).

6 We could thus say, misappropriating Raymond Williams somewhat, that "discursive matrices" and "structures of feeling" always presuppose one another. That would not be a problem for Sader, who speaks of "demands about social reproduction and symbolic recognition" as enjoying a "*virtual* existence," which is actualized in consciousness once they are articulated in language and become objects of reflection. See Sader, *Quando novos personagens*, 58.

7 Gabriel Feltran, "Formas elementares da vida política: Sobre o movimento totalitário no Brasil (2013–)," (blog), *Novos Estudos* (2020), http://novosestudos.uol.com.br/formas-elementares-da-vida-politica-sobre-o-movimento-totalitario-no-brasil-2013.

8 As for anti-intellectualism, if its meaning does not change, its source and reference points do: Among the upper class, religious authority often takes a back seat to repulsion to the supposed moral dissoluteness of universities, a contempt for knowledge without immediate economic utility, and the conspiracy theories spread by social media celebrities and influencers.

9 Verónica Gago, *Neoliberalism from Below: Popular Pragmatics and Baroque Economies*, trans. Liz Mason-Deese (Duke University Press, 2017), 36.

10 Gago, *Neoliberalism from Below*, 6.

11 Gago, *Neoliberalism from Below*, 11.

12 Rosana Pinheiro-Machado and Lucia Scalco, "From Hope to Hate: The Rise of Conservative Subjectivity in Brazil," *HAU: Journal of Ethnographic Theory* 10, no. 1 (2020): 21–2.

13 This is how obscure diplomatic-kook-turned-Bolsonaro-foreign minister Ernesto Araújo defines *globalism*. See Ernesto Araújo, "About," *Metapolítica Brasil* (blog), www.metapoliticabrasil.com. For a well-informed look into the role of YouTube in the rise of Bolsonarismo, see Max Fisher and Amanda Taub, "How YouTube Radicalized Brazil," *New York Times*, August 11, 2019, https://www.nytimes.com/2019/08/11/world/americas/youtube-brazil.html.

14 Theodor Adorno, *Aspects of the New Right-Wing Extremism* (Polity, 2020), 19, modified.

15 For a history of this process, see Camila Rocha, *Menos Marx, mais Mises: O liberalismo e a nova direita no Brasil* (Todavia, 2021).

16 Operation Car Wash was an investigation that uncovered a corruption scheme around the state oil company, Petrobrás, which had begun before PT came to power but was maintained under it and involved most of the major political parties in Brazil. The resulting scandal had a huge impact in both severely damaging the credibility of the Workers' Party and emboldening a then nascent far right. The judge and the prosecutor who became its figureheads would go on to have somewhat disappointing careers as right-wing politicians. Alongside several other decisions, Lula's verdict, on charges that were always less than unequivocal, was overturned once leaked conversations revealed that, among other miscarriages of justice, the two had been colluding to ensure the conviction of defendants.

17 Friedrich Hayek, *Law, Legislation and Liberty. A New Statement of the Liberal Principles of Justice and Political Economy* (Routledge, 1998), 2:97.

18 The story that became known as the "gay kit" was a disinformation campaign orchestrated by the religious right against the "Schools Without Homophobia" program introduced by the then–Minister of Education Fernando Haddad in 2010. The campaign, among other things, accused the government of distributing penis-shaped milk bottles to elementary schools. This was not only the first largely successful moral panic mobilized by the soon-to-be far right, setting the template for its future incursions in the "culture wars," but also the first time Bolsonaro stood out as a relevant leader in this milieu. It was also notable for PT's decision to drop the policy without putting up a fight, which would come

back to haunt it when Haddad ran against Bolsonaro in 2018 and all the false allegations that had not been dispelled at the time were put back in heavy circulation. See Carolina Evangelista, "Brazil Above Everything, God Above All," *Radical Philosophy* 2.09 (2020): 21–26.

19 Isabela Kalil, "Quem são e no que acreditam os eleitores de Jair Bolsonaro," Research Report, *Fundação Escola de Sociologia e Política de São Paulo* (2018), www.fespsp.org.br.

20 This is corroborated by Débora Salles's analysis of the discourse of the Bolsonaro campaign on Twitter using a methodology developed by Sara Walton and Brownyn Boon to apply Laclau's and Mouffe's insights to data analysis. Débora Salles, "The Twitter Effect: The Politics of Tweeting During the 2018 Brazilian Presidential Election" (PhD diss., Graduate Program in Information Science, Federal University of Rio de Janeiro, 2020).

21 The fact that the word evokes associations with sensual, even sexual, pleasure is no small part of that power: The suggestion that the exorbitant enjoyment possessed by some is the cause for the denial of enjoyment that its followers experience in everyday life has always been central to the far right. No surprise, then, that the Bolsonarista slogan *acabou a mamata* (*mamata* is over) would find itself echoed in the name of a Spanish ultraliberal far-right party, Se Acabó la Fiesta (the party is over).

22 Among the different types of Bolsonaro voter identified by Kalil, there were, for instance, the poor people who defended a "minimal state," which they explained as minimal intervention from the state in religious or moral matters rather than as the reduction of public services. See Kalil, "Quem são e no que acreditam," 20.

23 Aimé Césaire, *Discourse on Colonialism*, trans. Joan Pinkham (Monthly Review Press, 2001); W. E. B. Du Bois, *The World and Africa: An Inquiry into the Part Which Africa Has Played in World History* (International Publishers, 1965). See also Cedric J. Robinson, "Fascism and the Response of Black Radical Theorists," in *On Racial Capitalism, Black Internationalism, and Cultures of Resistance*, ed. H. L. T. Quan (Pluto, 2019), 149–59.

24 See Alberto Toscano, *Late Fascism* (Verso Books, 2023), 28ff.

25 Adrian Daub, "Psychozionism," *n+1*, July 3, 2024, www.nplusonemag.com/online-only/online-only/psychozionism.

26 See Érico Andrade, *Negritude sem identidade: Sobre as narrativas singulares das pessoas negras* (n-1, 2023).

27 See Pew Research Center, "Voting Patterns in the 2024 Election," Pew Research Center, June 26, 2025, www.pewresearch.org/

politics/2025/06/26/voting-patterns-in-the-2024-election; Júlia Barbon, "Datafolha: Lula lidera entre negros, e Bolsonaro, entre brancos no segundo turno," *Folha de São Paulo*, October 8, 2022, www1.folha.uol.com.br/poder/2022/10/datafolha-lula-lidera-entre-negros-e-bolsonaro-entre-brancos-no-2o-turno.shtml. That Trump's Latino vote could go from 28 percent in 2016 to 48 percent in 2024 is indicative of the preponderant weight of anti-Blackness in the racism he mobilizes.

28 This obviously does not apply to situations in which minority rule or ethnic exclusion does not need to seek majority consent, like apartheid South Africa or Israel and Palestine.

29 Richard Seymour, *Disaster Nationalism: The Downfall of Liberal Civilization* (Verso Books, 2024), 15.

30 Quinn Slobodian, *Hayek's Bastards: Race, Gold, IQ, and the Capitalism of the Far Right* (Zone Books, 2025), chap. 3.

31 Seymour, *Disaster Nationalism*, 194.

32 To name but an example, both the label "*gender ideology*" and the first stirrings of the international campaign against it are, as Verónica Gago reminds us, originally Catholic confections. See Gago, *Feminist International: How to Change Everything*, trans. Liz Mason-Deese (Verso Books, 2020), 212ff.

33 See for example David Smilde, *Reason to Believe: Cultural Agency in Latin American Evangelicalism* (University of California Press, 2007); Cecília Moreto Mariz, *Coping with Poverty: Pentecostal and Christian Base Communities in Brazil* (Temple University Press, 1994).

34 André Castro, *A luta que há nos deuses: Da teologia da libertação à extrema direita evangélica* (Machado, 2024), 152; see also Danièle Hervieu-Léger, "Sécularisation et modernité réligieuse," *Esprit* 106, no. 10 (1985): 50–62. Rolim made the tantalizing observation in the 1980s that informal workers tended to prefer evangelical churches over liberation theology's ecclesial base communities; see Francisco Cartaxo Rolim, *Religião e classes populares* (Vozes, 1980), 169.

35 Nancy Fraser, "From Progressive Neoliberalism to Trump—and Beyond," *American Affairs* 1, no. 4 (2017), https://americanaffairsjournal.org/2017/11/progressive-neoliberalism-trump-beyond.

36 See John B. Judis, *The Populist Explosion: How the Great Recession Transformed American and European Politics* (Columbia Global Reports, 2016), 10, Kindle.

37 Jason Hackworth, *Faith Based: Religious Neoliberalism and the Politics of Welfare in the United States* (University of Georgia Press,

2012), 45. This is in fact an important component in the constitution of a "neoliberalism from below," which Gago overlooks owing to the relatively marginal role played by evangelicalism in Argentina. It is only more recently that Milei, in a clear attempt to take a leaf out of the North American and Brazilian playbook, has begun courting evangelical churches, trying to bring them into politics more consistently.

38 See Melinda Cooper, *Family Values: Between Neoliberalism and the New Social Conservatism* (MIT Press, 2017).

39 This is what Foucault had in mind when he wrote that "a society made up of enterprise-units is at once the principle of decipherment linked to liberalism and its programming for the rationalization of a society and an economy." Michel Foucault, *The Birth of Biopolitics: Lectures at the Collège de France, 1978–1979*, trans. Graham Burchell (Palgrave, 2008), 225.

40 Jennifer Silva, *Coming Up Short: Working Class Adulthood in an Age of Uncertainty* (Oxford University Press, 2013), 155.

41 Silva, *Coming Up Short*, 150.

42 On the therapeutic narrative, see Silva, *Coming Up Short*, 114ff.

43 See Lauren Berlant, *Cruel Optimism* (Duke University Press, 2011). On the pathologies of chasing the mirage of individual sovereignty, see Gregory Bateson, "The Cybernetics of 'Self': A Theory of Alcoholism," in *Steps to an Ecology of Mind* (Ballentine Books, 1972), 309–37.

44 On the concept of negative solidarity, see Jason Read, "Negative Solidarity: The Affective Economy in Neoliberalism's Decline", ed. Ben Gook, *Libidinal Economies of Crisis Times: The Psychic Life of Contemporary Capitalism* (Transcript, 2024), 73–88.

45 A fascinating social history of public swimming pools in the United States establishes the connection between both historical moments in a clarifying manner. See Jeff Wiltse, *Contested Waters. A Social History of Swimming Pools in America* (University of North Carolina Press, 2010).

46 Bolsa Família (Family Allowance) is a cash transfer program introduced in Luiz Inácio Lula da Silva's first government in 2003 that has since come to be seen as an untouchable "third rail" in Brazilian politics. Although Bolsonaro railed against it while campaigning, in power he effectively tried to expand it (while simultaneously rebranding and disorganizing it so as to facilitate clientelism), especially after the COVID-19 pandemic and in the run-up to the 2018 elections.

47 On the combination of class anxiety, belief in meritocracy, and punitivism among Lula voters turned Bolsonaristas, see Pinheiro-Machado and Scalco, "From Hope to Hate," 27.

48 For an overview, see Tales Ab'Saber, "Ordem e violência no Brasil," in *Bala perdida: A violência policial no Brasil e os desafios para sua superação*, ed. Bernardo Kucinski et al. (Boitempo, 2015), 97–102.

49 See, for instance, Sérgio Buarque de Hollanda, *Roots of Brazil*, trans. G. Harvey Summ (Notre Dame University Press, 2012).

50 See Roberto Schwarz, "Misplaced Ideas: Literature and Society in Late Nineteenth-Century Brazil," *Misplaced Ideas: Essays on Brazilian Culture*, trans. and ed. John Gledson (Verso Books, 1992), 19–32.

51 It is worth remembering that Bolsonaro only became the frontrunner in 2018 after Lula was ruled out of the race. The Operation Car Wash (Lavo Jato) judge who convicted Lula, Sergio Moro, went on to become the minister of justice but resigned a year later, accusing Bolsonaro of trying to interfere with criminal investigations against his oldest son.

52 This is a slight *détournement* of an actual right-wing slogan, *direitos humanos para humanos direitos* (human rights for upstanding humans).

53 In the words of a well-known study of Brazilian stances toward transit, "to 'respect' connotes an option, and is therefore the more appropriate word for those who think themselves as superior," whereas "'to obey' is compulsory, and is therefore much more appropriate for those who have learnt to think of themselves or are classified and thought as inferior." Roberto DaMatta, *Fé em deus e pé na tábua: Ou como e por que o trânsito enlouquece no Brasil* (Rocco, 2010), 69, ebook. Roberto Andrés connects the growth of antisocial attitudes in traffic to the 255 percent rise in the number of motorized vehicles during the first four PT administrations, which the party held up as evidence of success in the fight against inequality. Roberto Andrés, "Jeitinho sobre Rodas," *Piauí*, no. 154 (2019): 32–5.

54 Corey Robin, *The Reactionary Mind: Conservatism from Edmund Burke to Donald Trump*, 2nd ed. (Oxford University Press, 2018), 10ff.

55 Wendy Brown, *In the Ruins of Neoliberalism: The Rise of Antidemocratic Politics in the West* (Columbia University Press, 2019), 173.

56 On the strict (versus "nurturant") father as metaphorical model for conservative politics, see George Lakoff, *The Political Mind: A*

Cognitive Scientist's Guide to Your Brain and Its Politics (Penguin Books, 2009), 77–81.

57 See Theodor Adorno, "Freudian Theory and the Pattern of Fascist Propaganda," in *The Essential Frankfurt School Reader*, ed. Andrew Arato and Eike Gephardt (Continuum, 1997), 125–28.

58 Adorno, "Freudian Theory," 136.

59 Alberto Toscano, "Notes on Late Fascism," *Historical Materialism* (blog), April 2, 2017 (italics in the original), www.historicalmaterialism.org/blog/notes-late-fascism#_ftn25.

60 Bruno Latour, *Down to Earth: Politics in the New Climatic Regime*, trans. Catherine Porter (Polity, 2018), 1.

CHAPTER 2

1 The figure of the zombie became so ubiquitous in post-2008 culture and political debate that it has even spawned a small industry of commentary attempting to explain that very ubiquity. As one of these commentators suggested, perhaps the reason for the undeads' popularity lies not so much in any unconscious fears they express but in the insights they offer into most people's everyday existence. See Chuck Klosterman, "My Zombie, Myself: Why Modern Life Feels Rather Undead," *New York Times*, December 3, 2010. See also: Chris Harman, *Zombie Capitalism: Global Crisis and the Relevance of Marx* (Haymarket Books, 2009); Turbulence, "Life in Limbo?," *Turbulence*, no. 5 (2009): 3–7; Jamie Peck, "Zombie Neoliberalism and the Ambidextrous State," *Theoretical Criminology* 13, no. 1 (2010): 104–10; Colin Crouch, *The Strange Non-Death of Neoliberalism* (Polity, 2011); Evan Calder Williams, *Combined and Uneven Apocalypse: Luciferian Marxism* (Zero Books, 2011); Mark Fisher, "How to Kill a Zombie: Strategizing the End of Neo-Liberalism," *OpenDemocracy*, July 18, 2013; Paul Krugman, *Arguing with Zombies: Economics, Politics, and the Fight for a Better Future*, (W. W. Norton, 2021). With new offerings as the series *The Last of Us* and the return of the *28 Days Later* franchise in 2025, the undead appear to be very much alive, as is the commentary; see Katy Waldman, "Our Age of Zombie Culture," *New Yorker*, August 9, 2025.

2 For a detailed (and exasperating) analysis of the rescue package in United States, see Robert Brenner, "Escalating Plunder," *New Left Review*, no. 123 (2020): 5–22. Another major effect of the pandemic was, of course, the further consolidation of the economic and political power of Big Tech, which has

since allied itself ever more openly with the right. For an early warning, see Naomi Klein, "New Screen Deal," *The Intercept*, May 8, 2020, https://theintercept.com/2020/05/08/andrew-cuomo-eric-schmidt-coronavirus-tech-shock-doctrine.

3 Against all odds, Bolsonaro's highest approval ratings (37 percent) and lowest rejection (32 percent) occurred during the pandemic, in the period between an initial drop in the number of COVID-related deaths in August 2020 and vaccines being made available in January 2021. The fact that it was only after the latter date that the two graphs changed trajectory shows that it was Bolsonaro's active opposition to vaccination, rather than his government's rhetorical and practical sabotaging of protective measures, that hurt him politically and, perhaps, eventually cost him his reelection bid.

4 The "expenditure ceiling" (more technically, the New Fiscal Regime) was the flagship bill of Michel Temer's caretaker government which took over from Dilma Rousseff in 2016. It established a limit for primary federal expenditure (including both discretionary and obligatory expenses but excluding public debt servicing) that was so stringent it had to be modified or broken every year since—five times in Bolsonaro's four-year term. Upon Lula's return to power in 2023, it was replaced with the New Fiscal Framework, which, while clearly a concession to financial markets preoccupied with disciplining the new government, has the advantage of being contracyclical, allowing for expenditure to grow with tax revenues and above inflation.

5 Will Davies, "The New Neoliberalism," *New Left Review*, no. 101 (2016): 121–34.

6 Michel Foucault, *The Birth of Biopolitics: Lectures at the Collège de France, 1978–1979*, trans. Graham Burchell (Palgrave Macmillan, 2008), 22.

7 Grim not only because it shows how many have internalized the idea that the government can let hundreds of thousands die if the cost of intervening is too high but also because it naturalizes future experiences and desensitizes toward them. As we have seen with the pandemic, countries with high mortality rates from causes like urban violence, such as Brazil and the United States, can easily accommodate to thousands of deaths per day. If risk can be the object of gradual habituation, perhaps, as Ulrich Beck speculated decades ago, future generations will be so used to pandemics that they will be able to live normally with them. See Ulrich Beck, *Risk Society: Towards a New Modernity* (Sage, 1992), 83.

8 "Truth lives, in fact, for the most part on a credit system. Our thoughts and beliefs 'pass,' so long as nothing challenges them, just as bank-notes pass so long as nobody refuses them. But this all points to direct face-to-face verifications somewhere, without which the fabric of truth collapses like a financial system with no cash-basis whatever." William James, "Pragmatism," in *Writings 1902–1910* (Library of America, 1987), 576–77.

9 Bruno Latour and Steve Woolgar, *Laboratory Life: The Construction of Scientific Facts* (Princeton University Press, 1986), 239ff. Drawing from the authors' own analogy between equiprobabilty and noise (information is predictability measured against a background of equally probable events) and Bateson's description of camouflage as "the opposite of communication," Letícia Cesarino analyzes far-right discourse as involving a reduction of signal/noise ratio (raising equiprobability through "firehosing" or "flooding the zone with shit," as per Steven Bannon's phrase); the breaking up of patterns and regularities in the signal (the flurry of activity that leaves opponents constantly scrambling to respond); and the introduction of similar patterns into the noise (the production of alternative accounts of the same events or facts). See Letícia Cesarino, *O mundo do avesso: Verdade e política na era digital* (Ubu, 2023), 196; Gregory Bateson, "Redundancy and Coding," *Steps to an Ecology of Mind* (Ballantine, 1972), 414.

10 In her commentary on an earlier version of this chapter, which was published in 2020, Naomi Klein appears to stop at this point when she summarizes what I call denialism as a "reflexive state of constant disbelief." My point, however, is that the disorientation produced by the proliferation of disinformation is only one half of the question—the other being, as we see next, the unconscious need to deny increasingly traumatic truths about the state of the world. See Naomi Klein, *Doppelgänger: A Trip into the Mirror World* (Farrar, Straus and Giroux, 2023), 224–25.

11 See Naomi Oreskes and Eric Conway, *Merchants of Doubt: How a Handful of Scientists Obscured the Truth on Issues from Tobacco Smoke to Global Warming* (Bloomsbury, 2010).

12 Louis, Althusser, "Ideology and Ideological State Apparatuses," *Lenin and Philosophy and Other Essays*, trans. Ben Brewster (Monthly Review Press, 1971), 162.

13 Wu Ming 1, *La Q di Qomplotto: QAnon e dintorni* (Alegre, 2021), 162–71. In that respect, if Naomi Klein is correct in pointing out that conspiracy theories find much of their material in our dim, disavowed awareness of the global economy's "Shadow

Lands"—zones of economic exploitation, extraction, illegality, and violence that exist in a permanent state of exception—we should also note that they contribute to their multiplication—by pushing behaviors like migration or some forms of sexuality further underground, for example, or by legitimizing repression against them, thus justifying the proliferation of things like detention centers and special prisons.

14 Richard Seymour, *Disaster Nationalism: The Downfall of Liberal Civilization* (Verso Books, 2024), 191.

15 Seymour, *Disaster Nationalism*, 9.

16 Seymour, *Disaster Nationalism*, 9.

17 On Brexit and self-harm, see Bertie Russell, "Brexit, Self-Harm, and a Method for Taking Control" (blog), Plan C, July 18, 2016, www.weareplanc.org/2016/07/brexit-self-harm-and-a-method-for-taking-control: "One reason people commit an act of self-harm is to obtain a *sense* of feeling control—it's a deeply emotional response to feelings of hopeless, isolation, that you're not listened to, and that there's nothing you can do to change anything. This is much more than a crude analogy being used to make a political point. It's to say that for many people, the referendum may have been played out at a deeply emotional level."

18 Theodor Adorno, "Remarks on the Authoritarian Personality," in *The Authoritarian Personality* (Verso Books, 2019), lii. The passage is worth quoting at length: "[E]nvy is certainly an aspect of prejudice, but people are not anti-Semitic because they are envious of the Jews. They are envious as such because of constant social pressure and the blatant contradiction between today's economic potentialities and their own deeply unsatisfactory existence. Eventually, their envy is directed against the Jews, following the line of least resistance. . . . It may be quite possible that even the most horrifying manifestation of discrimination, the Nazi policy of 'genocide', is deeply connected with the economic fact that today's form of economic organization proves incapable of reproducing the population living under such conditions."

19 See Theodor Adorno, "Freudian Theory and the Pattern of Fascist Propaganda," in *The Essential Frankfurt School Reader*, ed. Andrew Arato and Eike Gephardt (Continuum, 1997), 136–37.

20 As Sarah Stein Lubrano has recently argued, drawing from evidence in neuroscience and the social sciences, changing people's minds is far less dependent on rational argumentation than it is on the building and sustaining of interpersonal relations—something in which the left lags behind the contemporary far right

in all but a few types of social space. See Sarah Stein Lubrano, *Don't Talk about Politics: How to Change 21*st *Century Minds* (Bloomsbury, 2025).

AFFECTIVE INFRASTRUCTURES

1 See Jodi Dean, *Crowds and Party* (Verso Books, 2016); Lauren Berlant, "The Commons: Infrastructures for Troubling Times," *Environment and Planning D: Society and Space* 34, no. 3 (2016): 393–419; D. W. Kamish, "Infrastructure and the Black Panther Party: Toward an Infrastructural Politics," *Journal of African American Studies*, no. 25 (2021): 513–33. For a useful survey and discussion of the concept in these contexts and beyond, see Kai Bosworth, "What Is 'Affective Infrastructure'?," *Dialogues in Human Geography* 13, no. 1 (2023): 54–72.

2 Bosworth, "What Is 'Affective Infrastructure'?," 64.

3 Bosworth, "What Is 'Affective Infrastructure'?," 67.

4 See Ernesto Laclau and Chantal Mouffe, *Hegemony and Socialist Strategy*, 2nd ed. (Verso Books, 2001).

5 See Rodrigo Nunes, *Organisation of the Organisationless: Collective Action After Networks* (Mute, 2014), 22ff.

6 On the *ingenium*, which Shirley unsatisfactorily translates as "attitude to life," see Baruch Spinoza, *Ethics*, in *Complete Works*, trans. Samuel Shirley (Hackett, 2002), EIIIP31; Pierre-François Moreau, *Experience and Eternity in Spinoza*, trans. Robert Boncardo (Edinburgh University Press, 2021), 406ff. On transindividuality, see Gilbert Simondon, *Individuation in Light of Notions of Form and Information*, trans. Taylor Adkins (University of Minnesota Press, 2020).

7 See Roy Wagner, *The Invention of Culture* (Chicago University Press, 1981), 20. On equivocation as "the mode of communication par excellence between different perspectival positions," see Eduardo Viveiros de Castro, "Perspectival Anthropology and the Method of Controlled Equivocation," *Tipití: Journal of the Society for the Anthropology of Lowland South America* 2, no. 1 (2004): 5.

8 Gilles Deleuze and Félix Guattari, *Anti-Oedipus* (University of Minnesota Press, 1983), 29.

1 Since then, unusual spikes in financial trading occurring hours, or sometimes even minutes, before major announcements by the US government—notably during the conflict with Iran—have raised suspicions of systematic insider trading by individuals with access to the White House. See Nick Marsh, "The Insider Trading

Suspicions Looming over the Trump Presidency." BBC News, April 20, 2026.

CHAPTER 3

2 I thank Nancy Fraser for proposing this way of parsing my analysis at a debate on an earlier version of this chapter at the New School for Social Research, New York, on April 29, 2025.

3 Stuart Hall, "The Great Moving Right Show," *Marxism Today*, January 1979, 20.

4 Richard Cantillon, *Richard Cantillon's Essay on the Nature of Trade in General: A Variorum Edition*, ed. Richard van den Berg (Routledge, 2015).

5 Robert F. Hébert and Albert N. Link, *A History of Entrepreneurship* (Routledge, 2009), 8.

6 Joseph Schumpeter, *Capitalism, Socialism and Democracy* (Routledge, 2003), 83.

7 Ludwig von Mises, *Human Action: A Treatise on Economics* (Yale University Press, 1949), 253–54.

8 Gerard Radnitzky, "An Economic Theory of the Rise of Civilization and Its Policy Implications: Hayek's Account Generalized," *Ordo*, no. 38 (1987): 51.

9 Peter Drucker, *Innovation and Entrepreneurship* (Harper & Row, 1985).

10 See Nicholas Carnes and Noam Lupu, "It's Time to Bust the Myth: Most Trump Voters Were Not Working Class," *Washington Post*, June 5, 2017; Thomas Ogorzalek, Luisa Godinez Puig, and Spencer Piston, "White Trump Voters Are Richer Than They Appear," *Washington Post*, November 13, 2019.

11 In a highly financialized economy, the "key element shaping inequality is no longer the employment relationship, but rather whether one is able to buy assets that appreciate at a faster rate than both inflation and wages. Employment remains an important factor as it shapes the ability to do so (e.g., the ability to service a mortgage), but it is increasingly only one among other factors. Of course, income from work remains vitally important for many people as a way to access subsistence goods, but the important point is that by itself it is less and less able to serve as the basis of what most people would consider a middle-class lifestyle." Lisa Adkins, Melinda Cooper, and Martijn Konings, *The Asset Economy: Property Ownership and the Logic of Inequality* (Polity, 2020), 5.

12 Not only did tropes about "airports becoming more like bus stations" and "the children of maids going to Disney World" turn commonplace during the Worker's Party first turn in power, but they also later found in Bolsonaro's finance minister, Paulo Guedes, a politician always willing to repeat them in public. As Laura Carvalho suggested, the inflation of usually low-cost services like domestic work caused by rising living standards was key to souring the mood of the Brazilian middle class, breeding class hatred and sowing revolt against PT. See Laura Carvalho, *Valsa brasileira: Do boom ao caos econômico* (Todavia, 2018, 46–49). Another important moment in this process was the move to regulate domestic work in 2013.

13 Corey Robin, *The Reactionary Mind: Conservatism from Edmund Burke to Donald Trump* (Oxford University Press, 2018); W. E. B. Du Bois, *Black Reconstruction in America, 1860–1880* (Free Press, 1998). See also David R. Roediger, *The Wages of Whiteness: Race and the Making of the American Working Class*, revised edition (Verso Books, 1999).

14 According to Thomas Piketty, the improvement in wealth distribution "came entirely at the expense of the middle class, or more precisely, of those situated between the bottom 50 percent and the top 10 percent of the income distribution; those in the top 10 percent lost nothing and were able to maintain their position (which in Brazil's case is an unusually powerful one)." Thomas Piketty, *Capital and Ideology* (Bellknap, 2020), 957.

15 The term *concurseiro* refers to people, usually from the middle and lower-middle class, who spend a long time preparing for and taking exams of admission into public service (*concursos*), which is generally perceived as the safest path to a secure life.

16 While Murray Rothbard talked about *ideological entrepreneurs*—a coinage he credited to libertarian essayist Roy Childs—in the 1970s, the term appeared to hinge exclusively on an analogy between the tactical nous necessary to read a situation, find new paths, and exploit margins in both politics and business—an "art at which some people will be better than others." See Murray Rothbard, "Towards a Strategy for Libertarian Social Change" (April 1977), 23, www.davidmhart.com/liberty/AmericanLibertarians/Rothbard/Strategy/1977TowardStrategyLibertarianSocialChange.html. It is in a much the same way that "political entrepreneurship" is discussed in mainstream political science today, with political change being conceived as "the result of a tug-of-war between

mainstream parties seeking to protect their dominance and political entrepreneurs with innovating strategies to break this dominance." Catherine E. De Vries and Sarah B. Holbolt, *Political Entrepreneurs: The Rise of Challengers Parties in Europe* (Princeton University Press, 2020), 4. As I employ it here, the expression refers not to an analogy between business and politics—which has also been explored by Hardt and Negri—but an activity that is simultaneously both things and in which the two are necessarily intertwined. See Michael Hardt and Antonio Negri, *Assembly* (Oxford University Press, 2017). See also Alan Finlayson, "Neoliberalism, the Alt-Right and the Intellectual Dark Web," *Theory, Culture & Society* 38, no. 6 (2021): 167–90.

17 This does not mean that paramilitary structures have necessarily disappeared. In India, the one contemporary case that most resembles historical fascism—including in its obsession with racial purity—the Bharatiya Janata Party (BJP) relies on an intimate relationship with the Rashtriya Swayamsevak Sangh (RSS) movement for the capillarity of its on-the-ground political work and base building. In places like Brazil and the United States, on the other hand, this functioned has been downsized and outsourced to militias and groups like the Proud Boys and the Oath Keepers, which operate independently and according to their own purposes—primarily economic, in the case of Brazil. It should not surprise us that, like everything else, the way the far right organizes should also have come under neoliberal restructuring.

18 As I have argued elsewhere, the free enterprise approach to church building of Pentecostal pastors can be seen as a forerunner of the self-entrepreneurial marriage of commerce and a higher mission to be found among today's political influencers—many pastors having, of course, become political entrepreneurs in their own right over time. See Rodrigo Nunes, "The Pastor, the Swarm and the Movement," *Immanent Frame*, October 26, 2022, https://tif.ssrc.org/2022/10/26/the-pastor-the-swarm-and-the-movement.

19 Leo Löwenthal and Norbert Guterman, *Prophets of Deceit: A Study of the Techniques of the American Agitator* (Harper & Brothers, 1949), 129.

20 Rick Perlstein, "The Long Con: Mail-Order Conservatism," *Baffler*, no. 21 (2012). This thread would be taken up again in Rick Perlstein, *Reaganland: America's Right Turn, 1976–1980* (Simon & Schuster, 2020).

21 Quinn Slobodian, *Hayek's Bastards: Race, Gold, IQ, and the Capitalism of the Far Right* (Zone Books, 2025), 136.

22 Those who closely watched the 2015–16 protests for the impeachment of Dilma Rousseff will remember that support for a bill legalizing said pill was one of the more surprising elements in a very heterogenous set of demands.

23 Löwenthal and Guterman, *Prophets of Deceit*, 21.

24 Löwenthal and Guterman, *Prophets of Deceit*, 21.

25 Naomi Klein, *Doppelganger: A Trip into the Mirror World* (Farrar, Straus and Giroux, 2023), 125.

26 Schumpeter, *Capitalism, Socialism and Democracy*, 132.

27 F. A. Hayek, *Law, Legislation and Liberty: A New Statement of the Liberal Principles of Justice and Political Economy* (Routledge, 1982), 2:71.

28 Hayek, *Law, Legislation and Liberty*, 2:73. By reflecting on the social function of different discourses on society, Hayek was of course indirectly reflecting on his own role as a public intellectual. And this may ultimately explain why so many of his admirers perceive him as a staunch supporter of meritocracy even though he explicitly doubted it: they believe not in what he actually believed, but in what he believed was important for them to believe.

29 Hayek, *Law, Legislation and Liberty*, 2:116.

30 As a recent editorial on US Secretary of Health and Human Services Robert F. Kennedy Jr.'s Make American Healthy Again (MAHA) agenda underscores, its logic consists in substituting personal choice for large-scale, mandatory public interventions based on established science, which in practice "tends to replace the precautionary principle with exhortations for individuals to 'do your own research,' and sidelines scientific expertise in favour of 'wellness' hucksters and profiteers." Editorial, "The Guardian View on Peptides: Robert F. Kennedy Jr. Would Leave Public Health Policy to the Hucksters," *Guardian*, March 29, 2026, https://www.theguardian.com/commentisfree/2026/mar/29/the-guardian-view-on-peptides-robert-f-kennedy-jr-would-leave-public-health-policy-to-the-hucksters.

31 Ironically, the father of entrepreneurship studies himself, Richard Cantillon, made a fortune out of the Mississippi Bubble of 1717–20—the "heady years" in which "the very word 'millionaire' was coined." Murray Rothbard, *Economic Thought Before Adam Smith: An Austrian Perspective on the History of Economic Thought, Volume I* (Edward Elgar, 1995), 346. After liquidating his Mississippi Company holdings before the peak of the speculative wave for believing "the scheme was unsound and bound to fail," he was threatened with being sent to the Bastille by its

initiator, John Law. Anthony Brewer, *Richard Cantillon: Pioneer of Economic Theory* (Routledge, 1992), 6. Allegedly replying, "Hold on, I will not go and I will make your system succeed," he used the proceeds of his own shares to feed the mania by "advancing funds to English speculators who bought shares in the Mississippi Company that they subsequently pledged as collateral for their loans. Confident of the ultimate failure of Law's scheme, Cantillon sold the collateralized shares before the price of the stock broke, thus pocketing speculative profits in addition to the interest he collected on the loans he made. This practice provoked numerous lawsuits from his borrowers, but Cantillon successfully defended himself against their claims." Hébert and Link, *History of Entrepreneurship*, 8.

32 Marco Quiroz-Gutierrez, "Coca-Cola Loses $4 Billion in Market Value After Cristiano Ronaldo Shuns Coke," *Fortune*, June 16, 2021.

33 This impression is confirmed by the explosion in the last five years of TV shows, both fictional and documentary, dealing with such notorious fraud cases as those involving Fyre Festival, WeWork, Theranos, LuLaRoe, and OceanGate, or fake millionaire Anna Sorokin. If in chapter 2 we talked about the ubiquity of zombies in the imaginary of the last decade, perhaps now we are seeing the undead lose ground to scammers. What some of these examples of "faking it till you make it" show is that "faking it" can sometimes be an end in itself: the only way to enjoy the perks and admiration bestowed on someone who has "made it" for those to whom such a life would be otherwise inaccessible—even if criminal charges may beckon at the end.

34 This biblical verse (John 8:32) is a personal favorite of Jair Bolsonaro, to the point that it was often speculated it might be the only passage in the Bible that the self-professed Christian knew by heart.

35 Perhaps we should understand the positive valance of the *malandro* (hustler) in Brazilian culture as a tacit recognition of the fact that the trickster may be the one best positioned to navigate a society in which upward social mobility is all but blocked and even the free, at the time of slavery, depended on the favors of the powerful to get ahead. On the *malandro* as a figure that refers to the freemen of colonial society before its twentieth-century association with the urban underclass, see Antônio Cândido, "Dialética da malandragem," *Revista do Instituto de Estudos Brasileiros*, no. 8 (1970): 67–89.

36 A recent study by two economists advances a model, according to which, if the typical response for households in the face of objectives like home ownership and raising children is to "adjust by reducing consumption and increasing labor supply in order to stay on track," when such goals "become exceedingly difficult and are perceived as beyond realistic reach, households may cross a threshold at which they begin to give up on them entirely." This is reflected in greater consumption relative to wealth, reduced work effort, and the pursuit of "high-risk, high-return strategies—such as investing in cryptocurrencies—as a last resort." While focusing specifically on US data on house affordability, the authors make reference to the so-called *Sampo* ("giving up on three things") and *Satori* ("enlightened") generations in Korea and Japan, respectively, as well as China's *Tangping* ("lying flat") movement, as global examples of "a growing belief among young people that hard work no longer guarantees upward mobility." Seung Hyeong Lee and Younggeun Yoo, "'Giving Up': The Impact of Decreasing Housing Affordability on Consumption, Work Effort, and Investment," SRRN, November 19, 2025, http://dx.doi.org/10.2139/ssrn.5770722.

37 Jean Comaroff and John L. Comaroff, "Millennial Capitalism: First Thoughts on a Second Coming," *Public Culture* 12, no. 2 (2000): 313. Eyeing the donations that the sector could make toward his reelection campaign, Bolsonaro made online betting legal pending further legislation—then shunned the debate on how to regulate it. It was only at the very end of Lula's first year back in power, in December 2023, that a bill was passed in this regard, and even then, PT appeared to significantly underestimate the growing damage. A recent study by the National Confederation of Commerce observed that online betting in Brazil is especially popular among young low-income people and calculated that in the first half of 2024 alone it had already led 1.3 million people to insolvency. Confederação Nacional do Comércio, "Estudo do impacto econômico das bets," September 20, 2024, https://portaldocomercio.org.br/publicacoes_posts/estudo-do-impacto-economico-das-bets. In another study, 35 percent of respondents had said they had been forced to delay plans of going to university because of losing money online, a number that went up to 41 percent among those from families with a per capita income below the minimum wage. Bruno Alfano, "Brasileiros estão abrindo mão da graduação para gastar com bets e jogo do tigrinho, diz pesquisa," *O Globo*, September 19, 2024, https://oglobo.globo.com/brasil/

educacao/noticia/2024/09/16/brasileiros-estao-abrindo-mao-da-graduacao-para-gastar-com-bets-e-jogo-do-tigrinho-diz-pesquisa.ghtml.

38 The point could, to be sure, also be made of political entrepreneurs on the left.

39 I borrow the characterization of this alliance as "far right" and "far-out" from Naomi Klein, *Doppelgänger: A Trip into the Mirror World* (Farrar, Straus and Giroux, 2023), chap. 9. Quinn Slobodian and William Callison drew on the German term *Querdenken* to propose "diagonalism" as a name for the same phenomenon. See Quinn Slobodian and William Callison, "Coronapolitics from the Capitol to the Reichstag," *Boston Review*, January 12, 2021, www.bostonreview.net/articles/quinn-slobodian-toxic-politics-coronakspeticism. See also Letícia Cesarino, *O mundo do avesso: Verdade e política na era digital* (Ubu, 2022), chap. 4.

40 A recent study of Instagram influencers in Brazil identifies a tendency toward what it calls "career homogeneization": As commercial profiles grow in followership, they tend to move from offering products and services to offering courses on how to sell those products and services, then eventually to selling courses on digital marketing in general. Rosana Pinheiro Machado et al., 'Mídias sociais como plataforma de trabalho digital: Avaliando os impactos sociais, culturais e políticos da migração do mercado de trabalho para o Instagram," *Digital Economy and Extreme Politics* (2024), https://labdeep.com/wp-content/uploads/2024/12/Deeplab_Social-Media-as-Digital-Labour-Platform_PT_sem-links_13-12.pdf.

41 The word *viração*, which comes from the verb *virar-se* (to make ends meet, to do what it takes), is used by couriers to describe a reality in which no single source can provide sufficient income, and one is forced to circulate perpetually among a myriad different types of work or even between work and nonwork (government programs, training courses, and so on). Ludmila Abílio, "Uberization: The Periphery as the Future of Work?," in *Platformization and Informality: Pathways of Change, Alteration and Transformation*, ed. Aditi Surie and Ursula Huws (Palgrave McMillan, 2023), 157. Abílio proposes the term *subordinate self-management* to describe the reality that hides behind the entrepreneurial discourse around gig work.

42 Quinn Slobodian has written about the contemporary far right's origins in a "mutant strain" of neoliberalism seen, from the 1990s

onward, to be "doubling down on Social Darwinist principles of struggle in the market translated through hierarchical categories of race, nationality and gender." Slobodian, *Hayek's Bastards*, 69. But the ultimate source for that naturalization of competition lies, of course, in nineteenth-century thinkers like Herbert Spencer—who coined the term *survival of the fittest*, applied it to the struggle between races and classes, and made it into "the mechanism of progress via elimination of the weakest." Pierre Dardot and Christian Laval, *The New Way of the World: On Neoliberal Society* (Verso Books, 2014), 41.

CHAPTER 4

1 The integration between "troll armies" and governments is, of course, not unique to Brazil (nor to Russia, for that matter, despite what some would have us believe). A 2020 Oxford Internet Institute report identified seventy-six countries that had used disinformation and media manipulation as part of campaigns, and fifty-nine that had employed "state sponsored trolling" to attack political opponents. Samantha Bradshaw, Hannah Bailey, and Philip N. Howard, "Industrialized Disinformation: 2020 Global Inventory of Organized Social Media Manipulation" (working paper, Project on Computational Propaganda, 2021), 15, https://demtech.oii.ox.ac.uk/research/posts/industrialized-disinformation. Narendra Modi, Nayib Bukele, and Javier Milei, to name but three, have all been linked to stories suggesting they financially supported networks of bots and influencers; Milei even has an informal group of prominent online supporters that calls itself "Troll Ministry" whose online attacks inspire fear even in cabinet members. See Mauricio Caminos, "'Ministerio de Trolls': Cómo actúa el ejército virtual libertarios que tiene línea directa con el Gobierno," *El Diario*, December 7, 2024, www.eldiarioar.com/politica/ministerio-trolls-actua-ejercito-virtual-libertarios-linea-directa-gobierno_1_11882747.html.

2 As Will Davies notes, "The platformization of human life means that truth and falsehood, fact and rumor, become mere data points of equal value." Will Davies, "Stupidology", *n+1* , no. 15 (2025), www.nplusonemag.com/issue-51/politics/stupidology.

3 Paul Bloom and Matthew Jordan, "Are We All 'Harmless Torturers' Now?," *New York Times*, August 9, 2018. See Derek Parfitt, *Reasons and Persons* (Oxford University Press, 1996), chap. 3.

4 Richard Seymour, *The Twittering Machine: How Capitalism Stole Our Social Life* (Indigo, 2019), 94, ebook.

5 See Whitney Phillips, *This Is Why We Can't Have Nice Things: Mapping the Relationship Between Online Trolling and Mainstream Culture* (MIT Press, 2015).

6 Gregory Bateson, "A Theory of Play and Fantasy," in *Steps to an Ecology of Mind* (Ballantine, 1972), 177–93.

7 And, of course, also the left: The "dirtbag left" that emerged in the wake of Donald Trump's first electoral victory was to a large extent an attempt to deploy some of the same communication techniques in the benefit of a progressive agenda. That some figures who were originally associated with this scene subsequently drifted to the right follows a familiar pattern, in which positions initially adopted with ironic distance (the excoriation of "wokeism" and the ridicularization of some minorities, for example) gradually become incorporated as part of one's identity. This, as we shall see, is a characteristic effect of algorithmic recursivity on subjectivity.

8 Jay Yarrow, "Peter Thiel Perfectly Summarized Trump in Two Sentences," CNBC, November 9, 2016, www.cnbc.com/2016/11/09/peter-thiel-perfectly-summed-up-donald-trump-in-one-paragraph.html.

9 Before that, following an incident in which Bukele had sent in the military to coerce the Legislative Assembly into approving a loan to fund his national security plan, his supporters had responded to the hashtag #BukeleDictador (#DictatorBukele) on social media with #QueBonitaDictadura (#WhatALovelyDictatorship).

10 See Martin Pengelly, "DeSantis Aide Fired for Sharing Video Featuring Symbol Used by Nazis," *Guardian*, July 26, 2023.

11 A famous example of overidentification as a political-artistic practice can be found in the 1980s art movement known as NSK, or Neue Slowenische Kunst (New Slovenian Art), of which the industrial rock group Laibach was the best-known part. Instead of taking the more common position of criticizing the Yugoslav regime, NSK performed an adhesion to the state and nationhood so exaggerated that it exposed what was problematic about both in a way that was more uncomfortable—if also more ambiguous—than any dissident discourse. In time, the same tactic would be used against the liberal do-goodism of the "West." In Laibach's version of a Queen song, the music's martial air gave the well-meaning platitudes of the lyrics ("one flesh, one true religion") alarmingly fascist connotations. See Stevphen Shukaitis,

"Fascists as Much as Painters: Imagination, Overindentification and Strategies of Intervention," *Sociological Review* 59, no. 3 (2011): 597–615.

12 Paolo Gerbaudo, "Social Media and Populism: An Elective Affinity," *Media Culture & Society* 40, no. 5 (2018): 745–53.

13 Marcos Nobre calls these "digital parties" to highlight their strictly instrumental relationship with traditional parties, which they can easily discard (like Farage), occupy and leave (like Bolsonaro), or take over entirely (like Trump). See Marcos Nobre, *Limites da democracia: De junho de 2013 ao governo Bolsonaro* (Todavia, 2022), 205ff. They are distinct from the "platform parties" analyzed by Gerbaudo in that they do not try to create an institutional form for themselves but instead operate in the margins of the party system, seeking to influence and use it for its own purposes. See Paolo Gerbaudo, *The Digital Party: Political Organisation and Online Democracy* (Pluto, 2018).

14 See Ferenc Huszár et al., "Algorithmic Amplification of Politics on Twitter," *Proceedings of the National Academy of Sciences* 119, no. 1 (2022): e2025334119; Sandra González-Bailón et al., "The Advantage of the Right in Social Media News Sharing," *PNAS Nexus* 1, no. 3 (2022): pgac137; Sandra González-Bailón et al., "Asymmetric Ideological Segregation in Exposure to Political News on Facebook," *Science* 381 (2023): 392–98.

15 José Antonio Magalhães, *Tecnomia e demogramática: Direito e técnica no nomos das plataformas* (PhD diss., Graduate Programme in Law, Pontifical Catholic University of Rio de Janeiro, 2020), 247. See also José Antonio Magalhães, "Platforms as Law: A Speculative Theory of Coded, Interfacial and Environmental Norms," *Journal of Cross-disciplinary Research in Computational Law* 2, no. 1 (2023).

16 As Letícia Cesarino summarizes it, "At the scale of the user, the infrastructure is made to be experienced as individualized, liberating and even empowering. At the scale of the technical apparatus, it is highly centralized, little transparent and patently monopolistic, dominated by big corporations that grew in an unregulated way and with very low public accountability." Letícia Cesarino, *O mundo do avesso: Verdade e política na era digital* (Ubu, 2024), 96. Elsewhere, she adds that, since algorithmic influence works at three scales (technical infrastructure, embodied cognition, and the targeted intervention of influencers in the digital environment), opacity, "the basis of which is the technical alienation of users," occurs at all three: "covert tactical action, asymmetry

between platforms and users, and the confirmation biases proper to human cognition." *O mundo do avesso*, 210.

17 Yves Citton, *The Ecology of Attention*, trans. Barnaby Norman (Polity, 2017), 42, modified.

18 Herbert A. Simon, "Designing Organizations for an Information Rich World," in *Computers, Communications, and the Public Interest*, ed. Martin Greenberger (Johns Hopkins Press, 1971), 40–1.

19 Josef Falkinger, "Attention Economies," CES IFO Working Paper 1079 (2003), 2.

20 Citton, *Ecology of Attention*, 46.

21 See Manuel Castells, "Communication Power and Counter-Power in the Networked Society," *International Journal of Communication*, no. 1 (2007): 238–66.

22 Michel Foucault, *The Birth of Biopolitics: Lectures at the Collège de France, 1978–1979*, trans. Graham Burchell (Palgrave Macmillan, 2008), 148.

23 Rob Horning, "Facebook in the Age of Facebook," *New Inquiry*, April 19, 2012, https://thenewinquiry.com/facebook-in-the-age-of-facebook. He continues, "Doing what you want, and more of it, is more authentic than being consistent—but only if what you're doing is observable. . . . Being true to yourself is a private matter and thus irrelevant."

24 Erving Goffman, *The Presentation of Self in Everyday Life* (Pelican, 1971), 26.

25 Quantification is key to the economic functionality of attention: "To formulate an allocation problem properly, ways must be found to measure the quantities of the scarce resource; and these quantities must not be expandable at will." Simon, "Designing Organizations," 41. What digital platforms have done is to create metrics that make this quantification, which previously existed only in the form of things like viewership ratings or sales numbers, available to all; and to package them in mechanisms that are highly addictive. As Richard Seymour puts it, social media (or the "social industry," as he calls it) is an "addiction machine, which deploys the techniques of manipulation redolent of the 'Skinner Box' created by behaviorist B. F. Skinner to control the behavior of pigeons and rats with rewards and punishments. We are 'users,' much as cocaine addicts are 'users.'" Seymour, *Twittering Machine*, 16.

26 The analogy has been drawn, among others, by former Google design ethicist Tristan Harris and gambling ethnographer Natasha Dow Schüll. See Tristan Harris, "The Slot Machine in Your

Pocket," *Der Spiegel*, July 27, 2016; Mattha Busby, "Social Media Copies Gambling Methods 'to Create Psychological Cravings,'" *Guardian*, May 8, 2018. See also Adam Alter, *Irresistible: The Rise of Addictive Technology and the Business of Keeping Us Hooked* (Penguin Books, 2017); Seymour, *Twittering Machine*, chap. 2.

27 Enzo Rullani and Antonella Corsani, "Production de connaissance et valeur dans le postfordisme," *Multitudes*, no. 2 (2000): 100. See also Matteo Pasquinelli, "Immaterial Civil War," *European Institute for Progressive Cultural Policies*, November 2006, https://eipcp.net/policies/cci/pasquinelli/en.html.

28 See Rullani and Corsani, "Production de connaissance."

29 As Seymour writes, in a sensible counterpoint to addiction comparisons, "The more society becomes dependent on the social industry to achieve everyday goals, such as socializing, entertainment, job-seeking and romance, the more it becomes logical, not pathological, to use them often and to become anxious when cut off." Seymour, *Twittering Machine*, 55.

30 "The pre-digital system of experts provided a socially shared field of entropy control, in that it normatively fixed binary oppositions that organized reality, such as public-private and fact-fiction. Without this shared field, the old categories do not disappear, but become destabilized, oscillating and recombining in the terms of new matrices that are still in the process of emerging." Cesarino, *O mundo do avesso*, 76.

31 Saraiva devised the term out of an observation on how protest and campaign videos changed in the last decade: with the spread of social media, the outward-facing camera purporting to present an unmediated slice of true life was turned around to include the filmmaker or narrator as a protagonist in the story. See Leila Saraiva, *Só a luta cria vida: Estilhaços, barricadàs e faíscas de 2013* (doctoral thesis, Graduate Programme in Anthropology, University of Brasília, 2020), 201ff.

32 Um Grupo de Militantes na Neblina, *Incêndio: Trabalho e tevolta no fim de linha brasileiro* (Contrabando Editorial, 2022), 84.

33 As Táíwò highlights, eliteness is not an identity that would pertain to particular groups defined by wealth, education, social capital, and so forth, but "a relationship, in a particular context, between a smaller group of people and a larger group of people." Olúfẹ́mi Táíwò, *Elite Capture: How the Powerful Took over Identity Politics (and Everything Else)* (Pluto, 2022), 22.

34 Táíwò, *Elite Capture*, 22, 74.

35 Naomi Klein, *Doppelgänger: A Trip into the Mirror World* (Farrar, Straus and Giroux, 2023), 113.

36 The hermeneutics of ill will is a form of what Eve Kosofsky Sedgwick called "paranoid reading," in that it mobilizes essentially the same critical moves in order to preempt any meanings that would not be revelatory of a fault or violence; but it has the added element of a much more intense consciousness of being performed in front of an audience and against potential rivals. This makes its paranoia less instinctive and more instrumental. Whereas the main affective motivation of paranoid reading is defensive—to protect an imaginary reader from the hidden content it demystifies—ill will is equally driven by competition, and thus by the offensive desire to do harm to text and author. See Eve Kosofsky Sedgwick, "Paranoid Reading and Reparative Reading or, You're So Paranoid, You Probably Think This Essay Is about You," ed. Michèle Aina Barale, Jonathan Goldberg, Michael Moon, *Touching Feeling* (Duke University Press, 2003), 123–51.

37 See Cesarino, *O mundo do avesso.*

38 On this point, see Klein's remark on Steven Bannon: "The issues we are abandoning, the debates we aren't having, the people we are insulting and discarding. He is watching all of it, and he is stitching together a political agenda out of it." Klein, *Doppelgänger*, 12–22.

39 Klein, *Doppelgänger*, 57.

40 See danah boyd, *It's Complicated: The Social Lives of Networked Teens* (Yale University Press, 2014), 31ff. This phenomenon can dramatically alter not only the meaning of a message as it travels outside its intended audience but also the perception of that message among the audience for which it was originally meant. An example would be the story of *A vida de Tina* (The life of Tina), an Instagram account that makes satiric videos about a certain left-leaning, but often privilege-oblivious, segment of the São Paulo upper class. For as long as its content circulated mostly among people who were in on the joke—those who, like the creators themselves, belonged to or were adjacent to that social milieu—it could be seen as funny and punching up. Once the right picked up on it as an exposé of progressive hypocrisy, however, it was rejected by the left as friendly fire in the culture wars.

41 Luc Boltanski and Ève Chiapello, *The New Spirit of Capitalism*, trans. Gregory Elliott (Verso Books, 1999), 126.

42 Theodor Adorno, "Remarks on the Authoritarian Personality," in *The Authoritarian Personality* (Verso Books, 2019), lii–liii.

43 Anton Jäger, Hyperpolitics: Extreme Politicization without Political Consequences (Verso Books, 2025), 8.

44 That is how one ends up with initiatives as ill-conceived as Elon Musk's Department of Government Efficiency (DOGE), an example of government by *lulz* if there ever was one. And yet, while we can take DOGE as a paradigmatic case of hyperpolitical governance, we should observe that the justification for it is entirely embedded in the naturalization of bottom line–obsessive managerialism attained in the previous period. Like much of what passes for efficiency nowadays, it is merely a repetition of a repertoire established in the last four decades, sometimes farcical to the point of being highly inefficient. At the time of writing, it is clear that DOGE's claims to saving taxpayer money have been wildly inflated (even if exact figures remain unclear), and one estimate suggests that it may have caused $135 billion in costs with personnel alone. See Jessie Blaeser, "Just How Much Has DOGE Exaggerated Its Savings? Now We Have Receipts," *Politico*, August 12, 2025; Aimee Picchi, "DOGE Says It Has Saved $160 Billion. Those Cuts Have Cost Taxpayers $135 Billion, One Analysis Says," *CBS News*, April 28, 2025, www.cbsnews.com/news/doge-cuts-cost-135-billion-analysis-elon-musk-department-of-government-efficiency.

45 As cyberpunk luminary Bruce Sterling saw right after Donald Trump's first victory, "Bursts of popular viral fever appear, but very little statecraft gets accomplished. Old institutions are corroded or abandoned, yet no new ones are built." Bruce Sterling, "Notes on the 2016 US Election," *Texte zur Kunst*, November 11, 2016, www.textezurkunst.de/en/articles/bruce-sterling-us-election. But this observation also forces us to problematize Jäger's understanding of hyperpolitics as "politicization without consequences" arising from a deficit of institutionalization: for it is clear that, whereas movements from the left have failed to make much of a dent in institutional politics in the last decade, the far right, which in many places is itself far from being strongly institutionalized, has not encountered the same difficulty. What this shows is that, alongside the axes of politicization and institutionalization that Jäger takes into account, it is necessary to consider the permeability of institutions, which is itself variable over time and across the political spectrum; and if it is true, as this book suggests, that we are at a structurally-determined low point in what regards the receptivity of demands from below, "formalized political parties" on their own may not be enough to "return us to the superpolitical

1930s." Jäger, *Hyperpolitics*, xvii. In the end, it is the implicit assumption that there is a "normal" politics that we should go back to—the mass politics that existed from the mid-nineteenth to the mid-twentieth century—is what gives this diagnosis its melancholic note of expecting redemption from the very thing that it identifies as having becoming materially unlikely.

46 Elsewhere, I have tried to provide an account of the kind of "diffuse control" that bases can have over leaders in situations where there are no formal mechanisms of accountability, such as one finds online. These are, however, rather fragile, and tend in favor of greater autonomy for leaders and more dependency for the base over time. See Rodrigo Nunes, *Neither Vertical Nor Horizontal: A Theory of Political Organization* (Verso Books, 2021), 195–99. See also Paolo Gerbaudo's remarks on the propensity for what he deems "hyperleadership" in digital party formations in Gerbaudo, *Digital Party*, chap. 8.

OF MMA, ICE, AND MEN

1 An ethnography of this phenomenon, which placed it alongside proletarian expressions of masculinity such as the *baile funk* scene, can be found in Fátima Regina Cecchetto, *Violência e estilos de masculinidade* (Rio de Janeiro: Editora FGV, 2004).

2 In this, the new hipster culture harked back to the term's origins in the Black community of the 1940s; see Anatole Broyard, "A Portrait of the Hipster," *Partisan Review* (June 1948): 721–7. In the space of a decade, the word would go from denoting a Black countercultural figure to designating a white one modeled on the former; see Norman Mailer, "The White Negro," *Dissent* (Fall 1957), https://dissentmagazine.org/. Of the twenty-first-century hipster's aping of the "white working class" that would become one of the main (and most phantasmatic) characters in accounts of the rise of the far right, Mark Greif writes: "This recalled the seventies culture of white flight to the suburbs, and the most uncanny thing about the turn-of-the-millennium white hipsters is that symbolically, in their styles and attitudes, they seemed to announce that whiteness and capital were flowing back into the formerly impoverished city." Mark Greif, "What Was the Hipster?," *New York*, October 22, 2010, https://nymag.com/. But he also notes: "At the same time that hipsters were dressing like seventies-model Stanley Kowalskis, they were consuming culture that was considerably more anxious about machismo, heterosexuality, and maturity." It should be said that the relationship to an idealized, 1970s working

class was far more characteristic of North American hipsters than their counterparts around the globe.

3 "The /pol/ board would go on to become one of the most infamous alt-right internet spaces ever, launching the QAnon conspiracy theory, developing modern white supremacist symbols like Pepe the Frog, and directly inspiring at least one mass shooter." The revelation that 4chan creator Christopher Poole possibly set up /pol/ on the same day that he met Jeffrey Epstein, a marginal detail in the 3.5 million files of the investigation into the disgraced millionaire made public in early 2026, drew attention to the ties and interests connecting global elites, tech moguls, and people who played major roles in the rise of the contemporary far right, like Poole and Stephen Bannon. Kat Tenbarge, "Jeffrey Epstein Might Not Have Created /pol/, but He Helped Carry Out Its Mission," *The Verge*, February 12, 2026, https://www.theverge.com/tech/877903/jeffrey-epstein-4chan-pol-moot.

4 Mark Fisher, *Capitalist Realism: Is There No Alternative?* (Zero Books, 2009), 21ff. It is curious to recall that Fisher's famous passage on students constantly wearing headphones in class even if they were not playing anything was written at a time when the music would be coming from (rarer) MP3 players, not (ubiquitous) mobile phones. "Depressive hedonia," incidentally, also plays a role in the online gambling epidemic discussed in chapter 3.

5 Fisher, *Capitalist Realism*, 24. The phrase originally comes from Nick Land, in the days before his conversion into Neoreaction apologist. See Nick Land, "Cybergothic," *Fanged Noumena: Collected Writings, 1987–2007*, ed. Robin Mackay and Ray Brassier (Urbanomic/Sequence, 2012), 358.

6 Linda Stone, "Continuous Partial Attention," lindastone.net, November 30, 2009.

7 Richard Seymour, *The Twittering Machine* (The Indigo Press, 2019), 111 (ebook).

8 Seymour, *The Twittering Machine*, 94. As Seymour writes about the trolls who attack families and friends of deceased people online: "You have to 'get' pain in order to know how best to inflict it. If RIP trolls are magnetically drawn to grief, it might be because they can already imagine how they might feel about loss, how grief might affect them."

9 "There is an incentive to be a victim," claimed McInnes in a newspaper profile, before accusing the journalist of "victim-blaming" him for stereotyping Muslims. Simon Houpt, "*Vice* Co-Founder

Gavin McInnes's Path to the Far-Right Frontier," *Globe and Mail*, August 18, 2017, https://www.theglobeandmail.com/.

10 For the concept of the "patriarchal dividend"—"the advantage men in general gain from the overall subordination of women"—see Raewyn Connell, *Masculinities* (University of California Press, 2005), 2nd ed., 79ff.

11 Quinn Slobodian, *Hayek's Bastards: Race, Gold, IQ, and the Capitalism of the Far Right* (Zone Books, 2025), 126.

12 Justin Gilmore, "Incels: The New Politics of Indifference," *The Fair Observer*, November 7, 2019, https://www.fairobserver.com/.

13 It would be possible to rank different strands of the manosphere according to their hopes of being cared for—which is also to say, along the meritocracy-determinism axis. On one extreme, involuntary celibates and Men Going Their Own Way (MGTOW) appear as the least hopeful/most deterministic, utterly convinced of the impossibility of finding loving, reciprocal relationships, at least with women. This might be because of a fault mostly in female nature (MGTOW) or in their own (incels), At the opposite end of the spectrum, Pick-Up Artists (PUAs) are the most committed to meritocracy: Working on one's "game" can bring positive returns, and the difference between authentic and inauthentic care becomes immaterial when women see you as the best they could find. Given that natural determinism is a more demanding belief, cognitively as well psychologically, the vast majority, including Men's Rights Activists (MRAs), probably veer closer to this end.

14 On the poet and military adventurer D'Annunzio as a pioneer of Fascist symbology and ritual, see Michael Ledeen, *D'Annunzio: The First Duce* (Johns Hopkins University Press, 1977).

15 Benito Mussolini, *My Autobiography with "The Political and Social Doctrine of Fascism,"* transl. Richard Washburn Child (Dover, 2006), 230.

16 While the ever-evolving culture of internet forums has come up with several more categories identified by letters of the Greek alphabet, it is clear that these are subtypes of the original binary opposites rather than shades between them (a sigma is a type of alpha; delta, gamma, and omega are types of beta).

17 There certainly is work to be done on the figure of the "uncle" (Ho Chi Minh, Abdullah Öcalan, the *tiozão*) in politics, specifically as an alternative to the "father" (the Founding Fathers, Stalin, Kemal Atatürk, Getúlio Vargas).

18 The extreme homosociality of this world of "winners" has been expertly picked up on by the actor Bransen Gates in his lip-synced interpretations of Trump speeches on Instagram. By singling out various digressions heaping praise on or taking the measure of other men, then performing them with the mannerisms of gay flirtation, Gates highlights the extent to which this is an environment in which men perform for other men, including in their relationships with women.

19 Theodor Adorno, "Freudian Theory and the Pattern of Fascist Propaganda," in *The Essential Frankfurt School Reader*, ed. Andrew Arato and Eike Gephardt (Continuum, 1997), 127.

20 On hegemonic masculinity, see Connell, *Masculinities*, 37ff.

21 Klaus Theweleit, *Male Fantasies, vol. I: Women, Floods, Bodies, History* (University of Minnesota Press, 1987).

22 Anna M. Agathangelou and L. H. M. Ling, "Power, Borders, Security, Wealth: Lessons of Violence and Desire from September 11," *International Studies Quarterly* 48, no. 3 (2004): 519; see also Ashis Nandy, *The Intimate Enemy: The Psychology of Colonialism* (Oxford, 1988).

23 Cara Daggett, "Petro-Masculinity: Fossil Fuels and Authoritarian Desire," *Millennium: Journal of International Studies* 47, no. 1 (2018): 33, 41, 34.

CHAPTER 5

1 See Gregory Bateson, *Naven: A Study of the Problems Suggested by a Composite Picture of the Culture of a Papua New Guinea Tribe Drawn from Three Points of View* (Cambridge University Press, 1936), 176–87. Bateson differentiated between "symmetrical schismogenesis" (in which each group responds with equivalent behavior) and "complementary schismogenesis" (in which groups embody behaviors that complement each other), but acknowledged that the distinction is not always obvious and that relationships of one type contain elements of the other.

2 Keith T. Poole and Howard Rosenthal, "The Polarization of American Politics," *Journal of Politics* 46, no. 4 (1984): 1061.

3 Poole and Rosenthal, "The Polarization of American Politics," 1061.

4 Nolan McCarty, Keith T. Poole, and Howard Rosenthal, *Polarized America: The Dance of Ideology and Unequal Riches* (MIT Press, 2006).

5 "Political Polarization in the American Public," Pew Research Center, June 12, 2014, www.pewresearch.org/politics/2014/06/12/political-polarization-in-the-american-public.

6 Thomas E. Mann and Norman J. Ornstein, "Let's Just Say It: The Republicans Are the Problem," *Washington Post*, April 27, 2012.

7 Eleonora de Lucena, "Nova direita surgiu após junho, diz filósofo," *Folha de São Paulo*, October 31, 2014, www1.folha.uol.com.br/poder/2014/10/1541085-nova-direita-surgiu-apos-junho-diz-filosofo.shtml. See also Fabrício Brugnago and Vera Chaia, "A nova polarização política nas eleições de 2014: Radicalização ideológica da direita no mundo contemporâneo do Facebook," *Aurora* 7, no. 21 (2015): 99–129.

8 There were also those who refused the polarization diagnosis altogether. See Morris P. Fiorina, Samuel J. Abrams, and Jeremy C. Pope, *Culture War? The Myth of a Polarized America* (Longman, 2004).

9 See James Davison Hunter, *Culture Wars: The Struggle to Define America* (Basic Books, 1991).

10 Pablo Ortellado, "Guerras culturais no Brasil," *Le Monde Diplomatique Brasil*, no. 89 (2014).

11 Ortellado, "Guerras culturais no Brasil."

12 Ortellado, "Guerras culturais no Brasil."

13 Yascha Mounk, "How Labour Lost the Culture War," *Atlantic*, December 13, 2019.

14 On the "welfare queen" as a key rhetorical figure in transforming public perceptions of social security in the United States, see Ange-Marie Hancock, *The Politics of Disgust: The Public Identity of the Welfare Queen* (New York University Press, 2004); and Josh Levin, *The Queen: The Forgotten Life Behind an American Myth* (Little, Brown, 2019).

15 Michael Kazin, *The Populist Persuasion: An American History* (Cornell University Press, 1995), 224.

16 Stuart Hall, "The Great Moving Right Show," *Marxism Today*, January 1979, 14–20.

17 Melinda Cooper, *Family Values: Between Neoliberalism and the New Social Conservatism* (MIT Press, 2017).

18 Wendy Brown, *In the Ruins of Neoliberalism: The Rise of Antidemocratic Politics in the West* (Columbia University Press, 2019).

19 Nancy Fraser, *The Old Is Dying and the New Cannot Be Born: From Progressive Neoliberalism to Trump and Beyond* (Verso Books, 2019).

20 See Quinn Slobodian and Branden Söres, "From Neoliberal Globalism to Neoliberal Nationalism: An Interview with Quinn Slobodian," *Ephemera* 19, no. 3 (2019): 641–49. The belief that anti-globalism would represent a break with neoliberalism denotes

an exaggerated trust in the discourse—and a lack of attention to the actual practice—of both far-right governments and neoliberal ideologues themselves, who never shied away from regulatory structures or protectionist measures when it suited their ends. When the Bolsonaro government began, many still believed that the market libertarianism of finance minister Paulo Guedes made it unique among its peers. The following years will have hopefully disabused them of that notion.

21 A notable blind spot in the discourse emanating from North American political science is that, compared with places like Europe and Latin America, the party spectrum in the United States has always been rather narrow. The absence of a classic socialist or social democratic party helps explain why the richest country in the world for over a century has never even attempted to establish a universal public health care system, something that a much poorer country like Brazil has. In comparative terms, the center of US politics has always been asymmetrical, skewing more toward the right than they do in several other parts of the world.

22 On the contrary, in fact: Unlike the two major crises that preceded it, those of the 1930s (which led to the Keynesian social contract) and the 1970s (which led to the rise of neoliberalism), the 2008 crisis served as a pretext to deepen, rather than correct, the very mechanisms that caused it.

23 Although far from unanimous, the most influential version of the discourse on "left populism" that came out of this moment was that articulated by and under the influence of Laclau and Mouffe. See Ernesto Laclau, *Ernesto Laclau, On Populist Reason* (Verso Books, 2025); and Chantal Mouffe, *For a Left Populism* (Verso Books, 2018).

24 Rodrigo Nunes, "Junho de 2013 aconteceu, mas não teve lugar," *Revista do Instituto Humanitas Unisinos*, no. 524 (2018): 18.

25 Marcos Lisboa, "Descontrole," *Folha de São Paulo*, December 1, 2019.

26 I borrow the expression from Samuel Pessôa, "A crise atual," *Novos Estudos Cebrap*, no. 102 (2015): 5–10.

27 What happened in this 2015–16 period, however, was the precipitation of a shift to the right that had been in the making for some time, of which the first catalyst was the "gay kit" incident in 2011 (see chapter 1, note 18).

28 This argument, familiar to both conservatives and centrists, received a notorious version from the left in Angela Nagle, *Kill All Normies: Online Culture Wars from 4chan and Tumblr to Trump*

and the Alt-Right (Alresford, Zero Books, 2017). I see two major problems in Nagle's analysis: the identification between identitarianism and so-called identitarian or minoritarian activism, when the first is clearly a broader phenomenon, and the explanatory weight ascribed to online "social justice warriors" at the cost of larger, offline dynamics. In presenting the far right as the product of the radicalization of an "identitarian left" that has "gone too far," it ignores that what counts as "going too far" is always relationally defined: For someone with deeply entrenched prejudices, the mere visibility of an other (gay, trans, feminist, Black, Indigenous, . . .) may be experienced as "too much" and trigger a schismogenic reaction. In other words, the fact that someone feels that an other has "gone too far" does not necessarily make it the case.

29 I return to this point in the next chapter.

30 The idea that polarization is a product of the affective charge associated with identities rather than public policy issues is explored in Lilliana Mason, *Uncivil Agreement: How Politics Became Our Identity* (University of Chicago Press, 2018).

31 By assuming that everyone is as interested in maintaining a coherent political identity, the left often overestimates the consistency of other people's choices, projecting a complete worldview behind them, then being perplexed when it realizes that the assumption that people subscribe to a complete package of positions does not work. It is, in fact, perfectly possible for a person to be against homophobia and vote for the far right, for example; it suffices that their opposition to homophobia carry less weight for them than other factors underpinning their electoral choice.

32 See Richard Seymour, *Disaster Nationalism: The Downfall of Liberal Civilization* (Verso Books, 2024), 202.

33 On this point, see Pierre Charbonnier, *Affluence and Freedom: An Ecological History of Political Ideas*, trans. Andrew Brown (Polity, 2021).

34 See Jean-Baptiste Fressoz, *More and More and More: An All-Consuming History* (Penguin Books, 2025).

CHAPTER 6

1 Maurício Gomes Leite *apud* Eduardo Escorel, "O massacre de maio," *Piauí*, no. 128 (2017).

2 *A revolução brasileira* was the title of one of the most important books published in the aftermath of the coup, in which Marxist intellectual Caio Prado Jr. criticized the Communist Party's official interpretation of Brazilian reality and the political mistakes

that followed from it, pointing out the absence of revolutionary potential of the national bourgeoisie and laying out the tasks of a radical rupture to come. Caio Prado Jr., *A revolução brasileira* (Brasiliense, 1966).

3 To borrow an apposite turn of phrase from Celso Rocha de Barros, "O Brasil e a recessão democrática," *Piauí*, no. 139 (2018). Director Petra Costa also employs it in *Democracia em vertigem*.

4 José Padilha's Netflix series *O Mecanismo* (The Mechanism) offers a politically and artistically jejune fictionalization of the corruption investigation that led to Lula's conviction and was key to the institutional instability that provided the context for Rousseff's impeachment. After the judge who led the operation joined the Bolsonaro government, the director recognized he had been wrong to depict it as an idealistic and impartial investigation. José Padilha, "O ministro antiFalcone," *Folha de São Paulo*, April 16, 2019, www1.folha.uol.com.br/opiniao/2019/04/o-ministro-antifalcone.shtml. Another film, Rubens Rewald and Tales Ab'Saber's 2017 *Intervenção—amor não quer dizer grande coisa* (Intervention—love does not mean much), stands as something of an outlier in this list: A collage of videos made by right-wing YouTube influencers about an imminent military coup that existed only in their imaginations, it played a pioneering role in drawing attention to the growing ecosystem of far-right online political entrepreneurs.

5 Partial exceptions are *O muro*, which focuses on the street mobilizations for and against the impeachment, and *Já vimos esse filme*, whose point of view is more "peripheral" by virtue of being both set outside the centers of power in Brasília, São Paulo, and Rio de Janeiro—it was mostly shot in the southern city of Porto Alegre—and the only one that makes some effort to register what was going on outside the polarization between PT supporters and opponents.

6 Aristides Lobo, "Carta ao Diário Popular de São Paulo," November 18, 1889, *apud* Leôncio Basbaum, *História sincera da República: De 1889 a 1930* (Fulgor, 1968), 18. This passage went on to inspire a classic study of the lack of political participation in the early decades of the Brazilian republic; see José Murilo de Carvalho, *Os bestializados: O Rio de Janeiro e a república que não foi* (Companhia das Letras, 2004).

7 Much ink has been spilled about those events and their impact on Brazilian politics. For an overview, I refer the reader to André Singer, "Rebellion in Brazil: Social and Political Complexion

of the June Events," *New Left Review*, no. 85 (2014): 19–37; Rodrigo Nunes (org.), "Brésil: L'année qui ne s'achève pas," *Les Temps Modernes*, no. 678 (2014): 3–147; Marcos Nobre, *Limites da democracia: De junho de 2013 ao governo Bolsonaro* (Todavia, 2022); Roberto Andrés, *A razão dos centavos: Crise urbana, vida democrática e as revoltas de 2013* (Todavia, 2023); David Nemer, Augusto Jobim do Amaral, Pablo Ornelas Rosa, and Rodrigo Lopes Barro, *June Days: Reflections on a Decade in Changing Brazil* (SUNY Press, forthcoming).

8 The director's family is also the owner of one of the largest construction companies in Brazil, caught in the Car Wash scandal—a connection that the film mines both for material and behind-the-scenes access.

9 Ironically, Jair Bolsonaro subsequently shared the sequence from *O processo* on Twitter as if it were a video leaked directly from communist conspiracy headquarters, causing a stir among his followers.

10 For a collective effort to make sense of these dynamics, see Juan Grigera et al., "The Long Brazilian Crisis: A Forum," *Historical Materialism*, no. 27 (2019): 59–121.

11 Laura Carvalho, *Valsa brasileira: Do boom ao caos econômico* (Todavia, 2018), chap. 2.

12 Antonia Campos (2019) suggests that *Democracia em vertigem* be seen as "an anthropological incursion into the subjectivity of a specific social sector that saw in Lula's and Dilma's elections the crowning of a painful process of democratic struggles, and in their removal from power the end of democracy." While "it is true that PT and redemocratization were the outcome of struggles," and that the former's ousting was the result of antidemocratic maneuvers, the problem is that this sector has too narrow a perspective on reality, "and therefore cannot properly understand the experience of a huge part of the population who followed the process without much empathy." Antonia Campos, "*Democracia em Vertigem*: Um 'sonho curto' de um segmento social," *Veneta*, June 24, 2019.

13 Rocha's *Barravento* (1962) and *Deus e o diabo na terra do sol* (Black God, white devil) (1964), Pereira dos Santos's *Vidas secas* (Barren lives) (1963), and Ruy Guerra's *Os fuzis* (The guns) (1964) were among the most important films of this first phase.

14 Sérgio Martins has observed the same tendency in Brazilian painting of the period; see Sérgio Martins, *Constructing an Avant-Garde: Art in Brazil, 1949–1979* (MIT Press, 2013), 99ff.

15 See Spivak's analysis of the play of *Vertretung* and *Darstellung* in Marx's *Eighteenth Brumaire* in Gayatri Chakravorty Spivak, "Can the Subaltern Speak?," in *Marxism and the Interpretation of Culture*, ed. Cary Nelson and Lawrence Grossberg (University of Illinois Press, 1988), 275–78.

16 Karl Marx, *Karl Marx and Frederick Engels: Collected Works*, vol. 2, *The Eighteenth Brumaire of Louis Bonaparte* (International Publishers, 1979), 187.

17 Glauber Rocha, "Positif," in *Revolução do cinema novo* (Cosac Naify, 2004), 118. This meaninglessness has to do with the gesture's isolated character, not with a condemnation of violence. The director later adds that, at first, Martins "cannot accept violence, of course, because he is powerless, he has no organization for that," but "[a]t the time of his death, he knows that violence is the path to revolution." "Positif," 120.

18 Rocha, "Uma filosofia como autobiografia," in *Revolução do cinema novo*, 241.

19 Rocha, "Cahiers du cinéma," in *Revolução do cinema novo*, 195.

20 Rocha, "O transe da América Latina," in *Revolução do cinema novo*, 173. In the same interview, Rocha states, "I made the film with the aspiration that it would be a bomb, very deliberately attacking the prejudices of an academic, conservative left, which had a neurotic reaction against the film, and that was very positive." "O transe da América Latina," 171.

21 André Singer, Os sentidos do lulismo: Reforma gradual e pacto conservador (Companhia das Letras, 2012), 169–221.

22 Rosa Luxemburg, "The Russian Revolution," in *The Rosa Luxemburg Reader*, ed. Peter Hudis and Kevin B. Anderson (Monthly Review Press, 2004), 298.

THE ENCOUNTER OF BATMAN WITH THE PEOPLE

1 These gatherings, which were initially meant as being of an essentially social nature rather than as political occasions, quickly became a flashpoint in the highly volatile climate of the time. Attempts at repressing them sparked a conversation about racism and classism, access to the city, and the absence of leisure alternatives in deprived areas, and were seen as confirmation of some of the points made by the protests of six months earlier. For a look at this phenomenon, including its tension between being celebrations of consumption and raising questions about the occupation of public space, see Rosana Pinheiro-Machado and Lucia Scalco, "Les rolezinhos sont bons à penser: marques, consommation et

ségrégation dans la société brésilienne," *Les Temps Modernes*, no. 678 (2014): 60–72.

2 See chapter 6.

3 See, for example, Roberto Schwarz, "Culture and Politics in Brazil, 1964–1969," in *Misplaced Ideas: Essays on Brazilian Culture*, trans. John Gledson (Verso Books, 1992), 126–59; Celso Favaretto, *Tropicália: Alegoria alegria* (Ateliê, 1979); Ismail Xavier, *Allegories of Underdevelopment: Aesthetics and Politics in Brazilian Cinema* (University of Minnesota Press, 1997); and Christopher Dunn, "Tropicália: Modernity, Allegory and Counterculture," in *Tropicália: A Revolution in Brazilian Culture*, ed. Carlos Basualdo (Cosac Naify, 2005), 59–78.

4 Petista and Olavista are labels commonly used for, respectively, PT supporters and followers of Olavo de Carvalho. Leblon was the neighborhood in which the protest took place, one of the most exclusive in Rio de Janeiro.

5 Ernesto Laclau distinguishes populist logic, which consists in the construction of a collective identity around an antagonistic frontier between "us" and "them," from an institutionalist logic that tends to erase antagonism in favor of the possibility of an infinite chain of differences (anything and everything can potentially be included). See Ernesto Laclau, *On Populist Reason* (Verso Books, 2025), 81–2. This distinction allows us to grasp Lula's rhetorical tendency to oscillate between populism and institutionalism, emphasizing antagonism when addressing his party's base but relativizing it when speaking to the broader electoral coalition behind his success. That the discursive maneuver that PT attempted between 2013 and Dilma Rousseff's impeachment failed is evidence that this oscillation had, by then, been stretched to its limit, and the duality between internal and external discourse could no longer be maintained without one undermining the other. Cornered by the rise in anti-PT sentiment, the party resorted to a populist discourse, but this succeeded in galvanizing its supporters as much as it alienated those the party had managed to attract with an institutionalist appeal—and confirmed it as the "other" in the eyes of those who had passed over to the other side.

6 *Batalhador* (struggler) was the term proposed by sociologist Jessé Souza as an alternative to the "new middle class" that was widely discussed toward Lula's second term in power and Dilma Rousseff's first. Whereas PT claimed that years of economic growth and redistributive policies had catapulted a mass of poor people into the middle class, Souza pointed out that these late

arrivals lacked the accumulated social and cultural capital of their established counterparts, which made their class position not only different but more fragile in case the levels of consumption possible at the time could not be sustained. This distinction was vindicated later on, when the economic crisis stalled or inverted their upward social mobility, and some of them—especially in the Brazilian South and Southeast—switched their electoral allegiance to the right. See Jessé Souza, *Os batalhadores brasileiros: Nova classe média ou nova classe trabalhadora?* (UFMG, 2012).

CONCLUSION

1 André Singer and Fernando Rugitsky, "Slow Motion Lulismo," *New Left Review Sidecar*, January 8, 2024, https://newleftreview.org/sidecar/posts/slow-motion-lulismo.

2 Zack Colman, "Trump Is Transforming the GOP's Energy Policies—and Not All Conservatives Are Happy," *Politico*, July 22, 2025.

3 Stafford Beer, *The Heart of Enterprise* (Wiley & Sons, 1994), 10. As he puts it elsewhere, there is no point claiming that the purpose of a system is to something else if it constantly fails to do so.

4 On the passage from hypocrisy to cynicism in international relations signaled by the US kidnapping of Venezuela's Nicolás Maduro in early 2026, see Rodrigo Nunes, "The Mask Comes Off," *Boston Review*, February 4, 2026, https://www.bostonreview.net/articles/the-mask-comes-off/.

5 See Quinn Slobodian, "Speed Up the Breakdown," *New York Review of Books*, February 15, 2025. This is where I think Slobodian's otherwise on-point analysis of the meaning of DOGE does not go far enough. While right-wing accelerationism should certainly be considered as the most recent of the intellectual strains that converged into the creation of Elon Musk's merry band of vandals, it did not create the "real movement" of acceleration that simultaneously makes policies like that politically viable and is the resultant force of the convergence around them. If anything, it is a relatively niche attempt to rationalize it. See also Quinn Slobodian, *Crack-Up Capitalism: Market Radicals and the Dream of a World Without Democracy* (Penguin Books, 2023).

6 Yarvin writes that "if anyone can build anything like Patchwork, even a tiny, crude, Third World ripoff of Patchwork, it is all over for the democratic regimes" as we know them—which may well be true but is also blissfully oblivious to the fact that such a thing already exists in the militia-controlled peripheries of Rio

de Janeiro and in the parts of Mexico that are in the hands of drug cartels, for example. See Mencius Moldbug, *Patchwork: A Political System for the 21st Century* (Unqualified Reservations, 2008), chap. 1, www.unqualified-reservations.org/2008/11/patchwork-positive-vision-part-1.

7 At around the same time as I started developing this hypothesis, public security specialist Gabriel Feltran was speaking of *sistema jagunço* (henchman system) to describe pretty much the same thing, if from a somewhat different angle. Whereas the emphasis in "overseer capitalism" lies on the potential for the inclusion of overseers as major players into a viable political and economic arrangement that is beneficial for them as well as for capital, Feltran zooms in on the agency of "henchmen"—members of both public and private security apparatuses—as they become autonomous political and economic agents. Another important difference lies, of course, in the choice of words. Taking inspiration from Guimarães Rosa's classic novel *The Devil to Pay in the Backlands*, Feltran uses a term originally used to denote rural guns for hire, whereas I prefer to situate these contemporary figures more explicitly within the colonial history of law enforcement, choosing an earlier word that establishes an immediate connection to the plantation. See Gabriel Feltran, "Formas elementares da vida política: Sobre o movimento totalitário no Brasil (2013–)" (blog), *Novos Estudos* (2020), http://novosestudos.uol.com.br/formas-elementares-da-vida-politica-sobre-o-movimento-totalitario-no-brasil-2013.

8 On this genealogy, see Bruno Paes Manso, *A república das milícias: Dos esquadrãoes da morte à era Bolsonaro* (Todavia, 2020). Although Bolsonaro was in the army, the "basements" were a terrain of intense cross-fertilization among the military, the police, and organized crime, and he probably has an even stronger base in the police (which, it should be remembered, in Brazil is partially militarized) than he does in the armed forces.

9 As Peter Bloom points out, the growth of the security industry is inseparable from the need for securitization dictated by the subordination of all other forms of capital by finance: Speculation not only increases the need for social control, so as to ensure returns on investments, but also transforms risks into tradable assets and commodifies control itself, opening a vast market for "a global industry that thrives on the militarization of law enforcement, the normalization of surveillance, and the outsourcing of security functions to private entities." Peter Bloom, *Capitalism Reloaded:*

The Rise of the Authoritarian-Financial Complex (Bristol: Bristol University Press, 2025), 100.

10 This can be the case, of course, even when the connection to the security apparatus is absent. Confirming the tendency for the capitalist core to look more and more like the periphery, Trump's second term has attracted attention for its Banana Republic–level pay-to-play approach, in which a lavish jetliner gifted by a foreign country, "multimillion-dollar TV packages, real estate deals in Arab petrostates, dinners with the president going for $5m a pop, plum job offers for contributors to Trump's inaugural fund, cryptocurrency ventures attracting lucre from secret foreign investors, 'drill, baby, drill' enticements for oil and energy donations," as well as Trump-branded meme coins, mobile phone services, and even a "golden phone" all suggest the use of office to exchange favors and obtain personal gain. See Ed Pilkington, "'This Is the Looting of America': Trump and Co. Extraordinary Conflicts of Interest in His Second Term," *Guardian*, June 16, 2025. Five months into the new administration, an estimate suggested the North American president may have more than doubled his net worth since the start of his reelection campaign, but, as a specialist puts it, "Nobody in Trump's heartland sees this as damaging—it's what they expect a deal-maker to do." Edward Helmore, "'This Presidency Is a Brand-Franchise': Trump Has Taken the Commercialization of Politics to a New Level," *Guardian*, June 21, 2025.

11 Otto Kirchheimer, "In Quest of Sovereignty," *Journal of Politics* 6, no. 2 (1944): 161–62. The "racket society" could be understood as the counterpart, at the social level, of the political apparatus that Hungarian politician Bálint Magyar calls "mafia state", portraying it as "the privatized form of the parasitic state, the business venture of the adopted political family managed through the instruments of public authority." Bálint Magyar, *The Post-Communist Mafia State: The Case of Hungary* (CEU Press, 2016), 70-1. Although the latter term has become a go-to label for talking about much of the contemporary far right, especially since the start of Donald Trump's second term, Magyar clearly has in mind a situation more like Hungary's, in which the concentration of political and economic power around a single group or "political family" is much greater than elsewhere, and internal differentiation and competition is smaller than in Kirchheimer's model.

12 See Cory Doctorow, *Chokepoint Capitalism: How Big Tech and Big Content Captured Creative Labor Markets and How We'll Win*

Them Back (Scribe, 2022); Brett Christophers, *Rentier Capitalism: Who Owns the Economy, and Who Pays for It?* (Verso Books, 2022).

13 "But when the mechanism of coordination does not function any longer so as to guarantee fundamental agreements between the groups that contend for the power to make final decisions, the most powerful ones among them are compelled to resort to building a machine of violence that would enable them to suppress 'undesirable' groups and restrict competition among the 'desirable' ones. Agreement among a few groups is then reached through the medium of a paramount common interest in suppressing or restraining many others. Enforcement of the agreement is of necessity entrusted to the newly-built machine whose operators, 'practitioners of violence,' form new groups themselves, groups linked with each other through clusters of rackets. Old groups must share power with new groups. Initial agreements which originally insured coordination must be revised and a new compromise looked for." Kirchheimer, "In Quest of Sovereignty," 174.

14 See Ulrich Brand and Markus Wissen, *The Imperial Mode of Living: Everyday Life and the Ecological Crisis of Capitalism* (Verso Books, 2021).

15 Michel Foucault, "Film and Popular Memory: An Interview with Michel Foucault," trans. Martin Jordin, *Radical Philosophy*, no. 11 (1975): 27.

INDEX

X

Y

Z

ABOUT THE AUTHOR

RODRIGO NUNES is an associate professor of philosophy at the Pontifical Catholic University of Rio de Janeiro (PUC-Rio), Brazil, and a visiting fellow at the University of Essex. He has been a visiting professor and researcher at several institutions around the world, including Brown University, Goldsmiths, University of London, and the University of Wisconsin–Madison. He is the author of *Neither Vertical nor Horizontal: A Theory of Political Organization* (Verso Books, 2021) and *Organisation of the Organisationless: Collective Action After Networks* (Mute, 2014), as well as numerous articles published in *Les Temps Modernes*, *Radical Philosophy*, *South Atlantic Quarterly*, *Jacobin*, and *The Guardian*. He is a FAPERJ Scientist of the State of Rio de Janeiro grant recipient and an associate researcher at the Alameda Institute.

ABOUT HAYMARKET BOOKS

Haymarket Books is a radical, independent, nonprofit book publisher based in Chicago. Our mission is to publish books that contribute to struggles for social and economic justice. We strive to make our books a vibrant and organic part of social movements and the education and development of a critical, engaged, and internationalist left.

We take inspiration and courage from our namesakes, the Haymarket Martyrs, who gave their lives fighting for a better world. Their 1886 struggle for the eight-hour day—which gave us May Day, the international workers' holiday—reminds workers around the world that ordinary people can organize and struggle for their own liberation. These struggles—against oppression, exploitation, environmental devastation, and war—continue today across the globe.

Since our founding in 2001, Haymarket has published more than nine hundred titles. Radically independent, we seek to drive a wedge into the risk-averse world of corporate book publishing. Our authors include Angela Y. Davis, Arundhati Roy, Keeanga-Yamahtta Taylor, Eve Ewing, Aja Monet, Mariame Kaba, Naomi Klein, Rebecca Solnit, Mohammed El-Kurd, José Olivarez, Noam Chomsky, Winona LaDuke, Robyn Maynard, Leanne Betasamosake Simpson, Howard Zinn, Mike Davis, Marc Lamont Hill, Dave Zirin, Astra Taylor, and Amy Goodman, among many other leading writers of our time. We are also the trade publishers of the acclaimed Historical Materialism Book Series.

Haymarket also manages a vibrant community organizing and event space in Chicago, Haymarket House, the popular Haymarket Books Live event series and podcast, and the annual Socialism Conference.